Collins

mathspace

Teacher's Guide

Year 3

Contents

Introducing Mathspace

Mathspace is an exciting Numeracy resource offering flexibility and choice. The materials are designed to support your own teaching style, putting you at the centre of teaching and learning. With a straightforward structure, Mathspace offers:

• A wide variety of suggested activities for each National Numeracy Framework objective, allowing you to match appropriate activities to different groups of children;

• A wealth of pupil practice material for each objective, in the form of a concise, colourful pupil book and photocopiable differentiation worksheets;

• Powerful software, providing inbuilt differentiation with personalised learning paths for each pupil, allowing children to work independently, receiving consolidation and reinforcement according to their individual needs.

The **Teacher's Guide** contains structured unit plans for each Framework objective in a clear, easy-to-use format. Each plan contains a choice of discovery activities which allow children to acquire the building blocks for each mathematical concept through active exploration. Specific attention has been given to the plenary section in each plan, detailing common misconceptions and difficulties, and ways to overcome them.

The colourful **Pupil Book** provides pupil practice of the Framework objectives, in a clear, concise format. The **Differentiation Pack** provides further practice, support and extension work for the Framework objectives. All the material is linked to the unit plans found in the Mathspace Teacher's Guide for use after the discovery activities.

The **CD-ROM** offers diverse, entertaining interactive activities to help pupils achieve the Framework objectives. Ideal for independent use, the software responds dynamically to the success or failure of each pupil. It tracks pupils' progress, enabling them to begin working where they left off.

For each activity, help and remediation is provided, tailored to the specific error of a pupil. Pupils are also given different activities dependent on their ability level.

Teachers have direct access to pupils' progress with a range of individualised reporting functions. You can also run computer generated reports to review the progress of the whole class, allowing you to monitor how pupils are doing against your own and national targets.

How to use Mathspace

A. The Teacher's Guide

The Mathspace Teacher's Guide is a central component in the resource. Each double page spread contains a flexible unit plan, structured as follows:

Introduction
Each unit plan begins with a brief introduction to the concept or topic that is covered in the plan. This provides you with the mathematical background to the topic and information about how the concept fits into the context of the curriculum and the learning experience of your pupils.

Objectives
Two types of objective are included in each unit plan: the long-term National Numeracy Framework objectives addressed in the unit and the short-term goals of the particular activities suggested in the unit plan. The objectives from The Framework for Teaching Mathematics are bulleted, while the specific outcomes for the activities are marked with a dash. In order for the achievement of the pupils to be measurable, objectives are phrased in terms of what the children will be able to do by the end of each unit plan, rather than in terms of what they will know.

Key vocabulary
The key maths terms for the lesson are highlighted. These are drawn from the vocabulary recommended by the National Numeracy Strategy.

Materials
To aid preparation, the resources needed for the activities are listed on each unit plan. It is recommended that each pupil has their own small whiteboard. Where specific manipulatives are needed, they are provided as copymasters at the back of the Teacher's Guide, and are denoted by RM. The following resources and equipment are also used in various Mathspace activities and are assumed to be found in most classrooms.

- Large and small counters
- Pattern tiles
- Dot dice (1–6)
- Numeral dice (1–6)
- Blank dice
- Number lines 1–100
- Various dominoes
- Board games
- Construction material
- Blank playing cards
- Interlocking cubes
- Cuisinaire rods
- 0–9 cards
- 0–100 cards
- 100 number square
- 1–100 grids

- Number fans
- Money
- Money stamps
- Rulers
- Metre sticks
- Tape measures
- 2-D and 3-D shapes
- Pan balances
- Numbered beam balances
- Sand, water, pasta, rice
- Weights
- Weighing scales
- Containers
- Timers
- Clocks
- Stop watch

Oral and mental starter

Each unit plan offers two oral and mental maths activities designed to enable you to review with the children concepts encountered previously and warm up for the lesson at hand. These interactive starter activities increase pupils' ability to internalise information and to perform mental calculations rapidly and accurately. The starter activities, which take up the first five to ten minutes of each lesson, also enable you to spot and correct errors or misconceptions.

Main teaching

The main teaching in each unit plan comprises four discovery activities that address the goals of the unit plan. The first two activities are designed for group work, while the second two are designed for individual work. You should choose between two and four activities that are most appropriate for your class and that best suit your own individual teaching style. The discovery activities are structured in such a way that the children must actively explore the mathematical concept being taught in order to solve the problem or complete the task at hand. As a result, with some guidance from you, the teacher, the discovery activities enable pupils to discover the concepts themselves and create their own understanding.

As a result of this discovery process, pupils will engage in rich mathematical discourse with each other and with you both during and after the discovery activities. During these discussions, children will explore processes, draw conclusions and will be exposed to a variety of different strategies and methods for solving the same problem. You should moderate these discussions, helping organise the information so that you may pull it all together for the plenary session.

Plenary

Once the pupils have completed their discovery activities, either in groups or individually, the plenary pulls together the learning for the entire class. Each plenary presents a suggested activity that can be conducted with the whole class. This summarises the learning for the pupils, perhaps presenting it in a more formal manner, putting it in its mathematical context and introducing or reinforcing the correct mathematical vocabulary. Specific guidance is provided on the common errors or misconceptions that pupils make, with suggestions for remediation.

Homework suggestion

Suggestions for activities that pupils can easily do at home to reinforce the objectives are provided.

Related material

The related pupil practice material is always referenced on each unit plan. For each Teacher's Guide double page spread, there is a double page spread of practice activities in the Activity Books and a consolidation sheet, ideal for homework. For those struggling with a particular objective there is a support copymaster and an extension copymaster to challenge the more able. The related CD-ROM activity is also highlighted.

Assessment

Mathspace provides both aural and written assessment in test format similar to that of the National Tests. These assessments are designed to be carried out at the end of each half term, but may be used whenever a teacher feels confident that they have covered the topics. Each assessment has remediation resource references indicating the unit plan numbers and associated CD-ROM activities. These are provided so that you can use the activities in the unit plans to re-teach where necessary and use the CD-ROM to reinforce the skills learnt.

A sample Mathspace unit plan

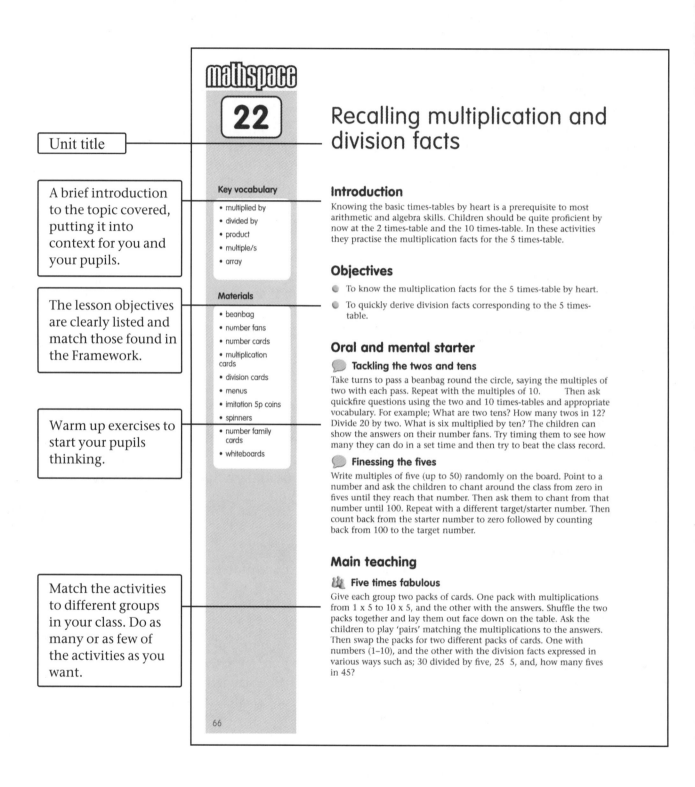

Unit title

A brief introduction to the topic covered, putting it into context for you and your pupils.

The lesson objectives are clearly listed and match those found in the Framework.

Warm up exercises to start your pupils thinking.

Match the activities to different groups in your class. Do as many or as few of the activities as you want.

mathspace

22

Recalling multiplication and division facts

Key vocabulary

- multiplied by
- divided by
- product
- multiple/s
- array

Materials

- beanbag
- number fans
- number cards
- multiplication cards
- division cards
- menus
- imitation 5p coins
- spinners
- number family cards
- whiteboards

Introduction

Knowing the basic times-tables by heart is a prerequisite to most arithmetic and algebra skills. Children should be quite proficient by now at the 2 times-table and the 10 times-table. In these activities they practise the multiplication facts for the 5 times-table.

Objectives

- To know the multiplication facts for the 5 times-table by heart.
- To quickly derive division facts corresponding to the 5 times-table.

Oral and mental starter

Tackling the twos and tens

Take turns to pass a beanbag round the circle, saying the multiples of two with each pass. Repeat with the multiples of 10.   Then ask quickfire questions using the two and 10 times-tables and appropriate vocabulary. For example; What are two tens? How many twos in 12? Divide 20 by two. What is six multiplied by ten? The children can show the answers on their number fans. Try timing them to see how many they can do in a set time and then try to beat the class record.

Finessing the fives

Write multiples of five (up to 50) randomly on the board. Point to a number and ask the children to chant around the class from zero in fives until they reach that number. Then ask them to chant from that number until 100. Repeat with a different target/starter number. Then count back from the starter number to zero followed by counting back from 100 to the target number.

Main teaching

Five times fabulous

Give each group two packs of cards. One pack with multiplications from 1 x 5 to 10 x 5, and the other with the answers. Shuffle the two packs together and lay them out face down on the table. Ask the children to play 'pairs' matching the multiplications to the answers. Then swap the packs for two different packs of cards. One with numbers (1–10), and the other with the division facts expressed in various ways such as; 30 divided by five, 25   5, and, how many fives in 45?

66

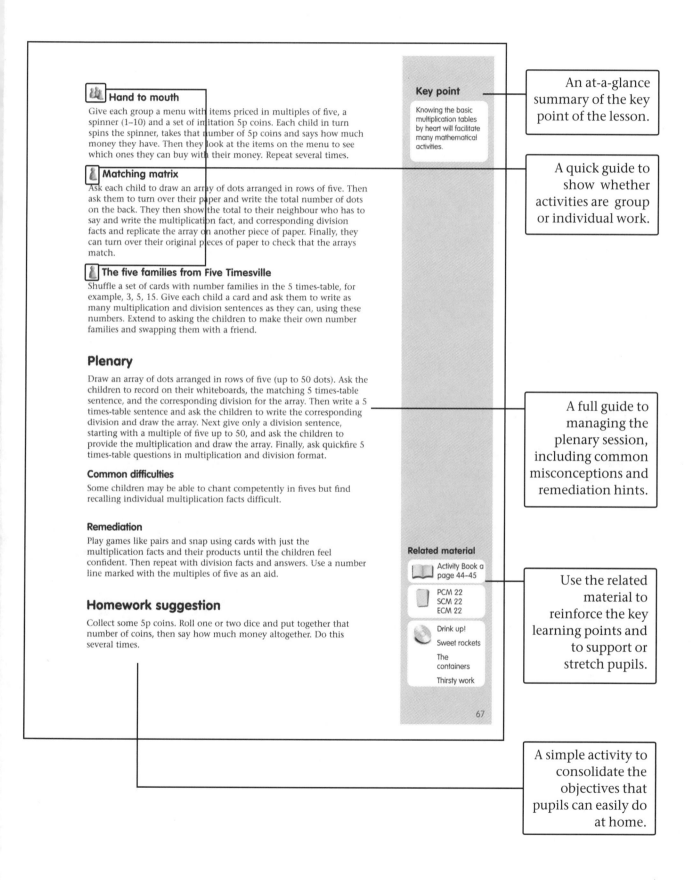

Hand to mouth

Give each group a menu with items priced in multiples of five, a spinner (1–10) and a set of imitation 5p coins. Each child in turn spins the spinner, takes that number of 5p coins and says how much money they have. Then they look at the items on the menu to see which ones they can buy with their money. Repeat several times.

Matching matrix

Ask each child to draw an array of dots arranged in rows of five. Then ask them to turn over their paper and write the total number of dots on the back. They then show the total to their neighbour who has to say and write the multiplication fact, and corresponding division facts and replicate the array on another piece of paper. Finally, they can turn over their original pieces of paper to check that the arrays match.

The five families from Five Timesville

Shuffle a set of cards with number families in the 5 times-table, for example, 3, 5, 15. Give each child a card and ask them to write as many multiplication and division sentences as they can, using these numbers. Extend to asking the children to make their own number families and swapping them with a friend.

Plenary

Draw an array of dots arranged in rows of five (up to 50 dots). Ask the children to record on their whiteboards, the matching 5 times-table sentence, and the corresponding division for the array. Then write a 5 times-table sentence and ask the children to write the corresponding division and draw the array. Next give only a division sentence, starting with a multiple of five up to 50, and ask the children to provide the multiplication and draw the array. Finally, ask quickfire 5 times-table questions in multiplication and division format.

Common difficulties

Some children may be able to chant competently in fives but find recalling individual multiplication facts difficult.

Remediation

Play games like pairs and snap using cards with just the multiplication facts and their products until the children feel confident. Then repeat with division facts and answers. Use a number line marked with the multiples of five as an aid.

Homework suggestion

Collect some 5p coins. Roll one or two dice and put together that number of coins, then say how much money altogether. Do this several times.

Key point

Knowing the basic multiplication tables by heart will facilitate many mathematical activities.

Related material

Activity Book a
page 44–45

PCM 22
SCM 22
ECM 22

Drink up!

Sweet rockets

The containers

Thirsty work

67

An at-a-glance summary of the key point of the lesson.

A quick guide to show whether activities are group or individual work.

A full guide to managing the plenary session, including common misconceptions and remediation hints.

Use the related material to reinforce the key learning points and to support or stretch pupils.

A simple activity to consolidate the objectives that pupils can easily do at home.

B. Mathspace Pupil Book

There is one Pupil Book for each year. The activities reinforce and build on the main teaching activities detailed in the unit plans in the Teacher's guide, offering pupils further practice and consolidation of the objectives.

This **lesson summary** panel is included on every spread and gives a summary of the key ideas in these activities

Clear and colourful **activities** motivate your pupils

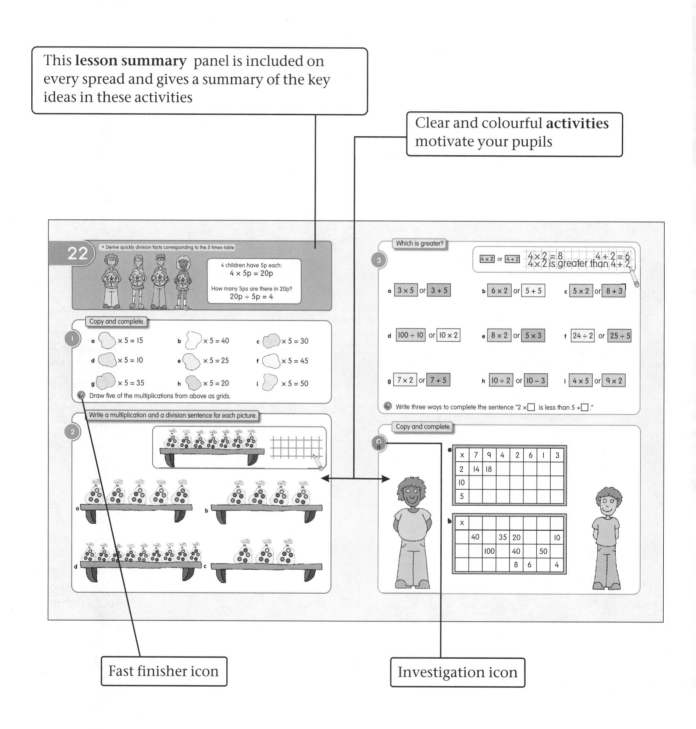

Fast finisher icon

Investigation icon

C. Differentiation Pack

Here are three photocopiable worksheets relating to the teacher's guide and pupil book on the previous pages.

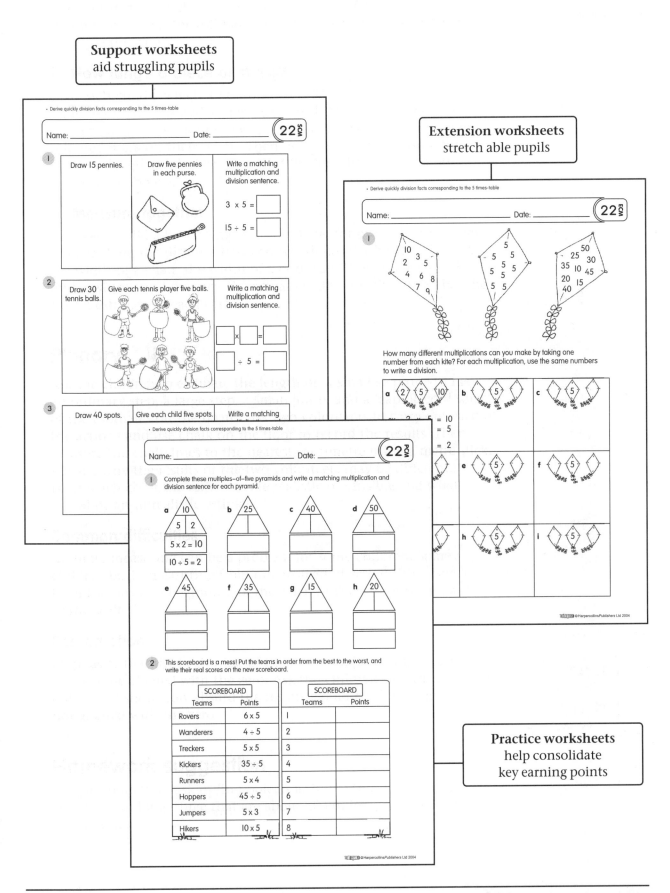

D. Mathspace CD-ROM

The Mathspace CD-ROM covers the entire National Numeracy Framework for Year 3, allowing students to practise skills in an enjoyable, interactive environment. Children follow a learning path tailored to their own individual needs. Teachers also have direct access to specific activities in order to provide pupils with support when needed.

The Mathspace software is ideal for independent use, as it responds dynamically to the success or failure of each pupil. It tracks pupils' progress, enabling them to begin working where they left off.

Exit

By clicking on Ziggy, children follow their own individualised learning path.

Clicking on the telescope allows you to review a specific objective by selecting an activity listed by Framework objective.

General features

The Mathspace interface is easy to use and is mastered in minutes.

Lights indicate the degree of success achieved in each activity

Green light – success on first try
Yellow light – success with help
Red light – failure

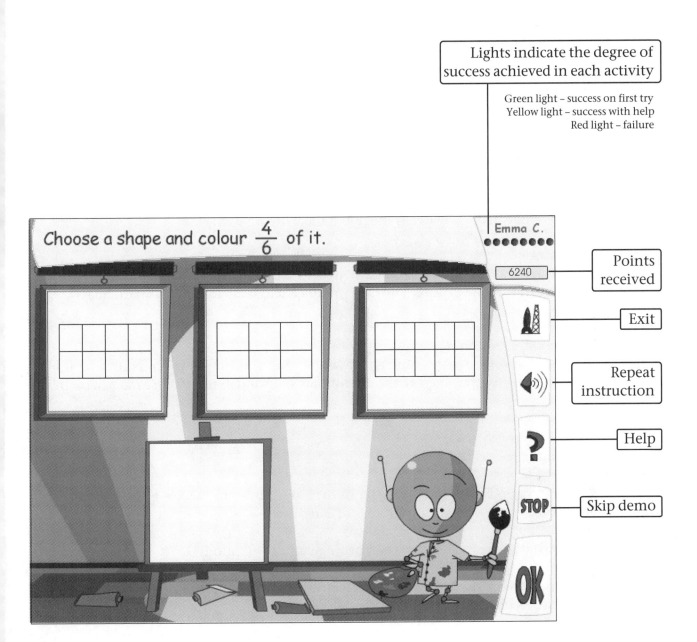

Points received

Exit

Repeat instruction

Help

Skip demo

The activities are structured in the same way so that pupils always understand what they have to do. Help and remediation is provided, tailored to the specific error of a pupil. The system provides the pupil with a clear indication of how they are progressing and encourages them to find the correct answer for themselves. It also means that a quick glance over a pupil's shoulder can tell you exactly how they are doing.

Activity cycle

Each activity is structured in the same way, so that pupils can focus on the mathematical concept presented each time.

Step 1 - Demonstration
At the start of each activity, Mathspace randomly generates a practice exercise for a particular Framework objective. The demonstration explains the objective and shows the pupil how to complete the activity.

Step 2 - Activity
The pupil is first presented with a repeat of the example shown in the demonstration to check their understanding of the task at hand. Mathspace then provides a number of randomly generated practice activities designed to help the pupil master the objective. If pupils encounter difficulty with particular activities, Mathspace will provide support activities, whereas enrichment activities will be provided if the pupils are working with ease.

Step 3 - Answer or help
Pupils can confirm they are happy with their answers by clicking the OK button. Alternatively, they can click Help if they are unsure. The help provided will be specific to the particular activity.

Step 4 - Evaluation and correction
Correct answers are rewarded with sound effects, entertaining animations and points. If pupils have answered incorrectly, they receive the appropriate help and explanation as to where they went wrong.

Learning manager

Mathspace provides pupils with individual paths of study. The software covers the entire National Numeracy Framework with hundreds of activities.

- **Core activities** are included in the learning paths of all pupils;

- **Support activities** are included in the learning paths of pupils experiencing difficulties with particular objectives;

- **Enrichment activities** are included in the learning paths of pupils working with ease.

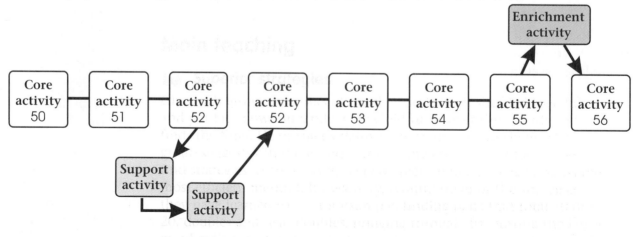

Reporting and assessment

The CD-ROM provides powerful reporting and assessment tools that allow you to follow the progress of the class and individual pupils, enabling you to fully tailor your lessons to the needs of your pupils.

1. The direct access screen

The direct access screen allows you to review quickly at a glance the progress of a pupil. The colouring of the icons shows how the pupils are doing over the range of activities. You may wish to review an activity with a pupil to provide prompt remediation in cases of difficulty. The pupil can then be returned to the main menu to resume learning on their individual learning path.

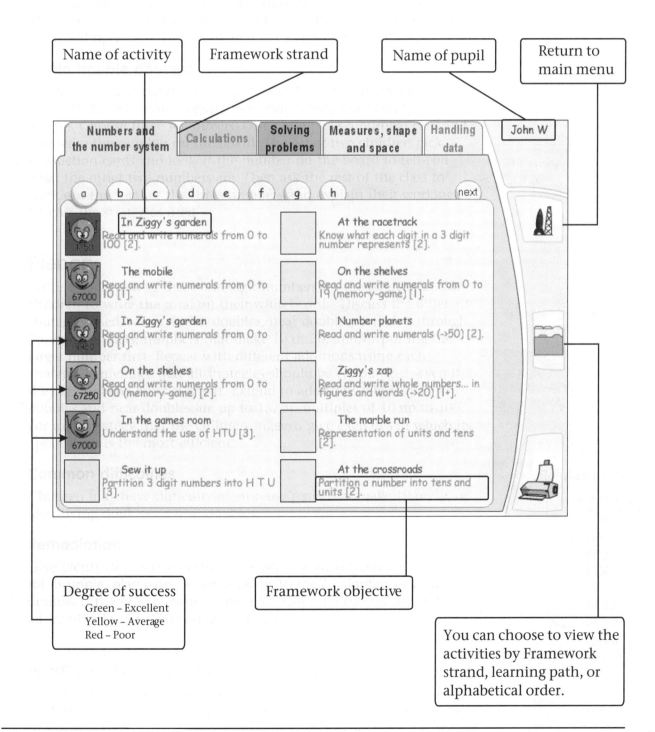

2. Progress reports

To help you assess your class in more detail, Mathspace provides four key reports. These computerised progress reports allow you to follow the progress and achievement of both the class as a whole and of individual pupils. The four reporting options are:

- Class distribution graphs
- Class progress reports
- Individual progress reports
- Intervention reports

Class distribution graphs
show where the pupils are in the path of the CD and give you a general picture of class progress.

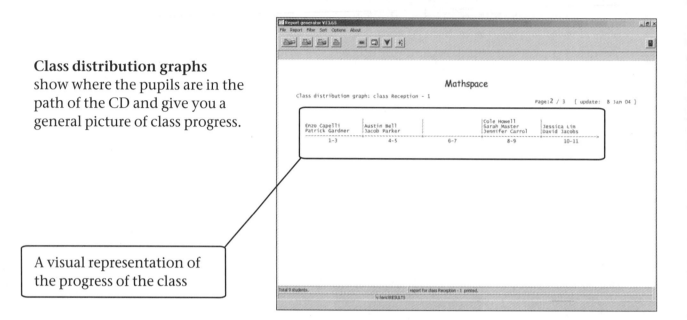

A visual representation of the progress of the class

Class progress reports
include the level achieved by each pupil on the last activity they completed and indicates the rate of class progress. The report gives each activity a score out of 10 (10 being the highest, 1 the lowest).

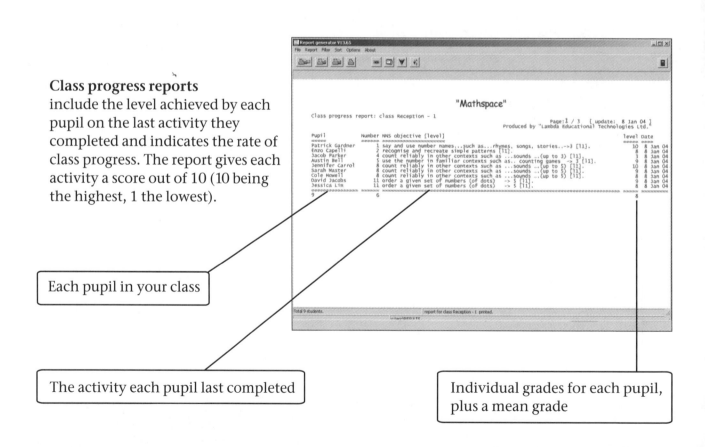

Each pupil in your class

The activity each pupil last completed

Individual grades for each pupil, plus a mean grade

Activity details, with indication of NC level

Number of times activity completed

Individual progress reports indicate the path followed by each pupil, the number of times they've attempted each activity and the level they've reached for each activity. Level A indicates a child working above the NC level indicated, level B at the level and level C below the level for the particular activity.

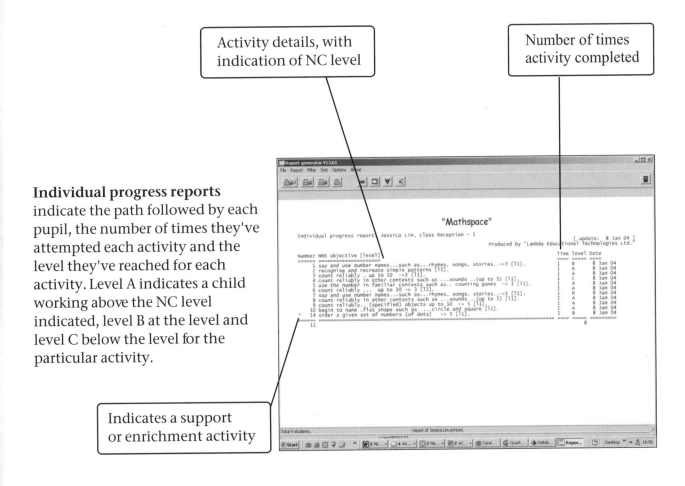

Indicates a support or enrichment activity

Intervention reports point out the rare cases of pupils that fail specific activities repeatedly, despite the computer help received. This allows you, the teacher, to provide focused remediation.

Identify any pupils who are failing specific activities repeatedly and may need extra support from you

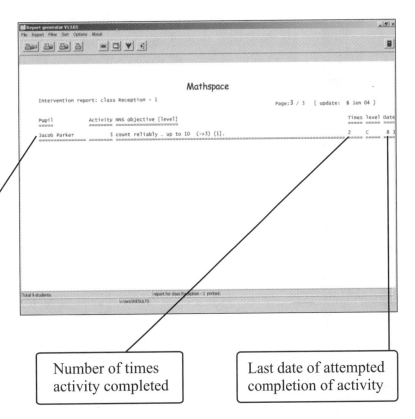

Number of times activity completed

Last date of attempted completion of activity

Year 3 NNS coverage

Unit	Plan	Strand	Topic	Objective
1	Hundreds, tens and units	Numbers and the number system	Place value and ordering	• Read and write whole numbers to at least 1000 in figures and words; • Know what each digit represents and partition three-digit numbers into a multiple of 100, a multiple of 10 and ones (HTU).
2	Place value	Numbers and the number system	Place value and ordering/ Counting, properties of numbers and number sequences	• Say the number that is 1, 10, or 100 more or less than any given two- or three-digit number; • Count on or back in tens or hundreds starting from any two-digit or three-digit number.
3	Estimation	Numbers and the number system	Estimating and rounding/ Counting, properties of numbers and number sequences	• Read and begin to write the vocabulary of estimation and approximation; • Give a sensible estimate of up to about 100 objects; • Count larger collections by grouping them.
4	Reading a labelled scale	Measures, shape and space	Measures	• Read scales to the nearest labelled division.
5	Number facts up to 20	Calculations	Rapid recall of addition and subtraction facts/understanding addition and subtraction	• Recall addition and subtraction facts for each number to at least 20; • Add three single-digit numbers mentally.
6	Addition	Calculations	Mental calculation strategies (+ and -)	• Use knowledge that addition can be done in any order to do mental calculations more efficiently; • Identify near doubles using doubles already known.
7	Addition strategies	Calculations	Mental calculation strategies (+ and -)	• Bridge though a multiple of 10, then adjust; • Add mentally a 'near multiple of 10' to or from a two-digit number.
8	Understanding addition and subtraction	Calculations	Understanding addition and subtraction	• Extend understanding of the operations of addition and subtraction; • Read and begin to write related vocabulary; • Use the +, - and = signs.
9	Money	Solving problems	Problems involving 'real life' money and measures	• Recognise all coins and notes. Understand and use £.p notation; • Solve word problems involving money.

Unit	Plan	Strand	Topic	Objective
10	Money problems	Solving problems	Making decisions/Problems involving 'real life', money and measures	• Choose and use appropriate operations to solve word problems and appropriate ways of calculating; • Find totals and give change, and work out which coins and notes to pay.
11	Drawing and measuring lines	Measures, shape and space	Measures	• Read and begin to write the vocabulary related to length; • Use a ruler to draw and measure lines to the nearest half centimetre.
12	Measuring length	Measures, shape and space	Measures	• Know the relationships between kilometres and metres and between metres and centimetres; • Suggest suitable units and measuring equipment to estimate or measure length.
13	Estimating and measuring	Measures, shape and space	Measures	• Record estimates and measurements to the nearest whole or half unit, or in mixed units.
14	Classifying shapes	Measures, shape and space/Solving problems	Shape and space/ Reasoning about numbers or shapes	• Classify and describe 2-D and 3-D shapes; • Identify right angles in 2-D shapes and the environment; • Investigate a general statement about familiar shapes by finding examples that satisfy it.
15	Position	Measures, shape and space	Shape and space	• Read and begin to write the vocabulary related to position, directions and movement.
16	Counting in tens and hundreds	Numbers and the number system	Counting, properties of numbers and number sequences	• Count on or back in tens or hundreds, starting from any two- or three-digit number.
17	Odd and even	Numbers and the number system	Counting, properties of numbers and number sequences	• Count on or back in twos starting from any two-digit number; • Recognise odd and even numbers to at least 100.
18	Solving mathematical problems and puzzles	Solving problems	Reasoning about numbers or shapes	• Solve mathematical problems or puzzles, recognise simple patterns and relationships, generalise and predict. Suggest extensions by asking, 'what if...?'; • Explain methods and reasoning orally and in writing.

Unit	Plan	Strand	Topic	Objective
19	Understanding multiplication	Calculations	Understanding multiplication and division	• Understand multiplication as repeated addition; • Extend understanding that multiplication can be done in any order.
20	Multiplication and division facts of two	Calculations	Rapid recall of multiplication and division facts	• Know by heart multiplication facts for the 2 times-table; • Derive quickly the division facts corresponding to the 2 times-table; • Derive quickly doubles of whole numbers to at least 20 and all the corresponding halves.
21	Multiplying by 10 and 100	Calculations	Mental calculation strategies (x and ÷)/ Rapid recall of multiplication and division facts	• Say or write a division statement corresponding to a given multiplication statement; • To multiply by 10/100 shift the digits one/two places to the left; • Know by heart the multiplication facts for the 10 times-table.
22	Recalling multiplication and division facts	Calculations	Rapid recall of multiplication and division facts	• Know by heart the multiplication facts for the 5 times-table; • Derive quickly division facts corresponding to the 5 times-table.
23	Solving problems	Solving problems	Problems involving 'real life', money and measures/Making decisions	• Solve word problems involving numbers in 'real life', money and measures using one or two steps; • Choose and use appropriate operations to solve word problems and appropriate ways of calculating; • Explain how the problem was solved.
24	Fractions	Numbers and the number system	Fractions	• Recognise unit fractions such as $\frac{1}{2}$, $\frac{1}{3}$, $\frac{1}{4}$, $\frac{1}{5}$, $\frac{1}{10}$ … and use them to find fractions of shapes and numbers.
25	More fractions	Numbers and the number system	Fractions	• Recognise unit fractions such as $\frac{1}{2}$, $\frac{1}{3}$, $\frac{1}{4}$, $\frac{1}{5}$, $\frac{1}{10}$ … and use them to find fractions of shapes and numbers.
26	Multiples of 100	Calculations	Rapid recall of addition and subtraction facts/mental calculation strategies (+ and -)	• Know by heart all pairs of multiples of 100 with a total of 1000; • Use known number facts and place value to add/ subtract mentally.

mathspace © Harpercollins*Publishers* Ltd 2004

Unit	Plan	Strand	Topic	Objective
27	Subtraction and addition	Calculations	Understanding addition and subtraction/Mental calculation strategies (+ and -)	• Extend understanding that subtraction is the inverse of addition; • Say or write a subtraction statement corresponding to a given addition statement, and vice versa; • Find a small difference by counting up from the smaller to the larger number.
28	Reading time to five minutes	Measures, shape and space	Measures	• Read the time to 5 minutes on an analogue clock and on a 12-hour digital clock, and use the notation 9:40.
29	Time problems	Solving problems	Making decisions	• Choose and use appropriate operations to solve word problems and appropriate ways of calculating.
30	Organising and using data	Handling data	Organising and using data	• Solve a given problem by organising and interpreting numerical data in simple lists, tables and graphs.
31	Comparing and ordering numbers	Numbers and the number system	Place value and ordering	• Read and begin to write the vocabulary of comparing and ordering numbers, including ordinal numbers to at least 100; • Compare two given three-digit numbers, say which is more or less, and give a number which lies between them.
32	Rounding numbers	Numbers and the number system	Estimating and rounding	• Round any two-digit number to the nearest 10 and any three-digit number to the nearest 100; • Read and begin to write the vocabulary of estimation and approximation.
33	Reading scales	Measures, shape and space	Measures	• Read scales to the nearest division;
34	Partitioning and recombining	Calculations	Mental calculation strategies (+ and -)	• Partition numbers into tens and units, then recombine; • Use known number facts and place value to add mentally.
35	Adding more than two numbers	Calculations	Understanding addition and subtraction/ Mental calculation strategies (+ and -)	• Extend understanding that more than two numbers can be added; add three or four single-digit numbers mentally; • Use known number facts and place value to add/ subtract mentally.

Unit	Plan	Strand	Topic	Objective
36	Money problems and investigations	Solving problems	Problems involving 'real life', money and measures	• Solve word problems involving numbers in 'real life' and money, using one or more steps; • Explain how the problem was solved.
37	Number operations	Solving problems	Making decisions	• Choose and use appropriate operations to solve word problems and appropriate ways of calculating.
38	Shapes and patterns	Measures, shape and space	Shape and space	• Make and describe shapes and patterns; • Relate solid shapes to pictures of them.
39	Right-angled turns	Measures, shape and space	Shape and space	• Make and describe right-angled turns; • Know that 90° equals a right angle; • Read and begin to write the vocabulary related to direction.
40	North, South, East and West	Measures, shape and space	Shape and space	• Recognise and use the four compass directions N, S, E, W.
41	Units of time	Measures, shape and space	Measures	• Use units of time and know the relationships between them; • Suggest suitable units to measure or estimate time.
42	Measuring mass	Measures, shape and space	Measures	• Measure and compare using the standard units of kilograms and grams; • Know the relationships between kilograms and grams.
43	Fraction problems	Solving problems	Reasoning about numbers or shapes/Problems involving 'real life', money and measures	• Solve mathematical problems or puzzles, recognise simple patterns and relationships, generalise and predict. Suggest extensions by asking, 'what if...?'; • Solve word problems using numbers in 'real life', money and measures.
44	Mass and weighing	Measures, shape and space	Measures	• Suggest suitable units and measuring equipment to estimate or measure mass; • Record estimates and measurements to the nearest whole or half unit, or in mixed units.
45	Investigating shapes	Solving problems	Reasoning about numbers or shapes	• Investigate a general statement about familiar shapes by finding examples that satisfy it.

Unit	Plan	Strand	Topic	Objective
46	Counting in steps of three, four and five	Numbers and the number system	Counting, properties of numbers and number sequences	• Count on in steps of 3, 4 or 5 from any small number to at least 50, then back again; • Describe and extend number sequences.
47	Solving puzzles	Solving problems	Reasoning about numbers or shapes	• Solve mathematical problems or puzzles, recognise simple patterns and relationships, generalise and predict; • Investigate a general statement about familiar numbers by finding examples that satisfy it.
48	Mental addition and subtraction	Calculations	Mental calculation strategies (+ and -)	• Use known number facts and place value to add/ subtract mentally; • Use knowledge that addition can be done in any order to do mental calculations more efficiently.
49	Understanding addition	Calculations	Understanding addition and subtraction	• Extend understanding that more than two numbers can be added; • Add three or four two-digit numbers with the help of apparatus or pencil and paper.
50	Understanding subtraction	Calculations	Understanding addition and subtraction	• Extend understanding of the operation of subtraction.
51	Doubling and halving	Calculations	Rapid recall of multiplication and division facts/ Mental calculation strategies (x and ÷)	• Derive quickly doubles of multiples of 5 to 100, and all the corresponding halves; • Use doubling or halving starting from known facts.
52	The 3 times-table	Calculations	Rapid recall of multiplication and division facts	• Begin to know the 3 times-table.
53	The 4 times-table	Calculations	Rapid recall of multiplication and division facts	• Begin to know the 4 times-table.

Unit	Plan	Strand	Topic	Objective
54	Understanding division	Calculations	Understanding multiplication and division / Mental calculation strategies (× and ÷)	• Understand division as grouping (repeated subtraction) or sharing; • Recognise that division is the inverse of multiplication; • Say or write a division statement corresponding to a given multiplication statement.
55	Word problems	Solving problems	Making decisions/Problems involving 'real life', money or measures	• Choose and use appropriate operations to solve word problems, and appropriate ways of calculating; • Solve word problems involving numbers in 'real life' and money, using one or more steps.
56	Recognising fractions	Numbers and the number system	Fractions	• Begin to recognise simple fractions that are several parts of a whole.
57	Equivalent fractions	Numbers and the number system	Fractions	• Begin to recognise simple equivalent fractions.
58	Comparing familiar fractions	Numbers and the number system	Fractions	• Compare familiar fractions; • Begin to recognise simple fractions that are several parts of a whole.
59	Bar charts	Handling data	Organising and using data	• Solve a given problem by organising and interpreting numerical data in simple lists, tables and graphs.
60	Pictograms	Handling data	Organising and using data	• Solve a given problem by organising and interpreting numerical data in simple lists, tables and graphs.
61	Comparing and ordering three-digit numbers	Numbers and the number system	Place value and ordering	• Compare two given three-digit numbers, say which is more or less, and give a number which lies between them; • Order whole numbers to at least 1000 and position them on a number line.
62	Estimating and approximating	Numbers and the number system	Estimating and rounding	• Read and begin to write the vocabulary of estimation and approximation.

mathspace © HarpercollinsPublishers Ltd 2004

Unit	Plan	Strand	Topic	Objective
63	Describing and extending number sequences	Numbers and the number system	Counting, properties of numbers and number sequences	• Describe and extend number sequences.
64	Add and subtract near multiples of 10	Calculations	Mental calculation strategies (+ and -)	• Add and subtract mentally a 'near multiple of 10' to or from a two-digit number; • Use patterns of similar calculations.
65	Mental calculations	Calculations	Mental calculation strategies (+ and -)	• Use known number facts and place value to add/ subtract mentally.
66	Working with three-digit numbers	Calculations	Mental calculation strategies (+ and -)	• Use known number facts and place value to add/ subtract numbers mentally.
67	More mental calculations	Calculations	Mental calculation strategies (+ and -)	• Use known number facts and place value to add/ subtract mentally.
68	Addition paper and pencil methods (1)	Calculations	Pencil and paper procedures	• Use informal pencil and paper methods to support, record or explain HTU + TU, HTU + HTU.
69	Addition paper and pencil methods (2)	Calculations	Pencil and paper procedures	• Use informal pencil and paper methods to support, record or explain HTU + TU, HTU + HTU.
70	Number problems and puzzles	Solving problems	Reasoning about numbers or shapes	• Solve mathematical problems or puzzles, recognise simple patterns and relationships, generalise and predict. Suggest extensions by asking, 'what if...?'
71	Capacity	Measures, shape and space	Measures	• Know the relationship between litres and millilitres; • Read scales to the nearest labelled and unlabelled division.
72	Measuring capacity	Measures, shape and space	Measures	• Record estimates and measurements to the nearest whole or half unit, or in mixed units; • Suggest suitable units and measuring equipment to estimate or measure capacity.

Unit	Plan	Strand	Topic	Objective
73	Symmetry and mirror lines	Measures, shape and space	Shape and space	• Identify and sketch lines of symmetry in simple shapes, and recognise shapes with no lines of symmetry; • Sketch the reflection of a simple shape in a mirror line along one edge.
74	Position and direction	Measures, shape and space	Shape and space	• Read and begin to write the vocabulary related to position, direction and movement.
75	Right angles	Measures, shape and space	Shape and space	• Recognise that a straight line is equivalent to two right angles; • Compare angles with a right angle.
76	Recognising multiples	Numbers and the number system	Counting, properties of numbers and number sequences,	• Recognise two-digit and three-digit multiples of 2, 5 or 10, and three-digit multiples of 50 and 100.
77	Investigating general statements	Solving problems	Reasoning about numbers or shapes	• Investigate a general statement about familiar numbers or shapes by finding examples that satisfy it. • Solve mathematical problems or puzzles.
78	Doubles and halves of multiples of 50	Calculations	Rapid recall of multiplication and division facts	• Derive quickly doubles of multiples of 50 to 500 and all the corresponding halves.
79	Three and four times-tables	Calculations	Rapid recall of multiplication and division facts/Mental calculation strategies/Understanding multiplication and division	• Begin to know the 3 and 4 times-tables; • Say or write a division statement corresponding to a given multiplication statement; • Recognise that multiplication is the inverse of division.
80	Mental multiplication and division	Calculations	Mental calculation strategies (x and ÷)	• Use known number facts and place value to carry out mentally simple multiplications and divisions.
81	Remainders	Calculations	Understanding multiplication and division	• Begin to find remainders after simple division; • Round up or down after division, depending on the context.

 mathspace © HarpercollinsPublishers Ltd 2004

Unit	Plan	Strand	Topic	Objective
82	Mental multiplication and division strategies	Calculations	Mental calculation strategies (x and ÷)	• Use doubling or halving, starting from known facts; • Use known number facts and place value to carry out mentally simple multiplications and divisions.
83	Multiplication and division word problems	Solving problems	Making decisions	• Choose and use appropriate operations to solve word problems and appropriate ways of calculating.
84	Fractions	Numbers and the number system	Fractions	• Compare familiar fractions.
85	Estimating fractions	Numbers and the number system	Fractions	• Estimate a simple fraction.
86	Partition into 'five and a bit'	Calculations	Mental calculation strategies (±)	• Partition into '5 and a bit' when adding 6, 7, 8 or 9.
87	Subtraction pencil and paper methods	Calculations	Pencil and paper procedures (±)	• Use informal pencil and paper methods to support, record or explain HTU – TU, HTU – HTU.
88	More pencil and paper methods for subtractions	Calculations	Pencil and paper procedures (±)	• Use informal pencil and paper methods to support, record or explain HTU – TU, HTU – HTU.
89	Using a calendar	Measures, shape and space	Measures	• Use a calendar.
90	Venn and Carroll diagrams	Handling data	Organising and using data	• Solve a given problem by organising and interpreting numerical data in simple lists, tables and graphs.

Hundreds, tens and units

Key vocabulary

- hundreds
- tens
- units

Materials

- number cards (0-9)
- whiteboards
- multibase hundreds, tens and units
- counters
- drawings of abacuses

Introduction

The activities in this unit plan introduce place value for three-digit numbers and show that the rules of place value for two-digit numbers also apply to three-digit numbers. These rules include: the value of a digit depends upon its position in the number; and, ten units in a given place equal one unit at the next, higher level. Various apparatus are suggested to model the working and as many examples as possible should be used.

Objectives

 To read and write whole numbers to at least 1000 in figures and words.

– To know what each digit represents and partition three-digit numbers into a multiple of 100, a multiple of 10 and ones (HTU).

Oral and mental starter

 Who's the hundred?

Sit the children in a circle and ask one child to choose a number card from a set of multiples of 10. The child has to predict who will be 100 if they count around the circle in tens, starting from the number on the card. Check the answer by counting, and repeat.

 Double figures

Describe two-digit numbers in a variety of ways, for example, 25, or two tens and five units, or 20 plus five. Ask the children to write the number in figures on their whiteboards.

Main teaching

 Multibase madness

Give each group a set of multibase hundreds, tens and units, and a set of three-digit number cards. The children take turns to choose a card and make that number with the multibase. Then ask each child to make a number higher than 100 with the multibase while the others record the number in figures.

👥 Complete cover up

Give each group a set of number cards (1-9) and some counters, and place a few three-digit numbers in the centre. The children take turns to pick a card from the pile. If the number matches one of the digits in any of the three-digit numbers, they cover that digit with the matching card and say what the digit represents, for example, three tens or four hundreds. The child who places the last card on a number has to read the whole number to win a counter. Then the child may move the cards on that number around to make different numbers. They win a counter for each three-digit number they can make and read. Repeat with different three-digit numbers in the centre. The child with the most counters at the end is the winner.

🔦 Abacus cadabra!

Give each pair of children a drawing of a three-prong vertical abacus without 'beads', and counters of three different colours to represent the beads. In turn, ask the children to place the beads on the paper to represent a number on the abacus, while their partner says the number and records it in figures.

🔦 Three card shuffle

Give each child a set of three number cards (1–9). How many three-digit numbers can they make and record? Ask for the highest and the lowest possible number for those cards.

Plenary

Write several three-digit numbers on the board. Ask volunteers in turn to read one of them and explain what each digit represents. Then write three-digit number words and ask all the children to write them in figures on their whiteboards. Ask questions about the numbers including the place value of individual digits and which are the highest and lowest three-digit numbers. Discuss what zero represents in a number and why it is necessary.

Common difficulties

Children may incorrectly record two zeros after the first digit of a three-digit number because it is a hundreds number.

Remediation

Show how the zeros are 'hidden' by layering the number cards for each value. For example, 236 has 200 on the bottom, 30 covering the two zeros of the 200, and 6 covering the zero of the 30.

Homework suggestion

Ask the children to find different numbers as they are travelling home or at home, and write the number in words. For example, house numbers, the number of a bus or number of pages in a certain book.

Key point

Any context, practical or theoretical, involving numbers greater than 10, requires an understanding of place value in order to give some meaning to the numbers.

Related material

Pupil Book
Page 4–5

PCM 1
SCM 1
ECM 1

At the racetrack
At the crossroads!
Payday

Place value

Key vocabulary

- hundreds
- tens
- units

Materials

- number word cards
- whiteboards
- number strips
- instructions for number strips
- paperclips
- washing lines
- pegs
- sets of number cards (0–9)
- one more, one less, 10 more, 10 less, 100 more, 100 less spinner

Introduction

The following activities utilise the knowledge of place value up to three-digits, learned in Unit plan 1. They focus on adding and subtracting 1, 10, and 100 to or from a given number, up to 999.

Objectives

 To say the number that is 1, 10, or 100 more or less than any given two or three-digit number.

 To count on or back in tens or hundreds starting from any two-digit or three-digit number.

Oral and mental starter

Cases of places

Prepare three separate sets of number word cards (zero to nine, multiples of 10, and multiples of 100). Ask three volunteers to pick one card from each pile. The rest of the class has to write the three-digit number made from the three cards, in figures on their whiteboards.

Two-digit tango

Ask a volunteer to choose a target number (1–100) and ask another volunteer to choose a starting number (30–80). Point at children randomly and give them one of the following instructions: add one, subtract one, add 10, or subtract 10 until you reach the target number. Then start again with different target and starting numbers.

Main teaching

Strip swap

Give each group six different number strips with the first number given, followed by five empty squares. Attach an instruction (1 more, 1 less, 10 more, 10 less, 100 more, or 100 less) to each strip with a paper clip. The children pass round the strips, filling in the next empty square according to the instruction attached to it. Then each group should check and correct their strip as necessary. Next, ask the groups to remove the instructions from the completed strips and swap strips with another group. Each group looks at the completed number strips and deduces what the instruction had been for each strip.

Laundry lark

Prepare number cards in sequences going up in ones, tens and hundreds. Give each group a number washing line and a shuffled set of sequence number cards. Ask the groups to peg their cards on the washing line in ascending or descending order. See which group can finish first. Swap cards and repeat.

 ### All in line

Working in pairs, one child gives instructions to count on or back in ones, tens or hundreds. The partner chooses a three-digit starting number but does not say what it is. He or she applies the instructions to the starting number and makes a number line. They check and then swap roles.

 ### Cover the changes

Give each pair of children a set of number cards (0–9). One child makes a three-digit number with three of the cards, reads the number and records it on a whiteboard. The partner changes the number by covering one of the digits with another card and reading the new number. They compare the new number with the original number on the whiteboard and decide how many hundreds, tens or units, were added or taken away. Repeat.

Plenary

Write a three-digit starting number on the board and ask a volunteer to spin a one more, one less, 10 more, 10 less, 100 more, 100 less spinner. Ask the children to write the next three numbers of the sequence obtained by applying the rule indicated on the spinner. Then ask simple word problems involving adding and subtracting one, 10 and 100. (See pupil book page 6).

Common difficulties

Some children may need to revise place value.

Remediation

Give further practice with place value cards and multibase. Revisit the activities in Unit plan 1 and, if necessary, ask the children to explain each step as they go along. Or ask them questions about the hows and whys of their working.

Homework suggestion

Ask the children to write three different digits (1-9). Set a challenge of writing as many different three-digit numbers as they can using the three single digits they wrote. Can they put the numbers in order from the smallest to the largest?

Key point

Proficiency in adding and subtracting one, 10 and 100 to or from different numbers up to 999, is a basic skill necessary for all levels of mathematics.

Related material

 Pupil Book Page 6–7

 PCM 2
SCM 2
ECM 2

 Name that number!
In the games room
Special delivery

mathspace

3

Estimation

Key vocabulary

- estimate
- nearly
- almost
- about
- more
- less
- approximately

Materials

- whiteboards
- twigs with leaves (or pictures of)
- dried beans
- bowls
- dot pictures
- large jar
- marbles

Introduction

Appropriate estimation shows an understanding of numbers as representations of quantity. These activities revise estimating the number of elements in a set. They introduce calculating the difference between the estimate and the actual number of elements in the set, and estimating the position of a point on a number line.

Objectives

 To read and begin to write the vocabulary of estimation and approximation.

 To give a sensible estimate of up to about 100 objects.

To count larger collections by grouping them.

Oral and mental starter

Chant and check

Sit the class in a circle. Give one child a starting number and ask what number another child, sitting four seats away, will say if you are counting in steps of 10. Chant round together to check. Then give one child a starting number, say 15, and ask, "Who is going to say 55, if we are counting in fives? Write that person's name on your whiteboard." Chant round the circle to check.

Branching out

Hold up a twig with leaves on it (or a picture of a branch with leaves). Ask the children to say whether there are more or less than x leaves on the twig. Count to check. Hold up another twig and ask them to tell you about how many leaves there are on the twig using the words, 'nearly' or 'about'. Write these words on the board and then count the leaves to check the answer. Repeat a few times with different twigs and see if the estimates are improving.

Main teaching

Full of beans

Divide the class into groups of four or five and give each group a bowl of dried beans. Each child takes a handful of the dried beans and puts them into a communal bowl. Each child then writes their estimation of how many beans there are in the bowl altogether. Discuss what strategies they used to estimate. What strategies can they use to count the actual amount? Ask them to count the actual amount and see how close they are. Whose strategy works the best?

Spots before my eyes

Give each child a copy of a random dot picture (or a printed text in a book from which to find the number of words). Divide the class into four groups, and assign three of the groups to circle the dots in sets of two, sets of five and sets of ten, respectively. Then ask all four groups to count the total number of dots. Discuss which method is the most effective.

Clap in time

Clap slowly and ask the children to make marks on a piece of paper, first in groups of two, in order to count the claps. Repeat with the children making marks in groups of five, and then groups of 10. Discuss which method is the easiest to count up afterwards.

Metre completer

Draw a blank metre stick divided into different coloured sections, on the board. Say and fill in the two end numbers. Ask the children to estimate where a certain number lies on the line. Ask how they can check and discuss the methods they might use. Then point to a spot about halfway along the stick and ask the children to estimate what the number is.

Plenary

Pass round a large jar of marbles. Ask the children to write down their estimates of how many marbles are in the jar. Discuss their strategies. Suggest the strategy, if necessary, of estimating one layer and then working out approximately how many layers there are. Then ask them to propose a way of counting. Ask volunteers to carry out each of the methods proposed. Discuss the efficiency and relative merits of each method.

Common difficulties

Children sometimes make wild guesses instead of estimates.

Remediation

Break the questions down into smaller quantities to estimate. Gradually increase the quantities to be estimated in order to demonstrate the relationship between the number and the quantities.

Homework suggestion

Ask the children to open a page of their reading book and estimate how many words there are on the page. Count and check. Then turn to the next page and ask whether they think there are more or less on this page and use this information to help estimate the number of words. Count and check how close their estimate is.

Key point

The ability to estimate sensibly before actual calculation is an invaluable skill, alerting pupils, at a glance, to answers that are obviously wrong.

Related material

 Pupil Book Page 8–9

 PCM 3
SCM 3
ECM 3

 Butterflies
Show time

4

Reading a labelled scale

Key vocabulary

- half
- and a half
- just more than
- just less than
- and a bit
- about
- centimetre/s

Materials

- objects of different sizes
- number fans
- tape measures
- rulers
- metre sticks
- different coloured counters
- wiggly line worksheets (RM 1)
- string
- coloured pens

Introduction

Measuring length started in Years 1 and 2 with direct comparison, progressing with the use of non-standard measuring units, until the need for uniform measuring units was recognised. The children were introduced to a basic standard unit, the centimetre, and they learned to measure using a centimetre ruler. In the following activities the children estimate lengths and measure them, reading a labelled scale to the nearest centimetre.

Objectives

 To read scales to the nearest labelled division.

Oral and mental starter

Compare and declare

Show two objects and ask which one is longer and which one is shorter. Continue by showing two different objects and, each time, ask questions of comparison using the following vocabulary pairs: wider/narrower, deeper/shallower, and thicker/thinner. Explain the vocabulary when necessary.

Unseen between

Draw a number line on the board with only the end numbers showing and the spaces in between blank. Ask the children to stand up and show you a number on their number fan that lies between these two end numbers. Start to fill in the missing numbers on the number line and ask the children to sit down when they see their number. If anyone is left standing at the end, it means that their number was not between the two given numbers. Repeat with different starting and end numbers.

Main teaching

Tailor-made

With one child as the model, ask the group to use a tape measure to find the different measurements they need to make a shirt: wrist, shoulder to elbow, elbow to wrist, collar, and neck to waist. They have to draw a large picture of the shirt and label the measurements. Draw a large table and ask each group to fill in their measurements. Compare and discuss the results on the table and ask the rest of the class to guess who the model was in each group.

👥 Tiddlywink trials

One child in the group flicks a red counter from a set starting point and each child estimates the distance of the flick to the nearest centimetre, recording their estimate on their whiteboard. Then one child measures the actual distance and another checks. They see whose estimate was the nearest. Repeat with different coloured counters and see if the estimates become more accurate. Ask why this might be the case.

♟ How long's a piece of string?

Give each child a wiggly line worksheet (RM 1), a piece of string, some coloured pens and a ruler. Ask the children to use the piece of string to measure each of the wiggly lines and make a corresponding coloured mark on their string. Then use the ruler to measure the different lengths. Ask them to record the lengths as x and a bit, nearly x, or about x.

♟ Measure together

Give each child a list of lengths to estimate, for example, the height of your chair, the distance between two desks, the height of a desk, the width of a chair, the width of a doorway. Then ask each child to find a partner and measure the actual lengths together. Who has the closest estimate in each case?

Plenary

Ask the children to estimate the length of: a small step (toe to heel), an ordinary step, a large step, a small jump, and a leap. Record some of the estimates on the board. Ask two volunteers to carry out each of the actions and use chalk on the floor to record the results. Then measure the chalk lines to the nearest centimetre using a metre stick. Discuss why the results of the two volunteers may be different. Discuss which of the estimates are realistic or sensible and what would be an unrealistic estimate.

Common difficulties

Accurate measuring can be a problem for some children. Some children begin measuring from one instead of zero on the scale, or from the physical beginning of the ruler, or even from the wrong end of the scale.

Remediation

Emphasise that the beginning of the line or object being measured needs to be aligned with the zero. Ask the children to measure a 1cm object and show how absurd the results would be if the ruler were not aligned with the zero.

Homework suggestion

Set the children a task to find objects at home that have a length of about 10 cm long, three that are about 20 cm long and three that are 30 cm long.

5

Number facts up to 20

Materials

- number cards (0–20)
- multiples of 10 to 100 number cards
- multiples of 100 to 1000 number cards
- interlocking cubes
- whiteboards
- number tracks (0–10)
- bingo cards
- a timer
- three dice

Introduction

These activities revise addition and subtraction number facts up to 20, concentrating on all pairs that make 20.

Objectives

- To recall addition and subtraction facts for each number to at least 20.
- Add three single-digit numbers mentally.

Oral and mental starter

 Snap happy

Give each child a number card (0–10). Ask the children to stand and hold up their cards. Ask a volunteer to pick a number card (0–10) from another pack that is shuffled and laid face down on the table. Then ask the volunteer to call out the number that he or she has picked. Ask all the children holding the number that totals 10 with the picked number to call out snap and sit down. When everyone has sat down, play again with multiples of 10 to make 100, and then again with multiples of 100 to make 1000.

 Winner at the wall

Ask two volunteers to stand back to back at the midway point between two accessible walls. Ask quick-fire addition and subtraction questions for facts up to 10. The first of the two to answer correctly, takes one step forward towards the wall he or she is facing. When one child reaches the wall they return to the middle to play against a new challenger while the other child sits down.

Main teaching

 It's a stick up!

One child in the group holds up a 'magic stick' of up to 20 inter-locking cubes. Each member of the group records the number of cubes in the stick on their whiteboards. The child holding the stick then hides it behind his or her back and snaps some of it off. They bring back one of the two parts and show the group. In order to find out the number of cubes that were snapped off the stick the children then have to write a subtraction sentence starting with the original number. The other part of the stick is brought out for them to check their answers. Repeat until all the children in the group have had a turn breaking the stick. Extension: Ask what pairs of numbers add up to 20.

👥 Total cover

Give each child a grid of six random numbers (0–10) and each group a set of number cards (0–20). Shuffle the number cards and place them face down in the middle. Give a target number up to 20. The children take turns to pick a card from the middle. If the card they pick and a number on their grid adds up to the target number, they cover that number on their grid and pick another card. If they cannot go, they return the card to the middle and the next child has their turn. The winner is the first to cover all their numbers. Play again with another target number. Make sure the target number is 20 in one of the rounds.

👤 The great cross out!

Give each child a bingo card with the numbers 0–20. Call out target numbers up to 20 and ask the children to cross out two numbers on their card that make the target. After each go they explain their choice of numbers to their neighbour. If the neighbour disagrees they can ask you to check the answer. Ask for all the different number combinations used and write them on the board. Extend the activity by asking for three numbers that make the target. After a few goes, some children may not be able to make every target with the numbers they have left. Allow them to be creative and use subtraction to reach the target. The first person to cross out all their numbers is the winner.

👤 Target trials

Write a target number up to 20 on the board. Set a timer for two minutes and see how many number sentences each child can write resulting in the target number. The number sentences can be addition or subtraction and include up to three terms. When the time is up, choose a volunteer to write their answers on the board. Ask if anyone can suggest any other number sentences. Repeat the activity and ask the children to see if they can beat their own record.

Plenary

Display a large number line up to 20. Ask two volunteers to each roll a die and the other children to write the total. Then ask which number they have to add to it to reach 20. Record the matching number sentences on the board. Repeat until all possible combinations have been rolled and then extend to rolling three dice. End with addition and subtraction fact questions up to 20.

Common difficulties

Some children still need physical representation to understand number facts, especially facts with three terms.

Remediation

Provide a lot of practice by using the starter activities in this book. Allow those who need it to use counters or cubes to represent their working.

Homework suggestion

Toss two 5p, two 2p and two 1p coins. Add up the values of those that land on heads and find the total. Write at least four different additions of any pairs of numbers that add up to the same total.

Key point

Knowing basic addition and subtraction number facts by heart makes mathematics easier and speeds up the calculation process. It enables the children to focus on the problem and other, higher mathematical considerations.

Related material

Pupil Book Page 12–13

PCM 5
SCM 5
ECM 5

In the recording studio

Ziggy's solar system

Ziggy's art gallery

35

Addition

Key vocabulary

- double
- near double

Materials

- number cards (0–20)
- spinners (1–15)
- spinners (1–10)
- instruction cards
- whiteboards

6

Introduction

These activities review the properties of addition, including the fact that it is commutative and that it can involve more than two numbers. The strategy of putting the larger number first to facilitate calculation is revised and the children are encouraged to use other strategies such as, doubles and near doubles, or looking for pairs that make 10 or 20 and doing these first.

Objectives

- Use knowledge that addition can be done in any order to do mental calculations more efficiently.
- Identify near doubles using doubles already known.
  - To add several numbers.

Oral and mental starter

 ### Guard of honour

Ask two children to stand up. Hold up a number card (0–10) and say the number aloud. The first child to say the number that is added to this number to make 10, wins the round. The other child sits down and is replaced with a different challenger and the competition continues. Repeat for numbers that total 20 using number cards from 0 to 20.

 ### Double spin

Spin a spinner (1–15) and ask the children to write the 'double' addition sentence and work out the total for example, 14 + 14 = 28. Extension: Ask them to write a 'near double' addition using the same number as part of the addition and write the total for example, 14 + 13 = 27, 14 + 15 = 29. Discuss the two different near doubles and how they are obtained. Spin again and repeat the activity.

Main teaching

 ### Superior strategies

Give each group three sets of number cards (0–9) shuffled together and put face down in a pile. One child turns over three cards and finds the total. He or she explains their method of working. The group suggests other methods for working out the result and tries to find strategies to apply to these particular numbers. They discuss the most efficient method. If necessary, remind them of the strategies they have learned so far, for example, finding pairs that total 10 or 20, doubles and near doubles, bridging through 10, putting the larger number first, and number facts.

👥 Double or quits

Divide the class into groups of four. Give each group one spinner (0–9) and a second spinner (0–15). One child spins the first spinner and two children take turns spinning the second spinner and they all write their results in pairs. The fourth child identifies any pair of numbers that are doubles or near doubles and then works out the total. If there are none, then the group discusses which strategies they could use instead.

♟ Answers for names

Ask each child to write an addition of three numbers, in which two of them add up to 10. They show their addition to their neighbour who has to say which pair equals 10 and what the total is. If they are correct, they write down whose addition they solved. Ask one child from each pair to change seats and continue with new additions. Then repeat with writing additions of three numbers, in which two of them add up to 20. How many names can each child collect?

♟ No trouble doubles

Prepare a pack of number cards (0–15) and a separate pile of instruction cards ('same again', 'one more', 'one less', and 'pick again'). Choose three volunteers. One child picks a number card and you write the number on the board. The other two children pick instruction cards and look at the number on the board to tell you what the other two numbers are. Then ask the rest of the class to work out the total of the three numbers and explain their working. Discuss the strategies used.

Plenary

Write an addition of three one-digit numbers on the board. Ask the children to write the total on their whiteboards. Discuss the different strategies used, for example, doubles, near doubles, bridging through 10, number facts, numbers that make 10 or 20, and/or putting the larger number first. Repeat with different additions using each strategy. Remember that all strategies should be encouraged, even if they are not the most efficient. Extend to additions where the doubles and near doubles are up to 15, or multiples of 10 up to 100. For each strategy that the children suggest, give exercises in which its application is the most efficient.

Common difficulties

Children may have difficulty identifying pairs that make 10 or 20, or identifying doubles or near doubles.

Remediation

Give plenty of practice in the above skills using different activities, for example, play pairs, where making 10 (or 20, double, or near double) is the requirement for the pair. Children should aim to know all number facts for 10 and 20 by heart.

Homework suggestion

Ask the children to write down their phone numbers including the dialling code and split them into groups of three. Ask them to add each set of three single digits together (and write which method they used).

Key point

A variety of addition strategies are useful for problem solving. Children need to know all of these in order to be able to decide which is the most efficient in any given situation.

Related material

📖 Pupil Book Page 14–15

PCM 6
SCM 6
ECM 6

💿 Target practice

Off the beaten track

Flower power

Addition strategies

7

Key vocabulary

- bridging
- multiples

Materials

- number cards (11–30)
- 100 squares
- coloured counters
- metre sticks
- whiteboards

Introduction

The children already know various strategies for adding two numbers together such as, addition facts, doubles, near doubles and bridging through 10. In these activities they revise adding and subtracting 9 and 11 using the mental strategy of adding or subtracting 10 and adjusting by one. They extend their knowledge to bridging through a multiple of 10 and adjusting by one, and to using this strategy for adding a one-digit number to a two-digit number.

Objectives

 To bridge through a multiple of 10, then adjust.

 To add and subtract mentally a 'near multiple of 10' to or from a two-digit number.

Oral and mental starter

💬 Round ups to ten

Hold up a two-digit number and ask the children to write down the number that needs to be added to reach the next multiple of 10. Repeat with other numbers.

💬 Make a break

Write a target two-digit number on the board. Go round the class asking children to say a pair of numbers that add up to this number. After a few proposals, change the target number.

Main teaching

Fine tuning

In groups of four, the children turn over a starting number card (11–30). First they add 10 to the starting number, then they add nine to it, and finally, they add 11 to the same original starting number. Ask them to discuss their strategies. Introduce the strategy of 'adding 10 and adjusting by 1'. Then they turn over another starting number card and one child says the number plus 10, the next child says the number plus nine, and the third child gives the number plus 11. The fourth child has to check and award a point for each correct answer. Swap roles and repeat several times. Then repeat the activity this time subtracting nine and 11 from the starting number.

The bridges of maths and counters

Give each group a 100 square and a spinner (1–9). Each child starts
with a counter on 100. They spin and subtract the number indicated.
If they have to pass a multiple of 10, they split the number to be
taken away so that they land on the multiple of 10 and then subtract
the remainder. For example, 57 – 8 is expressed as 57 – 7 = 50 – 1 = 49.
Each child wins a counter when they successfully bridge through 10
and the first to finish gets three extra counters. This activity can also
be used with addition, starting on the one.

 ## Crossing bridges

Give each pair of children a numbered metre stick or a laminated 0–100
number line. Write a two-digit number on the board and ask the
children to put a counter on that number as the starting spot. Then
complete the addition with a one-digit number, making sure the answer
involves bridging through 10. Ask the children to write the addition as
three numbers added together and find the total. For example, 36 + 9 is
written as 36 + 4 + 5 = 45. Ask a volunteer to use a number line to show
the bridging through 10 method. Repeat with subtraction.

Adjustment bingo

Each child writes down six two-digit numbers. Write a two-digit starting
number on the board and ask the children to add nine or 11, or subtract
nine or 11, and see if they can make one of the numbers in their list. If
they can, they write the number sentence under the number and cross it
out. The first to cross out all six numbers shouts, "Bingo!"

Plenary

Write a simple number sentence on the board, for example, 8 + 9. Ask
the children to suggest ways to work out the result. Some of the
strategies they know are: bridge through 10, near doubles, number
facts, write the larger number first and count on, adding 10 and
subtracting one. Repeat with more difficult questions involving a
two-digit number. Discuss and explain the strategies each time.

Common difficulties

Some children may still count up or back and not use any of the
other strategies. Children may still need concrete representation.

Remediation

Start with quickfire drill and practice of number facts of 10. Then give
extra practice adding a one-digit number without crossing a tens
boundary. Finally, talk through the methods again using a number
line and ask the children to draw each step with dots or by colouring
squares on a 100 square.

Homework suggestion

Ask the children to write three addition and three subtraction
number sentences that includes a one-digit number and a two-digit
number and involves crossing a multiple of 10. Ask them to write a
number story for one of their additions and one of their subtractions.

Key point

Developing mental
calculation strategies
facilitates and speeds
up problem solving.

Related material

 Pupil Book
Page 16–17

 PCM 7
SCM 7
ECM 7

 Balloon guns

On track

Name that
number!

Bring in the
hay!

8

Understanding addition and subtraction

Key vocabulary

- difference
- sum
- total
- altogether
- How many...?

Materials

- number cards (11–20)
- whiteboards
- number cards (30–60)
- bus tickets
- coins
- bingo cards
- counters
- counting apparatus
- price tags
- instruction cards

Introduction

Addition and subtraction are essential skills for solving many different kinds of problems including joining, combining, computing a difference and reducing. The following activities require the use of addition and subtraction in a variety of contexts, and consequently, extend the children's understanding of both these operations.

Objectives

- To extend understanding of the operations of addition and subtraction.
- To read and begin to write related vocabulary.
- Use the +, - and = signs.

Oral and mental starter

Method reminder

Ask a volunteer to take a number card (11–20) from a shuffled pack and use this as the target number. Ask the children to record on their whiteboards three numbers that make the target number. Ask for some answers and write them on the board. Discuss the most efficient strategy for adding each set of numbers. Repeat with different target numbers.

Count the ways

Write a target number (up to 20) on the board. Go around the class asking for any addition or subtraction sentence, with up to three terms, that makes the target number. See how many you can find for one number. If a number sentence is repeated either the child has to think again or start again with another target number.

Main teaching

What's the problem?

Give each group a set of number cards (30–60) and a set of instruction cards (find the difference, take away, subtract, find the sum, how many altogether, find the total, how many more/less). The children take two number cards and an instruction card. They have to use the three cards to devise a matching number sentence and then solve it using apparatus if necessary. Then they have to discuss the best strategy to use for that particular problem and why.

🚶 Fares please

One child in the group acts as the bus conductor. The others take turns to buy a ticket from a set price between 20p and 40p. They pay with a 50p coin and work out the change using complementary addition (counting up from the fare to the amount given). Extend to larger amounts and change from a £1 coin.

🧍 Problem bingo

Give each child a bingo card with two-digit numbers. Call the numbers in the form of addition and subtraction problems, using a range of different vocabulary. Make sure that the children have access to apparatus to help them work out the problems. If they have the answer on their card, they cover it with a counter. Check and discuss the strategies they use.

🧍 Inflation complication

Prepare a set of 'old' price tags with prices between 10p and 98p, and which are at least 11p apart in price. Prepare a second set of price tags that are 1p to 10p more than each of the tags in the first set. Give each child a set of each price tags shuffled together. Explain that all the original prices have gone up by 1p to 10p and a new set of price tags have been made, but the price tags have all been mixed up. The child has to match up the pairs of price tags and say by how much the price has gone up. Discuss the different ways of finding the pairs and finding the difference between the prices. Repeat the activity with the prices going down by having the 'old' price tags as the 'new' price tags and vice versa.

Plenary

Give simple problems similar to the ones proposed in the pupil book. Ask the children to explain the strategies they choose to solve the problems. Show that the same problem can sometimes be solved by using addition or subtraction. Discuss the different strategies available in each case and which are the most effective for any given situation.

Common difficulties

Some children have difficulty with the range of vocabulary. They may think that 'difference' means comparing the size of a number. Some children may count on including the final number instead of starting from the next number.

Remediation

Practise giving change in a shop which uses the counting on method. Use coins or counters to model the operation. Make a group of the smaller number and then add counters as you count on from the next number.

Homework suggestion

Ask the children to draw two columns and label them 'add' and 'subtract'. Ask them to write as many different words or phrases that belong in each column. They can use a thesaurus to help.

Key point

Understanding that addition and subtraction are useful in situations other than 'How many altogether' or 'How many are left?' enriches the children's knowledge of these basic operations.

Related material

 Pupil Book Page 18–19

 PCM 8
SCM 8
ECM 8

 What's the question?

Cinema problems

Country road

Alien quiz time

Key vocabulary

- pounds
- pence

Materials

- imitation coins up to £2
- imitation £5, £10, and £20 notes
- whiteboards
- blank cards
- pictures of sale items
- dice
- a spinner (1–15)

Money

Introduction

By now the children are familiar with coins but need to start working with notes in order to deal with higher denominations. The following activities revise the values of the different coins and the standard notations: £x.y and xp. £5, £10, and £20 notes are introduced at this stage and also word problems involving money.

Objectives

- To recognise all coins and notes.
- To understand and use £.p notation.
- To solve word problems involving money.

Oral and mental starter

Small change

Give all the children access to the full range of coins. Write a target amount on the board in pence. Ask which coins make up the amount using the fewest coins. Then repeat using amounts written as £s and p, up to £2.

The price is right

Give each child a blank card and ask them to write 'cheaper' on one side and 'more expensive' on the other. Hold up a picture of an item with its price written on the back. Ask one child to guess the price of the item and all the others to stand up and hold up their cards showing 'cheaper' or 'more expensive' according to what they think. Turn the picture around and all those who were wrong have to sit down. The others get a point. The first person with ten points is the winner.

Main teaching

Break the bank

Note: Before the main activities introduce the £5, £10 and £20 notes.

Ask the children in each group to nominate a banker. Give the banker a set of imitation £1 and £2 coins and some imitation £5 and £10 notes and one £20 note. The others in the group take turns to roll a die and collect that number of pounds in coins from the bank. Each time they make enough money to swap the coins for a note they make the transaction with the banker. When they have two £5 notes they have to swap them for a £10 note and so on. They write down how much they rolled each time. After four rolls they check how much by swapping with a partner who works out using coins how much their friend has. The first person to claim the £20 note is the winner and becomes the banker in the next round.

👥 Loadsa money!

Each child in the group takes a turn to roll three dice together. They arrange and record their three numbers so that they make the biggest three-digit number possible. This is the amount in pence. They then have to write the amount in £.p notation. Ask the group to compare and discuss their answers. Which combinations of notes and coins could they use to make the amounts? Which combination requires the fewest number of notes and coins for each amount?

👤 Cash combinations

Give all the children access to the full range of notes and coins up to £20. Ask them to choose an amount up to £50 and write it in £s and pence on their whiteboards. Ask a volunteer to write their amount on the board. Ask the others to work out which money they could use to make this amount. See how many different ways they can suggest and write the combinations on the board.

👤 The weight in your wallet

Give all the children access to the full range of notes and coins up to £20. Choose three volunteers to spin a spinner (1–15) and write their number on the board. Ask the children to take that many 1p coins for the first number, 10p coins for the second number, and £1 coins for the third number. How much money do they have? Ask them to write the amount in £s and pence. Then ask them to swap the coins for larger denominations where possible. How can they make the amount using the fewest notes and coins possible? Repeat with three different numbers.

Plenary

Show pictures of items priced up to £9.99. Ask the children to draw the notes and coins needed to buy the item on their whiteboards. Give the children access to notes and coins for working out. Extend to prices up to £50. Ask what the change would be from £10 for objects priced up to £9.99.

Common difficulties

Prices of £10 and over have a four-digit number of pence which children may find overwhelming.

Remediation

Model the amounts using an exchange activity where smaller amounts are swapped for bigger denominations until the whole amount can be 'seen' in £s and pence rather than just pence. Amounts over £10 pounds are not usually referred to in pence.

Homework suggestion

Find out by going to the shop with a parent, or looking in a shopping catalogue, three suggestions of items for each price: about £1, £2, £5, £10 and £20.

Key point

The £.p notation has real life relevance and is a useful tool towards fluency with decimal numbers.

Related material

Pupil Book Page 20–21

PCM 9
SCM 9
ECM 9

Changing money

At the checkout

Going shopping

43

Money problems

Key vocabulary

- operation

Materials

- whiteboards
- items for sale
- price cards
- cafe menus
- coins and notes
- word problems (RM 4)
- kiosk price list

Introduction

The children revised coins and learned about notes in Unit plan 9. The following activities focus on money problems, both written and in practical situations. The children are encouraged to check their results and not just trust the calculation, even if the result contradicts their intuition. They also practise finding totals and giving change while working out which notes and coins to use.

Objectives

 To choose and use appropriate operations to solve word problems and find appropriate ways of calculating.

 To find totals, give change and work out which coins and notes to use.

Oral and mental starter

Swings and roundabouts

Say amounts in pence (up to 999p) and ask the children to write on their whiteboards, that amount in £.p. notation. Then reverse the question, for example, how many pence is £1.25?

In the price range

Show an item and a possible price range, for example, a watch costs between £x and £y. Ask what the price could be? Show cards with amounts in pounds and pence and ask the children which amounts fit the criteria for the price of the watch. Repeat with other items and different price ranges.

Main teaching

 ### Self service

Give each group a cafe menu with prices in multiples of 5p, including those with a zero such as £1.05. Give each child £10 and ask them to order two of the same item. They have to write out their own bill and work out how much they have to pay. If necessary, the children may use coins to model the amount. The children have to explain and demonstrate to the group how they calculated the bill and the group checks that the results are correct. Then they have to compute the change they will get from their £10.

What's the problem?

Give each group a copy of RM4. Each child writes a number sentence for each problem and then they compare their answers. Have coins available for children to use. Ask if the group can check the results using an inverse operation or a different method.

Stamp duty

Give each child a set of coins and ask them to work out the amount of change they would get for each coin, when buying an 18p stamp. Ask them to explain their working methods to their neighbour and to draw the coins. Then ask them to write the calculations as number sentences.

Pound shop

With the children working in pairs, give each pair a price list of items for sale at the kiosk. Ask each child to make a list of things they can buy for exactly a pound. They have to write the matching addition sentence and then show their partner the coins for each item. They can check the total by swapping the smaller coins for higher denominations until they reach £1. Extend to a budget of £5 and then £10.

Plenary

Write a simple addition word problem involving money on the board, for example, Michael bought a hamburger for £1.50 and an orange juice for £1.10. Ask what the question could be, for example, How much did he pay? What change did he get from £5? Choose one suggestion, then ask one child to read the problem, another to identify the relevant information, and then ask all the children to solve the problem. Discuss the strategies used, especially how they checked their answers. Repeat with other simple money problems.

Common difficulties

Children often do not read the problem carefully or do not understand the question. Sometimes they do not choose an appropriate number operation. Some children may not understand the role of the zero in amounts such as £3.05.

Remediation

During the checking stage of a problem, carefully guide the children through all six stages of the method (read the problem, circle the question, find relevant information, develop a solving strategy and implement it - steps five and six from Year 2 method are now combined - write the answer, check it.) If needed, use graphical or concrete representation. Give practice making up amounts with a zero in them, using coins. Then extend to adding the amounts and recording results. Give coins of amounts with a zero and ask them to count and record the total.

Homework suggestion

Ask the children to find an old receipt for less than £20. Ask them to work out what coins or notes they could use to pay the bill and how much change they would expect to receive.

Key point

Problem solving is one of the most important and most interesting topics in mathematics. Developing good habits and learning to work systematically without skipping stages is invaluable at higher levels of problem solving.

Related material

Pupil Book Page 22–23

PCM 10
SCM 10
ECM 10

In Ziggy's shop

Drawing and measuring lines

Key vocabulary

- centimetre/s
- half
- length

Materials

- whiteboards
- pencils
- centimetre rulers (with half centimetres marked)
- bookmarks
- cardboard strips
- drawing paper

Introduction

Unit plan 5 focused on measuring length in centimetres. The following activities extend this knowledge to measuring and drawing line segments to the nearest half centimetre.

Objectives

 To read and begin to write the vocabulary related to length.

To use a ruler to draw and measure lines to the nearest half centimetre.

Oral and mental starter

 Measuring up

Ask the children to each take a pencil and measure and record its length to the nearest centimetre. Then ask them to swap pencils with their neighbour and measure and record the length of their neighbour's pencil. The children compare their measurements and if there is a difference they measure again, checking how they position the ruler and how they read the answer. Ask questions to elicit the longest and the shortest pencils measured.

Comparative I spy

Choose an object from around the room. Write some comparative adjectives on the board, such as: narrower, wider, longer, shorter, deeper and shallower. Then hold up an object and say, *"The object I am thinking of is ... than this."* The child who guesses correctly chooses the next object.

Main teaching

 Bookmark lark

Give each group a set of bookmarks with lengths of exact half centimetres. Ask the children to measure each bookmark and notice precisely where the measurement falls between two whole centimetre values. The group needs to find a way to record the measurements. Discuss their propositions and introduce the notation x.5 cm for half centimetres.

👥 Measure for measure

Give each group a pencil case containing pencils of different lengths. Each child measures one pencil, draws a line that is the same length to the nearest half centimetre then records its length on the back of the paper. They then order the lengths. Finally, they lay out the pencils using the proposed order and see if they were accurate.

👤 Kite flying

Ask each child to draw a kite using four straight lines and a wiggly tail. Ask them to measure the lenghts of the sides, and to label the measurements to the nearest half centimetre (written as x.5 cm). They can use a piece of string to measure the tail. Then they swap drawings with a partner and check the measurements on their partner's kite. Are their results the same?

👤 Triangle tangles

Ask each child to draw two sides of a triangle with lengths of 4 cm and 5 cm. Ask them to join the two open ends to form a triangle. Then have them measure the third side to the nearest half centimetre. Did they all get the same length? Can they look at the triangles and say why not? Repeat with sides of 2 cm and 5 cm, and with 3 cm and 7 cm.

Plenary

Write various lengths in whole and half centimetres on the board. Ask the children to draw two lines using these lengths, one that is in whole centimetres and one that ends in half centimetres, and label them. Collect all the papers and redistribute them randomly. Ask the children to check the measurements of all the lines on the paper they have. There is no need to know who drew the original lines on each paper. The papers can also be double checked to make absolutely sure.

Common difficulties

Children may not measure from the zero. They may have problems handling the ruler, measuring and drawing all in one operation.

Remediation

Emphasise that we measure from the zero. Ask the children to draw a 1 cm line and see if it looks the same as 1 cm on the ruler. Work with the children showing them exactly how to hold a ruler, where to position their hands, and how to make sure the pencil stays against the ruler edge.

Homework suggestion

Ask the children to find and measure to the nearest half centimetre five small objects at home, then draw lines with a ruler that they think are the same length as the objects and check their measurements.

Measuring length

Key vocabulary

- metre/s
- kilometre/s
- length
- distance

Materials

- whiteboards
- rulers
- tape measures
- metre sticks
- stopwatch or timers

Introduction

The following activities introduce the metre and the kilometre for measuring lengths greater than those for which centimetres are appropriate. The children start to consider which unit of measurement is suitable to measure any of the objects and distances in their environment. Explain that we like to work with small numbers so it is more convenient to measure in metres when a length is hundreds of centimetres long. The children also learn to take the units into account so that even if the number is larger, it does not mean that the length is greater, for example, 2 m is longer than 150 cm.

Objectives

 To know the relationships between kilometres and metres and between metres and centimetres.

– To suggest suitable units and measuring equipment to estimate or measure length.

Oral and mental starter

 I measured the window in metres

Play a variation of 'I went to market'. Go round the class saying an object and whether you measured it in metres or centimetres (or you could say, "*... using a metre stick/a tape measure/a ruler.*"). Each child says all the examples that came before and then adds on their own. When a mistake is made in the chain, the next child starts again with one example.

 What's my line?

Ask each child to draw a line on their whiteboards, measure it with a ruler and label the length in centimetres. Ask them to find another child and compare to see if their line is longer, shorter or the same length as their own. When they return to their seats, ask volunteers to say who they found. Ask them both to hold up their whiteboards so that the class can check.

Main teaching

 Wider and wider

Ask each child in the group to write on their whiteboards their own estimate of the width of the classroom in metres and centimetres. The group measures together choosing their measuring instrument. Whose estimate was the nearest? Discuss the different ways of measuring and their relative advantages. Repeat with a different length to measure.

👥 Gone walkabout

Mark out 10 m in the playground and ask the groups to walk this distance, counting their steps. Ask them how many steps they think would be needed to walk 100 m. Ask one volunteer to walk this number of steps while the rest of the group count in tens to find the actual distance, for example 400 steps was between 8 and 9 metres. Ask them to choose a volunteer to walk the hundred metres (10 m ten times) and the rest of the group time them. Then ask how many steps would be needed to walk 1000 m. Explain that 1000 m is 1 km. How long do they think it would take to walk 1 km? Finally take the class on a half kilometre walk around the playground with a number of children timing how long it takes.

♟ Hop, skip and a jump

In the hall or playground, ask each child to do a hop, skip and a jump starting from the same starting line. Then ask them to suggest the units to measure the distance and explain their choice. Repeat with two hops, skips and jumps.

♟ Local landmarks

If possible, walk half a kilometre around the playground with the class and time how long it takes. Return to the classroom and draw the school and some local landmarks (the park, leisure centre, shops, church,) on the board, with the distances roughly to scale. Draw a line between the school and each place and ask the children to guess how far each one is from the school. Discuss the distances in terms of the length and how long it takes to get there by car or walking. Write in the real distances in metres and ask how many kilometres this would be. Discuss which notation is more convenient.

Plenary

Write two measurements using different units and ask the children to compare them, for example, 150 cm and 2 m, or 3 km and 2500 m. What would be their first step towards solving such a problem? Write some lengths, in centimetres, metres, and kilometres, on the board and ask the children to suggest objects or distances that are about these lengths.

Common difficulties

Children may not have developed their own concepts of distance sufficiently to be able to suggest appropriate units of measurement. They may have difficulty expressing and comparing the same measurement with different units.

Remediation

Discuss instances where distances are recorded in real life, for example, on motorway signs. Walk various distances (10 m, 100 m, 1 km,) with the children. Show that 1 m = 100 cm and 1 km = 1000 m by lining up multibase where one cube represents 1 m.

Homework suggestion

Ask the children to find example/s of 'objects that have lengths or heights of...' or 'two places that have a distance between them of...'. for the following measurements: 1 cm, 10 cm, 1 m, 10 m, 1 km, 10 km.

Key point

Choosing the appropriate unit to measure objects and distances is a basic scientific skill.

Related material

Pupil Book
Page 26-27

PCM 12
SCM 12
ECM 12

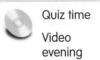
Quiz time
Video evening

Estimating and measuring

Key vocabulary

- centimetre/s
- metre/s
- mixed units

Materials

- rulers
- metre sticks
- tape measures
- charts
- ribbons
- whiteboards
- area labels

Introduction

The previous unit plan focused on the three main measuring units. In the following activities the children learn to estimate lengths and check by exact measuring. They also learn to write a length expressed in mixed units, for example, 3 m 40 cm.

Objectives

- To record estimates and measurements to the nearest whole or half unit, or in mixed units.

Oral and mental starter

Grand handspans

Ask each child to draw around their hand and then draw a line, using a ruler, from the tip of their little finger to the tip of their thumb. Ask them to measure and label the line in centimetres to the nearest half centimetre. Then ask them to find a partner and check each other's measurement. Extension: Prepare cards with lines of different lengths drawn on them. Give each child a line card. Ask the children to measure their line and then find someone who has a line that is either half or double their length. Another pair checks if that pair is correct.

One foot up, one foot down is how you get to London Town

Write centimetres, metres and kilometres on the board. Ask: *"What would you use to measure the distance from Newcastle to London?"* The children write the appropriate unit on their whiteboards and hold them up. Discuss the answers and repeat with other lengths and distances.

Main teaching

Triple long jump

Ask one child in the group to jump as far as they can. Ask the other children to estimate the length of the jump and then estimate what the length would be if the same child jumped three times. They record their estimates in centimetres. Ask the child to jump three times and the group measures the distance in metres and centimetres. They convert their estimates to centimetres and see who was closest to the actual distance. Discuss the methods used to estimate, measure and convert.

👥 Strength in length

Give each group a recording chart with headings: 'less than 1 m', '1 m–2 m', '2 m–3 m', and 'more than 3 m'. Ask the children to look around the room and find objects that belong in each column. Then ask them to measure the different lengths and see if they were correct. Ask them to record each length in mixed units.

♟ Flog it!

Put different length ribbons in a bag. Conduct an estimate auction. Draw out a ribbon, show it to the children and discuss what they think the starting bid should be. Then ask them to bid in half centimetre bids and to record the bid they make. They each have one bid. If they think someone else has the right bid, they write down the name of the bidder. When the bidding stops ask a volunteer to measure the ribbon and see who had the correct bid and who else wrote down that bidder's name.

♟ Areas of estimation

Label four areas of the room: 0–0.5 m, 0.5 m–1 m, 1 m–1.5 m and more than 1.5 m. Hold up an object and ask the children to stand in the area where they think the label correctly describes the length. Then ask one child to measure the object to the nearest half metre. Next, all the children in the right area give an estimate to the nearest centimetre, using mixed units. The child with the nearest estimate wins a point. If no one stood in the correct corner to begin with, you win the point.

Plenary

Ask the children to estimate in centimetres the width of the classroom. Then ask volunteers to measure it in any way they choose (with a helper if necessary). Compare the methods and the results. Ask the children to record their measurements in centimetres and in mixed units, metres and centimetres. Then write a three-digit length in centimetres on the board. Ask the children to record it in mixed units. Repeat with a length in mixed units which the children record in centimetres. Then repeat with other lengths.

Common difficulties

Estimation of lengths and distances is quite complex for many children. Converting length to or from mixed units is often difficult.

Remediation

The more practice the children have estimating lengths and distances, and then checking the actual measurements, the more accurate their estimates will become. Let the children measure with different equipment, for example, using metre sticks and rulers.

Homework suggestion

Draw a plan of a room in your house and write your estimate to the nearest cm in mixed units of the length height and width of the room and of different objects – windows, doors etc.

Classifying shapes

Key vocabulary

- pentagon
- hexagon
- octagon
- semi-circle
- circular
- pentagonal
- hexagonal
- octagonal
- prism
- hemisphere

Materials

- squares of paper
- 2-D shapes
- 3-D shapes
- whiteboards
- feely bags
- property cards
- quadrilaterals
- prisms
- geo-strips
- statement cards

Introduction

These activities focus on the revision of 2-D and 3-D shapes. The children learn to identify their main properties, and especially, to recognise right angles.

Objectives

● To classify and describe 2-D and 3-D shapes.

● To identify right angles in 2-D shapes in the environment.

● To investigate general statements about familiar shapes by finding examples that satisfy it.

Oral and mental starter

 Right angle hunt

Give each child a piece of paper. Ask them to fold it carefully to form a right-angled corner. Then ask them, with a partner, to find right angles in the classroom. How many different examples can they find? Give the children a time limit and then compare the findings.

 All ship shape

Place a collection of familiar 2-D and 3-D shapes, labelled with numbers, on your table. Say: *"Record the number of the sphere on your whiteboards."* Repeat with the other shapes. Then pass round one of the shapes. Ask the children to show you the number of faces, edges or sides, corners and right angles.

Main teaching

 Matching properties

Give each group a set of 2-D shapes in a feely bag, including pentagons, hexagons, octagons, semi-circles and different four-sided shapes (quadrilaterals). Prepare a set of cards with the properties of the 2-D shapes in the bag, for example, half of a circle, no right angles, four straight sides, five equal sides, and three vertices. Ask the children, in turn, to take a shape out of the bag and match it to one of the cards. Repeat with 3-D shapes. Include a prism and a hemisphere. Use clues such as, a sphere cut in half, a triangular face at each end and a circular flat face.

Describing the details

Give the group a set of various quadrilaterals. Ask the children to look at the shapes carefully and write their own descriptions for each shape. Then compare and discuss their answers with another group. What do they notice? Repeat with a set of various prisms.

Technical writing

Give each child a set of geo-strips. Ask them to make a 2-D shape with five or more sides and then to write a set of instructions for another child to make the same shape. Swap instructions and see if the other child is able to follow them accurately.

Detective work

Give each child a statement card about shapes with right angles to investigate. For example, all four-sided shapes have right angles or, all squares are rectangles. Can they find shapes that prove or disprove the statement? How do they know they have the right answer?

Plenary

On the board, draw a decision tree with empty boxes for the questions and 'yes' and 'no' arrows coming out of the top of each box. One child thinks of a shape, the others ask questions to elicit yes/no answers until they arrive at the name of the shape. For example: Is it a 3-D shape? No. Does it have straight sides? Yes. Does it have a right angle? Yes. Does it have four sides? No. Does it have three sides? Yes. Is it a triangle? Yes. Repeat with other shapes.

Common difficulties

Some children may need help to recognise the different types of prisms. They may be familiar with the vocabulary 'semi' to describe a half shape but not 'hemi'. They may encounter difficulty investigating general statements about shapes.

Remediation

Demonstrate the cross section and the end faces by cutting a prism in different places. Give the children a set of prisms with spheres, hemi-spheres and cylinders to sort and match to labels. Begin with very simple general statements, for example, rectangles have four right angles.

Homework suggestion

At home or in the shop look for boxes and cartons that are different prisms. Cut the empty cartons open and count and record the faces and edges.

Key point

Experience of and knowledge about shapes and their properties develops children's spatial awareness. Children need to develop strategies to check the truth of basic mathematical statements and to be aware that statements can and should be checked.

Related material

 Pupil Book Page 30-31

 PCM 14
SCM 14
ECM 14

 At the amphi-theatre

Shape table

Arty shapes

mathspace

15

Position

Key vocabulary

- grid
- row
- column
- co-ordinates
- horizontal
- vertical

Materials

- squared paper
- coins
- island maps
- whiteboards
- masking tape
- direction cards

Introduction

During Year 2, children learned the basic vocabulary of position, direction and movement, and how to describe the relative positions of objects on a grid. These activities revise the above and extend it to simple co-ordinates, and position vocabulary such as horizontal, vertical and diagonal. As a first step, children learn how to find the co-ordinates of squares in questions where the columns are labelled with letters and rows with numbers.

Objectives

- To read and begin to write the vocabulary related to position, direction and movement.

Oral and mental starter

 Grid gala

Use floor tiles or masking tape to mark out a large squared grid on the floor. Mark one of the squares as the 'start' square. Ask a few children to stand on random squares in the grid. Each player has a partner who remains sitting and who, in turn rolls a die for the number of steps to move and picks up a direction card (turn right, turn left, forwards, backwards) in order to tell their partner how to move. Which player lands on (or is nearest to) the start square?

 Mathematical statues

Mark out a large grid on the floor, enough for one square per child. Ask all the children to stand on one square. Play a version of 'Musical statues' where the children walk round while there is music and then stand still in a square when the music stops. Can they find their original place on the carpet when the music stops? If yes, how did they work it out?

Main teaching

 Instruction noughts and crosses

Divide the class into groups of four. Give each group a large, blank grid. The children in the group divide into two teams and play giant noughts and crosses. Each go, one teammate gives an instruction to their partner for placing their nought or cross on the grid. The first team to make three (or four) marks in a line, wins. Can they decide on a way to label the rows and columns to make it easier to give instructions?

Coin matrix

Place coins in different squares on a 5x5 grid. Ask the group to discuss how they would describe where the coins are and design their own system of co-ordinates. If necessary, introduce the notion of labelling rows and columns. Ask the children to test their system by giving each other co-ordinates on which to place coins.

Island maps

Give each child a copy of a desert island map drawn on squared paper. Ask them to draw a hut, a tree, a boat, and a treasure chest in four different squares. They then sit with a partner, with their maps hidden from each other, and take turns to guess which squares the features are on. How can they refine their guesses?

Copycat patterns

Each child colours in squares on a piece of squared paper, to make a pattern. They then give instructions for another child to make the same pattern. Can they find a way to mark the rows and columns?

Plenary

Draw an 8x8 grid on the board and label the horizontal axis with letters A to H and number the vertical axis 1 to 8. Draw different coloured butterflies in different squares. Ask the children to help the yellow butterfly escape from its cage by recording its co-ordinates on their whiteboards and holding it up. Introduce the convention that you read the horizontal axis before the vertical one (read the column label before the row - B 4, not 4 B). Repeat with the other butterflies until the grid is clear.

Common difficulties

Children are used to moving around on a grid but some may have difficulty defining the position of objects using two co-ordinates. Some often invert the row and the column and, despite the fact that, at this level (letter, number), the error has no impact, it will be critical later.

Remediation

Teach the technique of pointing to the position of the object then tracing back to each axis to find its label. Emphasise the conventional order of recording co-ordinates ('along the corridor and up the stairs').

Homework suggestion

Make a grid and design a game of 'battleships'. Write the co-ordinates for the position of each ship.

Key point

Describing and finding the position of a square on a grid of squares, with the rows and columns labelled, is the first step towards learning co-ordinates.

Related material

 Pupil Book
Page 32-33

 PCM 15
SCM 15
ECM 15

 Space battle

mathspace

16

Counting in tens and hundreds

Key vocabulary

- hundreds
- tens
- units
- ones

Materials

- whiteboards
- three-digit number cards
- bingo cards
- counters

Introduction

Unit plans 1 and 2 introduced place value up to three-digit numbers, and counting on and back in ones, tens, and hundreds, to a given number, up to 999. The following activities allow the children to practise counting on or back in tens or hundreds from any two or three-digit number. The concept of place value is reinforced by observing where and how the change is represented in the new number.

Objectives

 To count on or back in tens or hundreds, starting from any two or three-digit number.

Oral and mental starter

What's my number?

Use three numbers to write six three-digit numbers on the board and ask volunteers to describe each one in terms of how many hundreds, tens and units each has. Then ask each child to write their own three-digit number. Ask one child to describe his or her number in terms of how many hundreds, tens or units it has (they can describe it in any order to make it more difficult). The other children write the number on their whiteboards and hold it up.

Passed it!

Sit the children in a circle and give each child a three-digit number card. Ask them to pass the cards round the circle until you say stop. Then say a rule: one, 10 or 100 more or less. Ask the children to hold up their cards and, in turn, say their new number, according to the rule. Start passing the cards round again and repeat.

Main teaching

👥 Stepping stones

Ask each group of children to draw five stepping stones on the ground to make a path. In turn, each child picks a three-digit number card (between 101 and 500) and jumps from one stepping stone to the next, counting on 100 for each jump and announcing the new number. Repeat with counting on 10, then with a start number between 501 and 999 and counting back 10 and 100.

The line up

In groups of four to six, one child stands out of earshot. The others stand in a row and choose a starting number (up to 999). They then count on or back in ones, tens or hundreds until each child has a number. The other child comes back and is told the starting number and the third child's number. He or she says what all the missing numbers are and the number they are counting in. Repeat until all the children have had a turn saying the missing numbers. If there are more than three children in the line up, they can make it more difficult by giving the starting number and the fourth or last number.

Calculation bingo

Give each child a bingo card with ten three-digit numbers in pairs, where in each pair only one digit is different (number of ones, tens or hundreds). Make statements of the type: five tens more, or, three hundreds less. The children may put a counter over the two numbers that make a pair of numbers that match the definition, if they have such a pair on their bingo card.

Solve and show

Ask questions of the type, four hundreds less than 765, or five tens more than 145. Ask a volunteer to show how he or she did the calculation on the board.

Plenary

Write a three-digit starting number on the board and give a rule for counting on or back in ones, tens or hundreds. Go around the class counting according to the rule, up to 999 or down to zero. Repeat with different instructions and a different starting number.

Common difficulties

Children sometimes do not understand the rule or instruction and, for example, will count on 10 in the middle of a 'count on in hundreds' sequence.

Remediation

Build a number line, write the rule and chant up/down the line with the children. If a child still finds it difficult, use concrete representation using multibase 100 blocks or 10 interlocking cubes and counting the total each time.

Homework suggestion

Play heads and tails – start with a two or three-digit number then toss a coin ten times. Each time you land on heads, add 10, each time on tails, subtract 10. Repeat, adding/subtracting 100.

Key point

Proficiency in counting up or back in ones, tens and hundreds, to or from three-digit numbers, reinforces the place value system, and facilitates problem solving and complex calculation.

Related material

 Pupil Book Page 34-35

 PCM 16
SCM 16
ECM 16

 Special delivery

The number screen

On wheels

Odd and even

Key vocabulary

- odd
- even

Materials

- number cards (1–20)
- squared paper
- whiteboards
- spinners (5–9)

Introduction

These activities revise the basic properties of odd and even integers learned in Year 1 and Year 2. The basic properties are: even numbers pair off with no leftover; counting in twos from an even number produces only even numbers; counting in twos from odd numbers produces only odd numbers; the sum of an odd and an even number is always an odd number; the sum of two odd or two even numbers is always even. The children also learn to find all the odd or even numbers within a set range.

Objectives

● To count on or back in twos starting from any two-digit number.

● To recognise odd and even numbers to at least 100.

Oral and mental starter

 Pontoon parody

Tell the children, whoever reaches 21 on the count wins the point. Pick a starting number from a set of number cards (1–11). Count around the class with each child saying a number that is one or two more than the last. The winner picks the next card and starts the count for the next round.

 Even in a minute

Count in twos around the class, from zero, and see how high they can go in a minute without making any mistakes. Then start at one and see how high they can go in a minute. Repeat and see if the class can beat its own record.

Main teaching

 Bold folds

Each child measures and cuts out paper strips of different lengths (1-10) from squared paper. Ask the children to fold the strips in half and see how many squares are on each side of the fold for each strip. Ask them to make a table showing this information. Which number of squares fold exactly in half and which have to share one of the squares between both sides? Repeat the activity with a selection of strips up to 50 squares long. What do the children notice about the numbers that fold exactly in half and those which do not? Can they find a rule for the two sets of numbers? Introduce if necessary, the rule odd numbers end in 1, 3, 5, 7, or 9; even in 0, 2, 4, 6, 8.

What are the odds?

Divide the class into pairs. One child chooses odd, and the other even. Each child is dealt six cards (1–20). Each one chooses a card and puts it face down in front of them. They find the total. If the total is even the 'even' childs wins the point, if odd, the 'odd' child wins the point. After several rounds, ask each pair to find the rules that predict when the 'even' child would win and when the 'odd' child would. Discuss the answers.

Dividing the odds

Ask four volunteers to choose four random single-digit numbers and write them on the board. Ask the children to make as many different two-digit numbers as they can using these numbers and then split them into groups of odd and even numbers. How did they know which number went into which group?

Even better

Ask two volunteers to each spin a spinner (5–9) twice, to make a two-digit number between 55 and 99. Ask the children to find all the even numbers that lie between the two numbers. Repeat with other pairs of numbers. Discuss how to solve this problem.

Plenary

Write a two-digit number on the board. Ask the children to record on their whiteboards, the next three even numbers, or the next three odd numbers. Show a three-digit number in which the units digit is hidden. Say that it is an odd number. Ask the children to record the different possible numbers and discuss them. Repeat with an even three-digit number.

Common difficulties

Some children may have difficulty understanding general statements about numbers.

Remediation

Give many positive examples of the rule, and show that it always works, no matter what numbers you use.

Homework suggestion

Look for and write down ten car registration numbers and say if the three-digit number is an odd number or an even number. Please note: this will not work for the newer style of car registrations.

Related material

 Pupil Book
Page 36-37

 PCM 17
SCM 17
ECM 17

 Sea captain
Ziggy

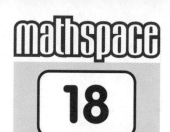

Solving mathematical problem and puzzles

Materials

- number fans
- whiteboards
- train sheets
- counters
- dominoes
- number cards (1–20)
- playing cards

Introduction

These activities utilise all the mathematical skills children have learned so far and apply them to solving mathematical problems and puzzles. At every stage, children are required to explain their chosen strategy and show their working. They should be encouraged not to rub out errors, but rather to see mistakes as valuable links in their chain of thoughts and ideas.

Objectives

- To solve mathematical problems or puzzles, recognise simple patterns and relationships, generalise and predict. Suggest extentions by asking, 'what if...?'
- To explain methods and reasoning orally and in writing.

Oral and mental starter

Odd and even

Ask quick fire questions about odd and even numbers, for example, what is the next odd number before/after 17? Or, what even number comes between 26 and 30? Or, if you add two odd numbers, is the answer odd or even? Ask the children to show their answers on their number fans.

Small change

Ask the children to draw on their whiteboards, the fewest number of coins they can use to make a given amount. Include pounds and pence.

Main teaching

Note: *For all the activities in this unit plan, ask the children to show you their working even if the strategy they use does not solve the problem. Emphasise that they do not need to rub out attempts that do not work and that it is their thought processes that are important.*

The number train

Give each group an outline of a train with three carriages. Explain that the two outer carriages can hold a maximum of eight passengers altogether, they have to hold the same number each, and they have to have one less than the centre carriage. How many different ways can they put people on the train? How many people will be on the train each time? What is the most and the least number of people the train can hold? Can they find a rule? Repeat with a maximum of 12 passengers in the outer two carriages. If necessary, suggest that the children use counters to represent passengers.

Domino dilemma

Give each group a set of dominoes. Ask the children to find pairs of dominoes that total 9, and to list their results. Can they see a pattern? How many pairs did they find?

 Count the ways

Working with a partner, give each pair a set of number cards (1–20). Give a target number and ask the children to find how many ways they can make the target using each card only once. Repeat with a different target number and then repeat with each pair choosing a target number of their own. For each target number, ask if they can make the total with only even or only odd numbers?

Rules and regulations

Ask the children to record on their whiteboards and hold up a three-digit number that fulfills the criteria: the hundreds digit is odd and the others are even. What numbers can they make? Discuss the possible answers. Repeat with other similar rules and constraints.

Plenary

Show a set of playing cards and say the rule is that the number cards, from 2 to 10, are worth their own number, and the picture cards (Jack, Queen and King) are worth 10. The ace can be either 1 or 11. Ask the children to draw on their whiteboards, two possible ways to make 21 with only three cards. Write some of the suggestions on the board. Ask volunteers to explain their strategy. Ask the children to try to find rules and apply them to find other ways to make 21. Extend to making 21 using four cards.

Common difficulties

Some children dislike showing working out that may be incorrect. They may have difficulty working systematically and applying a strategy in a logical order without skipping examples.

Remediation

Work with the children on possible solutions that do not solve the problem but that you then keep for reference. Show how to apply a strategy and how to work systematically. Then give a different, but very similar, problem to solve.

Homework suggestion

Roll two then three dice several times and see what even totals you can make.

Key point

Solving mathematical problems and puzzles necessitates the use of meaningful mathematics at a higher level.

Related material

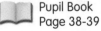 Pupil Book
Page 38-39

 PCM 18
SCM 18
ECM 18

 Flower power
In the maths lab

Understanding multiplication

Key vocabulary

- multiplication
- times
- product

Materials

- dice
- whiteboards
- interlocking cubes
- squared paper

Introduction

The following activities present multiplication as repeated addition and also as describing an array. Simple multiplication problems are introduced at this stage.

Objectives

- To understand multiplication as repeated addition.
- To extend the understanding that multiplication can be done in any order.

Oral and mental starter

Double double die

Ask a volunteer to roll two large dice. Ask the children to write the double of the total amount thrown, on their whiteboards. Then ask them to hold up their whiteboards to check the results.

Incremental counting

Count in threes round the class starting from zero. Write some numbers on the board from the threes sequence and ask the children which numbers are missing. Repeat for counting in tens and fives.

Main teaching

Multi-towers

Give each group a box of interlocking cubes and a die. Ask one child to build a tower of up to 10 cubes. Ask another child to roll the die to find a number from one to six. All the children have to make towers that are that many times as high as the first tower. Ask them to discuss the strategies they used to work out how many cubes they needed in their towers. Discuss repeated addition, multiplication and how the answer in a multiplication is called the product. Emphasise the fact that multiplication is possible only if the numbers added are all equal.

👥 Chocolate products

Give each group different sized 'bars of chocolate' represented by grids on squared paper. Ask the children to find the total number of squares in each bar. Discuss the different strategies, and the efficiency of multiplication.

♟ Colour the times

Write a multiplication on the board. Ask the children to colour in a rectangle on squared paper to represent the multiplication sentence. Ask them what the product is. Then ask if there is another way to represent the same rectangle using a different multiplication. Discuss the suggestions and repeat with other multiplications.

♟ Multi methods

Write a simple multiplication problem on the board. For example, a group of children are sitting in three rows with four children in each row. How many children are there altogether? Ask the children to explain the way they solved the problem. Discuss the strategy of multiplication. Revise the stages of problem solving, including writing the answer and checking it. Then repeat with other simple multiplication problems.

Plenary

Draw a 6 x 4 grid on the board. Ask the children to find out how many squares there are altogether. Discuss the methods they used. Then emphasise the use of multiplication and elicit the benefits of multiplication over repeated addition. Give simple multiplication problems (see pupil book for examples), asking volunteers to present the different stages of the solution.

Common difficulties

Children sometimes become confused using multiplication. For example, they solve 2 x 6 as 2 + 6, giving the answer as 8 instead of 12, or they write 6 x 6 instead of 2 x 6, giving the answer as 36.

Remediation

Allow the children to draw the multiplication as an array on squared paper and then count the squares. Or, ask them to represent the multiplication using counters or cubes.

Homework suggestion

Write down the names of the people in your household, and count the letters in each name. Now draw an array to find the product of the number of letters multiplied by the number of people in your household.

Related material

 Pupil Book Page 40-41

 PCM 19
SCM 19
ECM 19

 Ball machine
Tooty fruity

Multiplication and division facts of two

Key vocabulary

- times
- multiplied by
- divided by

Materials

- blank cards
- interlocking cubes
- imitation coins
- spinners marked 'double', 'half'
- priced merchandise (22p–40p)
- blank bingo cards with six squares
- spinners (1–20)

Introduction

These activities revise doubling and halving, and emphasise the connection between the two operations. The children learn the 2 times-table by heart and how to quickly derive the corresponding division facts. These skills will be useful in further study of fractions and more difficult multiplication work.

Objectives

- To know by heart multiplication facts for the 2 times-table.
- To derive quickly division facts corresponding to the 2 times-table.
- To derive quickly doubles of whole numbers to at least 20 and all the corresponding halves.

Oral and mental starter

In the puddle

Sit the children in a circle and go around chanting the 'one frog' chant whereby each child in turn chants one phrase. The sequence is: *"one frog," "two eyes," "four legs," "kerplunk!", "in the puddle."* The next child says, *"two frogs,"* and the sequence continues with: *"four eyes," "eight legs," "kerplunk!", "kerplunk!", "in the puddle", "in the puddle."* Continue adding one frog each time until someone makes a mistake. When this happens, the next child starts from the beginning with, *"one frog"*. See how many frogs you can count up to.

Who's on two?

Sit the children in a circle and ask: *"If we start with Harry and Harry says 'two', who is going to say 12 when we are counting in twos?"* Repeat with different children starting and different multiples of two.

Main teaching

Hidden halves

Each child in the group thinks of an even number (2–40), writes it down on a blank card and turns the card over. Remembering their number, they then make a tower of cubes of that number and split the tower into two equal towers, putting one away and the other in the middle of the table. The children take turns to pick up a tower and say the double. The child with that number written on their card can turn it over to verify the answer and bring out the matching tower. Ask the group to write the corresponding operations for each pair of towers.

Shopping spree

Give each group a spinner marked 'double' and 'half' and each child, a set of imitation coins to the value of £1. One child in the group is the shopkeeper with items priced 22p to 40p. The children take turns to spin the spinner and then buy an item from the shop at double or half the price, according to the spinner. If there is nothing left that they can afford, they miss a go. When all the money is spent, see who has had the most successful shopping spree.

 ### Double or halve

Give out bingo cards with six empty squares. Ask the children to write an even number, between two and 40, in each square. Then ask a volunteer to spin a spinner (1–20). Play bingo where the children cover the double of the number shown on the spinner. For variation the children write six numbers from one to 20, and the spinner has even numbers (2–40). In this game, the children cover the half of the number shown on the spinner. You could also ask the children to write the corresponding operations or elicit them and write them on the board.

Tuppence a bag

Put the price list from a sweet shop on the board, where the prices are multiples of two. Ask the children how many 2p coins they need to pay for each item. Ask them to write a matching multiplication and division to show how they worked this out. Ask volunteers to present their answers and explain the connection between the multiplication and division.

Plenary

Write the 2 times-table on the board and chant it through with the children. Then give quickfire questions of multiplication, and division facts within the 2 times-table. Ask if anyone would like to try and say the 2 times-table off by heart (without looking at the board).

Common difficulties

Some children may have difficulty learning the division facts of two.

Remediation

Give plenty of practice of halving, then explain that dividing by two is the same as halving. Ask the same questions but in the form of division questions. If necessary show concrete representation using cubes or counters.

Homework suggestion

Look for 10 even house numbers in your street, work out and write down half of each and then double each half to check.

Key point

Linking halving and doubling helps children divide by two and reinforces mental links between operations.

Related material

 Pupil Book
Page 42-43

 PCM 20
SCM 20
ECM 20

 Red roofs

Flower
numbers

Down on the
farm

21

Multiplying by 10 and 100

Key vocabulary

- place holder
- times
- multiply by
- hundreds
- tens
- units
- times-table

Materials

- number cards (1-10)
- number cards (multiples of 10 up to 100)
- interlocking cubes
- multiplication cards for 10 times-table
- multibase
- H U chart
- plastic coins

Introduction

These activities focus on multiplying by 10 and 100 and demonstrate the result as a shift of numbers by one or two places to the left. The children learn to add zeros as place holders. To bring relevance to the activities, contexts are used that the children are already familiar with, such as the 10 times-table and the relationship between metres and centimetres.

Objectives

 To say or write a division statement corresponding to a given multiplication statement.

 To multiply by 10/ 100 by shifting the digits one/ two places to the left.

To know by heart the multiplication facts for the 10 times-table.

To know the relationship between meters and centimetres.

Oral and mental starter

💬 T.T.T.

Write the 10 times-table on the board. Chant it together as you point to each line. Clean the board and say; *"The product is 60. What did I multiply 10 by?"*. Ask the children to write the answer on their whiteboards and hold them up. Ask that many children to stand up and count together in steps of 10 to reach the product.

💬 Tenfold partners

Prepare enough number cards (1–10, and multiples of 10 up to 100) for one per child. Give out the cards and ask the children to find their 'times 10' partner. Shuffle the cards and repeat.

Main teaching

👥 Playing with zeros

Give each group towers of 10 cubes and multiplication cards in the 10 times-table. Each child takes a multiplication card, shows the correct number of towers and says the answer. Then they try to write a division sentence using these three numbers. Discuss how they worked it out. Repeat with multibase 100-cubes and multiplication cards (1–9 x 100). Ask what they notice about the pattern of the digits in each case.

Place holder seeker

Give each group a box of multibase, number cards (1–9), and give each child an H T U chart. The children each take a number card and write the number in the units column on their chart. Then they multiply the answer by 10 and write the answer in the chart. Then they multiply the number by 100 and write that answer in the chart (they may use the multibase to help work out the calculations). Ask them to compare their results and discuss what they notice about the numbers. Explain how multiplying by 10 or 100 causes the digits to shift one or two places to the left and how a zero is used as a place holder.

Mix 'n' match methods

Write up to five distances in metres (1 m–9 m) on the board and ask the children to write the measurements in cm. For each answer, ask the children to write a matching multiplication sentence. Then write up to five distances in centimetres (100 cm–900 cm) on the board and ask the children to write the measurements in metres. Again, ask them to write a number sentence for each answer. Discuss the methods used and ask volunteers to come up and demonstrate each method. Which method is the most efficient?

Decimal currency

Give all the children access to plastic coins. Hold up an item with a price tag (1p–9p) and ask them to write in pence how much one would cost, how much 10 would cost, and how much 100 would cost. They may use the plastic coins to help them work out the answers. What do they notice about the digits in the prices? Ask them to work out 10 times the price and then 10 times again. What do they notice? Then hold up an object with a two-digit price tag and ask how much one would cost, and how much 10 would cost. What do they notice about the results?

Plenary

Give the children prices of items in £s. Say how many of each item are bought (10 or 100), and ask for the total amount that has to be paid. Repeat, giving the total and ask the children to find out the quantity bought. Then write a set of three numbers (such as 3, 30 and 300) on the board, but not in the right order. Point to one of the numbers and ask which number is 10 times larger/smaller, or which is 100 times larger/smaller. Repeat with other number sets of a similar type.

Common difficulties

Zero is understood as 'nothing' when it is used as a number representing an amount, but it has to be understood as a place holder when it is used as a digit in a larger number.

Remediation

Explain the place value system again. Use cubes or an abacus for concrete representation.

Homework suggestion

Ask at home for an old receipt from the supermarket, choose some of the prices and work out what 10 of each item would cost.

Recalling multiplication and division facts

Key vocabulary

- multiplied by
- divided by
- product
- multiple/s
- array

Materials

- beanbag
- number fans
- number cards
- multiplication cards
- division cards
- menus
- imitation 5p coins
- spinners
- number family cards
- whiteboards

Introduction

Knowing the basic times-tables by heart is a prerequisite to most arithmetic and algebra skills. Children should be quite proficient by now at the 2 times-table and the 10 times-table. In these activities they practise the multiplication facts for the 5 times-table.

Objectives

- To know the multiplication facts for the 5 times-table by heart.
- To derive quickly division facts corresponding to the 5 times-table.

Oral and mental starter

 ### Tackling the twos and tens

Take turns to pass a beanbag round the circle, saying the multiples of two with each pass. Repeat with the multiples of 10. Then ask quick fire questions using the two and 10 times-tables and appropriate vocabulary. For example, What are two tens? How many twos in 12? Divide 20 by two. What is six multiplied by ten? The children can show the answers on their number fans. Try timing them to see how many they can do in a set time and then try to beat the class record.

 ### Finessing the fives

Write multiples of five (up to 50) randomly on the board. Point to a number and ask the children to chant around the class from zero in fives until they reach that number. Then ask them to chant from that number until 100. Repeat with a different target/starter number. Then count back from the starter number to zero followed by counting back from 100 to the target number.

Main teaching

 ### Five times fabulous

Give each group two packs of cards, one pack with multiplications from 1 x 5 to 10 x 5, and the other with the answers. Shuffle the two packs together and lay them out face down on the table. Ask the children to play 'pairs' matching the multiplications to the answers. Then swap the packs for two different packs of cards, one with numbers (1–10), and the other with the division facts expressed in various ways such as 30 divided by five, 25 ÷ 5, and, how many fives in 45?

Hand to mouth

Give each group a menu with items priced in multiples of five, a spinner (1–10) and a set of imitation 5p coins. Each child in turn spins the spinner, takes that number of 5p coins and says how much money they have. Then they look at the items on the menu to see which ones they can buy with their money. Repeat several times.

 ### Matching matrix

Ask each child to draw an array of dots arranged in rows of five. Then ask them to turn over their paper and write the total number of dots on the back. They then show the total to their neighbour who has to say and write the multiplication fact, and corresponding division facts and replicate the array on another piece of paper. Finally, they can turn over their original pieces of paper to check that the arrays match.

The five families from Five Timesville

Shuffle a set of cards with number families in the 5 times-table, for example, 3, 5, 15. Give each child a card and ask them to write as many multiplication and division sentences as they can, using these numbers. Extend to asking the children to make their own number families and swapping them with a friend.

Plenary

Draw an array of dots arranged in rows of five (up to 50 dots). Ask the children to record on their whiteboards, the matching 5 times-table sentence, and the corresponding division for the array. Then write a 5 times-table sentence and ask the children to write the corresponding division and draw the array. Next give only a division sentence, starting with a multiple of five up to 50, and ask the children to provide the multiplication and draw the array. Finally, ask quick fire 5 times-table questions in multiplication and division format.

Common difficulties

Some children may be able to chant competently in fives but find recalling individual multiplication facts difficult.

Remediation

Play games like pairs and snap using cards with just the multiplication facts and their products until the children feel confident. Then repeat with division facts and answers. Use a number line marked with the multiples of five as an aid.

Homework suggestion

Collect some 5p coins. Roll one or two dice and put together that number of coins, then say how much money there is altogether. Do this several times.

Key point

Knowing the basic multiplication tables by heart will facilitate many mathematical activities.

Related material

 Pupil Book Page 46-47

 PCM 22
SCM 22
ECM 22

 Down on the farm

Ziggy's space journey

Solving problems

Materials

- whiteboards
- word problems (RM5)
- apparatus for graphical and concrete representation

Introduction

In Years 1 and 2, the children learned how to solve word problems using the seven-step strategy. This year two of the steps have been combined so that strategy is now: reading and understanding the problem, identifying the question, finding the relevant information, develop a solving strategy and implementing it (if necessary, building a graphical representation), writing the answer, and checking it. These activities revise word problem solving, with emphasis on ways to check the answer.

Objectives

- To solve problems involving 'real life' numbers, money and measures using one or two steps.
- To choose and use appropriate number operations and ways of calculating to solve problems.
- To explain and record how the problem was solved.

Oral and mental starter

Conversion immersion

Ask the children to write on their whiteboards how many pence there are in £3.65, £4.08, and £9.30. Then ask for 712p, 605p and 992p in £ and pence notation. Ask other conversion questions such as what is £4 in pence? Or, what is 6m in centimetres? And, what is 400cm in metres?

Solving with the six-step strategy

Write the following word problem on the board and work through the six-step strategy as outlined in the introduction. (Also see Unit plan 10, remediation). There are 23 books on the top shelf of a bookcase and 8 books on the lower shelf. How many books are there altogether?

Main teaching

Pricey problem

Give each group the following word problem: *"The price of a mobile phone is £125. Its price is £30 higher than last week. What was its price last week?"* Ask the groups to present their solutions. Discuss graphical representations, strategies and checking methods. Also emphasise misleading vocabulary. In this example, the price was higher but to find the solution involves subtracting.

👥 Applying the six-step

Give each group a copy of RM 5. Give one set to each group. Each group solves each problem using the six-step problem solving method. Ask them to present some of their answers and explain each step of the method. Ask them, specifically, to say how they checked the results at the end.

♟ Two-stage how do you do

Set a two-stage problem and ask the children to solve it. For example, Measure the length of your rubber to the nearest centimetre. Work out the length of five rubbers? Ask: *"How did you work it out?"* and, *"How can you check your answer?"*

♟ Present a problem solved

Ask the children to solve a simple word problem, such as: *"Jack has £49. He wants to buy an MP3 player which costs £95. How much more money does he need, to buy the MP3 player?"* Ask volunteers to present the way they understood the problem, the strategy they used to solve it, and their checking methods.

Plenary

Write a simple word problem on the board. For example: *"39 Year 2 pupils and 28 Year 3 pupils went to the shopping centre. After half an hour, 25 pupils left to go back to school. How many pupils remained at the shopping centre?"* Ask the children to solve the problem and record their answers. Then ask them to check their answers and record the way they checked. Ask six volunteers to talk through each of the six steps of the six-step strategy. At each step, ask if any other child has a different way of applying that step. Emphasise how to look and check that the answer makes sense and how to use different methods of checking, for example, inverse operation.

Common difficulties

Children often need a graphical representation of the problem. Pupils sometimes cannot see how it is possible to check the answer.

Remediation

Suggest a variety of apparatus to represent a problem, such as cubes, coins, counters, a number line, pictures, tables or graphs. Show how to begin from the answer to check it. For example, 42 (remaining pupils) + 25 (pupils who left) = 67, which is the total number of pupils who went to the shopping centre (39+28).

Homework suggestion

Write a number sentence for the following word problem. Show how you work out the answer by showing your method and how you check your answer. *"Jerry has 57p. He takes 9p out of his money box. How much does Jerry have left?"*

Key point

Developing good problem solving habits and learning to work systematically without skipping stages, especially checking the answer, are among the most valuable skills for mathematics and real life.

Related material

 Pupil Book Page 48-49

 PCM 23
SCM 23
ECM 23

 What's the question?

The lottery

Country road

Ask the robot!

mathspace

24

Fractions

Key vocabulary

- fraction/s
- unit fraction/s
- half
- halves
- third/s
- quarter/s
- fifth/s
- sixth/s
- tenth/s

Materials

- paper shapes
- grids on squared paper
- number cards
- fraction cards
- cubes
- counters

Introduction

These activities introduce the topic of fractions. Fractions at primary school level have two main representations: a) one or more parts of a unit divided into equal parts ($\frac{2}{3}$ represents two slices of a pizza that has been divided into three equal parts) and b) a part of a set of identical elements ($\frac{2}{3}$ represents 8 marbles out of 12 marbles). It is important that the children read the fractions aloud as they often read them incorrectly. The activities also address frequent mistakes and misconceptions about fractions.

Objectives

To recognise unit fractions $\frac{1}{2}$, $\frac{1}{3}$, $\frac{1}{4}$, $\frac{1}{5}$ and $\frac{1}{10}$, and use them to find fractions of shapes and numbers.

Oral and mental starter

Shaded shapes

Show pictures of different shapes divided into quarters and halves with different fractions shaded – include some shapes that are not equally divided. Ask the children to record the shaded areas on their whiteboards using the correct notation $\frac{1}{4}$ or $\frac{1}{2}$ if possible.

Hidden halves

Draw a 5 x 2 grid on the board. Write the numbers 1 to 10 in the boxes and cover them with their doubles. Then ask the children to say the half of each number and reveal the number underneath to see if they are correct.

Main teaching

Naming and sharing

Give each group a set of shapes including circles, squares, rectangles and diamonds. Ask the children to draw lines to divide each shape into two equal parts. Discuss and compare the results with other groups. Revise the concept of half and the $\frac{1}{2}$ notation. Given that a shape divided into two equal parts contains two halves, ask what would be a good name for each part of a shape divided into three, four, five, or 10 equal parts. Give each group a set of circles representing pizzas or cakes. Ask the children to choose a number card (2, 3, 4, 5, or 10) and decide how to divide each of the circles equally between that number of children. What fraction will each child receive? Give them a set of unit fraction cards to choose from. Can they do the same activity with a square or rectangular shaped cake or pizza?

The whole nine counters

Give each group sets of arrays drawn as grids on squared paper (more than one of each size), and a set of cards with unit fractions matching the arrays, for example: $\frac{1}{3}$ of 9, $\frac{1}{4}$ of 12 and $\frac{1}{10}$ of 20. Ask the children to take turns to choose a fraction card, find the appropriate array and colour the fraction on the array. Then they can shuffle the arrays and the fraction cards and use them for a game of 'snap' or 'pairs'.

 A fraction of the work

Give out paper shapes and ask the children to divide them into halves, thirds, quarters, fifths, or tenths. Ask them to label each part of each shape and then show the finished work to their neighbour who has to check that they are equally divided. Discuss how they labelled each section and how they can check each fraction (by folding, measuring, or matching with same-sized parts).

Set slice

Ask each child to lay out 12 cubes set out in rows. Then ask them to lay out a set with half of the cubes. Repeat with a third, a quarter and a sixth. Then repeat with sets of different amounts (for example, 20 cubes) and ask for different fractions ($\frac{1}{5}$ and $\frac{1}{10}$). Emphasise fraction notation: $\frac{1}{2}$, $\frac{1}{3}$, $\frac{1}{4}$, $\frac{1}{5}$ and $\frac{1}{10}$.

Plenary

Ask the children to colour half of a shape. Check that all the shapes are divided equally. Emphasise that the two parts are only halves if they are equal. Ask the children each to lay out a set of eight counters and then show you half of the set. Repeat with other fractions, with the children showing what part of a shape it is and what part of a set. Explain the meaning of the denominator as the number of parts into which the whole was equally divided. Explain the numerator as the number of parts taken or shown from the whole.

Common difficulties

Some children may not understand the concept of dividing a shape or number into equal parts with fractions other than halves and quarters.

Remediation

Demonstrate equal division into halves with apparatus such as cubes. Show that one part is one of two same-size parts. Then extend to other unit fractions. Prepare some shapes divided into three or four parts, some equally and some not. Ask the children to say which are divided into halves or quarters and which are not.

Homework suggestion

At tea-time, see if you can find different fractions, for example, $\frac{1}{2}$, $\frac{1}{4}$, $\frac{1}{5}$, $\frac{1}{3}$, $\frac{1}{10}$ of pizza.

More fractions

Key vocabulary

- half/ halves
- third/s
- quarter/s
- fifth/s
- tenth/s
- fraction
- unit fraction

Materials

- divided shapes
- shaded grids
- cubes
- fraction/number cards
- coloured counters
- number cards (1–20)
- blank cards
- squared paper strips

Introduction

Unit fractions were introduced in the previous unit plan. In the following activities the children further their knowledge of recognising the unit fractions: $\frac{1}{2}$, $\frac{1}{3}$, $\frac{1}{4}$, $\frac{1}{5}$, and $\frac{1}{10}$, and use them to find fractions of numbers. They discover that there are many ways to represent a fraction, such as shading different parts of a shape, and taking different subsets of a set.

Objectives

 To recognise the unit fractions: $\frac{1}{2}$, $\frac{1}{3}$, $\frac{1}{4}$, $\frac{1}{5}$, and $\frac{1}{10}$, and use them to find fractions of shapes and numbers.

Oral and mental starter

 Shapely halves

Prepare pictures of shapes dividing them into two sections, some equal and some not. Hold up the shapes one at a time and ask the children to vote on whether each one is divided into halves or not. Check. Repeat with quarters, thirds, fifths and tenths.

Part partners

Prepare grids with unit fractions coloured in different ways. Give each child a grid and ask them to find a partner with the same fraction coloured on their grid. Ask them to record and name the fraction on a whiteboard and hold it up.

Main teaching

 Splitting cubes

Prepare sets of number/fraction cards using the unit fractions $\frac{1}{2}$, $\frac{1}{4}$, $\frac{1}{3}$, $\frac{1}{5}$, and $\frac{1}{10}$, and numbers that divide evenly by the fractions, for example, 12 or 15. Give each group cubes and a set of number/fraction cards. In turn, each child takes that number of cubes, builds the fraction representation and says how many cubes represents the unit fraction. The other children check each answer.

👥 Fraction dominoes

Ask the children to make cards for a game of 'fraction dominoes'. Give each child five blank cards and ask the children to divide them into two halves. On one half they can either draw a grid or a shape and colour it in to represent $\frac{1}{2}$, $\frac{1}{3}$, $\frac{1}{4}$, $\frac{1}{5}$, or $\frac{1}{10}$. On the other half they write a fraction, but **not** the fraction that corresponds to the drawing on the same card. Then they play 'fraction dominoes' in which a fraction can be laid down next to a pictorial representation of the same fraction.

♟ Counter play and fraction say

Give each child a bowl of different coloured counters and a number. Ask the children to use the counters to divide their number into equal sets of different colours. They record what the unit fraction is and how many it is, for example, $\frac{1}{4}$ of 20 is 5. Choose different volunteers to ask a question based on what they found out, for example, 'What is $\frac{1}{4}$ of 20?'. The other children can use their counters to work out the answer.

♟ Number splits

Divide the class into pairs. Give each pair a set of number cards (1–20) and cubes or counters. Ask them to pick a card and represent the number with cubes or counters. Ask them to investigate how many different ways the number of cubes can be split – in half/quarters/thirds etc. The children can record their results with drawings. They say what number each unit fraction is of the number on their card, for example, $\frac{1}{3}$ of 18 is 6.

Plenary

Give each child a strip of paper divided into 20 equal squares. Ask them to investigate how many different fractions they can fold the strips into so that each part has only whole squares. Elicit all the possible unit fractions and ask the children to check each fraction before you write it on the board. Then give out strips of different numbers of squares. Make a display of the folded strips and ask the children to describe them as, for example, a strip of 20 squares folded into quarters. Each quarter is 5 squares.

Common difficulties

Some children may be able to find simple fractions of numbers such as, $\frac{1}{4}$ of 4, but not of larger numbers such as $\frac{1}{4}$ of 16 or 20.

Remediation

Demonstrate by sharing the cubes into four equal piles, then record by colouring parts of strips of the same number of squares or by drawing and circling.

Homework suggestion

Take 10 toy cars or lego pieces, find as many different fractions as you can by dividing them into equal groups, draw and say the fraction. Repeat with different amounts.

mathspace

26

Multiples of 100

Key vocabulary

• multiple

Materials

• number cards (0–10)
• washing line and pegs
• multiples of 10 and 100 cards
• laminated blank cards
• felt tip pen
• items priced in multiples of £100
• whiteboards
• large number line marked in hundreds

Introduction

The place value system of numbers is built in base 10. Knowing pairs of multiples of 10 that add up to 100, and pairs of multiples of 100 that total 1000 by heart, are invaluable tools for rapid mental calculation. They also facilitate the use of the four basic operations: addition, subtraction, multiplication and division.

Objectives

● To know by heart all pairs of multiples of 100 with a total of 1000.

● To use known number facts and place value to add or subtract mentally.

Oral and mental starter

 Decimal laundry

Peg on a washing line a set of multiple of 10 cards in order but with some missing. Ask volunteers to come up and write the missing numbers on laminated blank cards with a felt tip pen, and peg them on the line in the correct places. Repeat with multiple of 100 cards up to 1000.

 Partners for 10

Give each child a number card (0–10). Ask them to find a partner so that their numbers total 10. Repeat several times with the emphasis on speed. Then repeat with multiples of 10 cards with the children finding a partner to make 100.

Main teaching

 A grand budget

Give each child in the group £1000 with which they have to buy two objects priced in multiples of £100. Each child chooses two different objects, write out their own bill and work out the total amount they need to pay. Ask one child to be the shopkeeper. Say that each child has a special £1000 note to pay with. Ask the shopkeeper to give each child the correct change according to his or her bill.

🔖 Tens to a hundred

Give each group cards with multiples of 100 to play a version of 'Pairs'. The children take turns picking up two cards, keeping them if the two numbers revealed total 1000, returning them to the table if not. Repeat with other target numbers (for example, 900, 600, …).

🔖 Many multiples

Each child thinks of and writes two different multiples of 10 on two cards. Write a multiple of 10 on the board. Any child who can add their two numbers together to make 100 scores a point. How do they know if they can or not? Who can collect the most points? Repeat with multiples of 100 and a target of 1000.

🔖 1000 snap

Give each pair of children two sets of number cards (multiples of 100 up to 1000) shuffled together. Ask the children to divide the pack between them and then they each place their cards in a pile, face down, in front of them. In turn, each child turns over their top card and places it on their own discard pile in the middle (so that there are two piles of upturned cards). They say "snap!" if the two upturned cards total 1000. The first child to say "snap!" correctly, takes both discard piles and puts them, face down, under their own pile. If a wrong call is made, the other child takes both the upturned piles. Repeat the activity with other "snap" numbers, for example, 200, where the children can use either addition or subtraction to make the number.

Plenary

Write a multiple of 100 on the board. Ask the children to record on their whiteboards, the addition of that number and the multiple of 100 that totals 1000. Repeat using other multiples of 100 as the target number. Then give target numbers in multiples of 100 and ask the children to write subtraction sentences starting with 1000. Finally give a multiple of 100 as the target number and ask the children to record an addition or a subtraction of multiples of 100 that has a sum or difference of that number. Ask volunteers to explain their working using a number line, saying how many steps along the number line were taken.

Common difficulties

Some children may not be able to relate their knowledge of number facts of 10 to multiples of 100.

Remediation

Use multibase when finding the different totals in order to make the connection.

Homework suggestion

Arrange a set of ten 10p coins (or buttons each representing 10p) in different ways in two piles. Write the combinations that make £1 each time. Now do the same with £1 coins, or buttons each representing £1. Write the combinations that make £10.

Key point

Knowing pairs of multiples of 100 that total 1000, by heart, is an invaluable tool for rapid mental calculation. It also facilitates the use of the four basic operations.

Related material

Pupil Book
Page 54-55

PCM 26
SCM 26
ECM 26

On track
The recording studio

27

Subtraction and addition

Materials

- dice
- imitation coins
- number cards
  (up to 100)
- price cards
- bingo cards

Introduction

These activities focus on the rule that addition facts have corresponding subtraction facts and that given an addition, you can deduce the matching subtraction. These links between addition and subtraction facilitate problem solving.

Objectives

 To say or write a subtraction statement corresponding to a given addition statement.

 To extend understanding that subtraction is the inverse of addition.

To find a small difference by counting up from the smaller number.

Oral and mental starter

💬 Big Chief Running Total

Each child takes a turn to roll the die. They add their score to the running total, which started at one. The child who reaches or passes 100 becomes Big Chief Running Total. Repeat in reverse, starting from 100 and subtracting the die roll down to one. The child who reaches or passes one, becomes Little Chief Running Total.

💬 Plenty for twenty

Put a box of imitation coins on each table and tell the children that they each have 20p to spend. The first child thinks of an item to buy that costs less than 20p and states the price. The next child says the amount they will receive in change from their 20p piece, and the third child finds the fewest coins that will make that change. Repeat round the class until all the children have had a turn. Make sure they think of different prices each time.

Main teaching

Two-digit dilemmas

Give each group a pair of two-digit numbers whose total does not involve bridging through 10, for example, 21 and 45, or 34 and 26. The children record as many additions and subtractions as they can, using these two numbers. Discuss the results and methods used by each of the groups.

Something spent, something saved

Each child in the group picks a number card (10–20) and collects that number of imitation £1 coins. Then they each roll a die to see how much change (in pounds) they have left after going shopping. Now ask them to work out how much they spent and check their answers using a different operation. Ask the group to discuss how they can do this. Then see if they can do this starting with amounts of money in pounds and pence. For this they need a set of cards with prices where the number of pence ends in 6, 7, 8 or 9, in order not to cross the tens number when subtracting up to 6.

Within five bingo

Working in pairs, give each child a bingo card with numbers between 50 and 100 (or ask them to write their own). They take a card from a set of number cards (45–100). If the number is within five of a number on their bingo card, they write the subtraction sentence and work out the answer. Ask them to check the answer. Discuss ways of doing this. Encourage the counting up method.

Family matters

Give each pair a set of three number cards that make a number family, for example, 3, 8, and 11. Ask the children to write as many addition and subtraction sentences as they can, using these numbers. Ask them how they can check their answers. Extend by giving them a set of cards with a starter number (11–20) and a total (20–40). Ask them to find the other 'family' member and then show all the possible additions and subtractions using the three numbers. Finally ask each child to make up a number family for their partner to do.

Plenary

Write two close numbers between 100 and 1000. Ask the children to find the difference. Discuss the methods used. Explain the counting up method and its efficiency when applied to close numbers. Then write two two-digit numbers and their sum (without bridging 10), for example 45, 22 and 67. Ask the children to write the two additions and two subtractions using these numbers.

Common difficulties

Children cannot always easily find all the four possible number sentences for a number family.

Remediation

First explain how to find the additions by explaining that the order of the numbers does not change the result, so we already have two number sentences. Secondly, show that for subtraction, one can subtract the first number from the total, or the second number. Doing both of these options gives us another two number sentences. If necessary, show concrete examples using cubes or counters.

Homework suggestion

Think of a set of three numbers that make a number 'family' (start with an addition sentence and use the three numbers) and write down all the addition and subtraction sentences you can make with your numbers.

Related material

 Pupil Book Page 56-57

 PCM 27
SCM 27
ECM 27

 In the recording studio

Windmill wonders

Cinema problems

Key vocabulary

- minute/s
- hour/s
- analogue
- digital
- a.m.
- p.m.

Materials

- analogue clock faces
- whiteboards
- daily event cards
- coins
- dice
- digital time cards
- time line

Reading time to five minutes

Introduction

In previous years, children have learned to read the time to the quarter hour on analogue and digital clocks. These activities revise basic time notions and extend the children's knowledge to reading the time to the nearest five-minute division.

Objectives

 To read the time to five minutes on an analogue clock and on a 12-hour digital clock.

Oral and mental starter

Beanbag to beanbag

Count round the class in steps of five, forwards then backwards, from different starting numbers, up to, and back from 60. Before each count, choose the children to start and finish by throwing a 'starting beanbag' and a 'finishing beanbag' of different colours.

Time conversion

Give each child an analogue clock face. Write a 12-hour digital starting time on the board and ask the children to show that time on their clocks. Then ask them to show new times, for example, half (or quarter of) an hour later (before) or earlier (after) than the starting time. Repeat with different starting times, including half and quarter hours. Then say times in words and ask the children to write the digital format on their whiteboards.

Main teaching

Morning, noon and night

Give each group a set of daily event cards with o'clock, half and quarter hour times. Ask the children to place the events in the order in which they happen. Which happen in the morning and which happen in the afternoon? Can they suggest ways to distinguish between morning times and afternoon times? Introduce a.m. and p.m. Then ask how many minutes in an hour and ask the value of each division on an analogue clock. Explain that each division represents five minutes. Ask the groups to set, and hold up, different times in digital format and on analogue clocks.

What's the time Mr Wolf?

Give the wolf in each group an analogue clock face with a movable minute hand. 'Mr Wolf' stands at the front and shows the time as o'clock time. The rest of the group asks, *"What's the new time Mr Wolf?"* Mr Wolf spins the minute hand and replies by showing the time on the clock, for example, *"ten past two"* The children advance by two paces (two lots of five minutes), counting; *"five past two, ten past two"* Then they ask again. If the time lands on an o'clock, they are chased back home by the wolf. Repeat with different children as the wolf.

Five minute turns

Working in pairs, the children take turns to set an analogue clock to a starting time. The second child spins a coin. If it lands on heads, they move the long hand on by five minutes. If it is tails, they move it back. They say the new analogue time and record it in digital format. Which times are shown on the 'past' side of the clock face, which times are shown on the 'to' side?

Five minute chances

Give each pair of children an analogue clock, a die and a set of cards with digital times at five-minute intervals. Ask them to take a card and set the clock hands accordingly. Then they roll the die and move the hands on by that number of five minutes. What time is it now? They each record the new time, in both words and digital format, and check each other's work.

Plenary

Display a time line marked in hours (with a.m. and p.m.). Set the starting time, for example, 11.00 a.m., and ask how many steps of five minutes there are from this time to, say, 12.00 p.m. Roll a die marked: 5, 10, 15, 25, 40 and 55 representing minutes. Ask for the time that many minutes earlier or later than the hour on the time line. Ask the children to record the new time, and say it aloud in both formats, analogue and digital. Then ask what time it will be five/10 (up to 30) minutes later.

Common difficulties

Some children confuse the numbers on the analogue clock for the number of minutes, for example, reading 10:35 as 10:07.

Remediation

Show on a big analogue clock, that it takes five minutes to move from one number to the next. If necessary, ask the children to count aloud to 60 for each minute.

Homework suggestion

Label a clock face showing the things you can do during one hour at home that take 5, 10 or 15 minutes each and draw them next to the times you start each one.

Key point

Reading time is a basic everyday skill, and reading the five minute divisions drills the 5 times-table.

Related material

 Pupil Book
Page 58-59

 PCM 28
SCM 28
ECM 28

 The train station

At the airport

29

Time problems

Key vocabulary

- a.m.
- p.m.
- minute/s
- hour/s
- analogue
- digital

Materials

- a.m. and p.m. cards
- spinner (1–12)
- analogue clock faces
- whiteboards
- activity cards
- sports day summaries
- die

Introduction

In these activities the children apply their knowledge of measuring time to solve simple, 'real life', word problems, mainly through mental calculation.

Objectives

- To choose and use appropriate operations to solve word problems, and appropriate ways of calculating.

  – To solve time problems.

Oral and mental starter

Before noon, after noon

Give each child an a.m. or a p.m. card. Choose one child to spin a spinner (1–12) to find an o'clock time and say an activity that usually happens around that time. The rest of the class hold up their a.m. or p.m. cards according to when the activity is most likely to take place. Repeat with other children taking turns to spin the spinner.

Who's on the hour?

Sit the class in a circle. Give each child an analogue clock face. Choose an o'clock time, and go round the class, each child adding on five minutes. The children set their clocks to their time, and hold it up as they say the new time. Repeat, but start by asking the children who they think will say the next o'clock and to write that child's name on their whiteboards. When they reach o'clock, ask who guessed correctly.

Main teaching

Note: the children should show all the strategies they used (timelines, counting in fives, operations, calculations) and checking methods.

What time's teatime?

Give each group cards with jobs and/or events and the duration of each. For example, visit the dentist – 40 minutes, lunch – half an hour. Say, *"all the activities have to be completed before tea!"*. The children put the cards in the order they want to do the activities and decide what time to start in the morning. They then work through the day recording the starting and finishing times of each activity. When they finish, they have tea! What time is teatime for each group? Repeat, giving the starting time as 9:05 a.m. and make sure the a.m./p.m. barrier is crossed. Extension: Give the finishing time and the children find the start time.

What a sport!

Give each group a summary of a school sports day. Ask them to write their own word problems based on the information, for example, The 1000 m race began at xx.yy and finished at ww.zz. How long did it take? Or, the sack race began at xx.yy and lasted ww minutes. When did it finish? They pass their word problems to another group who solve them and discuss checking methods.

 ### Time teasers

Write a time statement on the board, for example, 40 minutes before 9.00 a.m. Ask the children to work out the time referred to. Ask volunteers to tell the class the strategy they used to find the answer and to present their working on the board. Repeat with other time statements using p.m. and 'after', as well.

In an hour or less

Write a digital time on the board including a.m. or p.m. Ask a volunteer to roll a die and multiply the number by five to represent a number of minutes. Ask the children to write the starting time on their whiteboards, add the number of minutes, write the new time, and hold up their results. Check and remediate. Then ask the children to make up a word problem using the time and duration, for example, 'At 7.35 a.m., I brushed my teeth for five minutes. What time did I finish?' or, 'The lady went into the shoe shop at 4.30p.m., tried on shoes for 25 minutes and left without finding any she liked. What time did she leave?'. Choose volunteers to read out their word problems.

Plenary

Write the following, or a similar problem, on the board: 'Sandra started her homework at 5.30 p.m. and finished at 7.00 p.m. How long did it take her?' Ask one child to read the problem and another to say it in their own words. Ask a third child to identify the question, another to say the relevant data, and others to propose a strategy. All the children try to solve the problem and record their answers on their whiteboards. Discuss how the answers could be checked and ask each child to check their neighbour's number sentence.

Common difficulties

A frequent mistake is to round off answers to the nearest hour, instead of carrying over the minutes to the next hour. In times longer than an hour, some children forget to add the hour as well as the minutes.

Remediation

Use an analogue clock to show that the duration went over the hour. Explain the steps, for example, one and a half hours from 5.30 p.m.: from 5.30 to 6.00 is half an hour, and from 6.00 to 7.00 one more hour which makes an hour and a half.

Homework suggestion

Look at the clock to see the time when you go out to play or to the shops and look again when you get back. Say how long you were out by counting in five minute bands.

Key point

Solving time word problems involves the integration of many basic skills and enhances mathematical reasoning.

Related material

 Pupil Book Page 60-61

 PCM 29
SCM 29
ECM 29

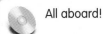 All aboard!

Organising and using data

Key vocabulary

- data
- survey
- frequency
- list
- table
- graph
- block graph

Materials

- whiteboards
- 2-D shapes
- feely bags
- imitation coins
- dice
- reading books
- squared paper

Introduction

In Year 2 the children began to organise and interpret data using the following tools: graphs, lists, tables and pictograms. In these activities they begin to carry out their own surveys, and learn about the concept of frequency. They also encounter the random phenomena, for example, two children tossing a coin x times do not necessarily have the same results.

Objectives

🔵 To solve a problem by organising and interpreting data from simple lists, tables and graphs.

– To collect data efficiently, to make a simple frequency table, and to discuss the outcomes.

– To collect data for simple surveys, such as 'what is your favourite sport?'

Oral and mental starter

 Even odder!

Ask the children to write a sequence of five numbers (1-30) in steps of three, on their whiteboards. Explain that they should circle the odd numbers in blue and the even in red. Check with a partner. Repeat with sequences in steps of one, two, four, five, and 10. What do they notice about the pattern of odd and even numbers each time?

 Picto-birthdays

Build a pictogram with twelve rows, one for each month by asking each child to come and draw a smiley face in the month he or she was born. Then ask questions about the information gathered. For example, *"In which month were most children born?"* and, *"How many children in the class were born in February?"*

Main teaching

 Shape sort

Give each group a set of 2-D shapes in a feely bag. Ask the children to take turns picking out shapes until there are none left in the bag. Then ask them to design a list, table, or block graph to show how many of each shape each child picked and how many of each shape there was in the bag. Ask them to think of questions that they can answer using the information found. Can they think of ways to represent the data on a graph besides a simple block graph? Ask how the tables/graphs would change if each child had twice as many of the same shapes.

👥 The coin change

Give each group a bag of mixed imitation coins and ask each child to take out a handful of coins. Each child then finds their own way to sort their coins and makes a table showing how they did this. Then they think of questions to ask each other about the amount of each type of coin collected. They ask the questions and use the tables to find the answers. Can they think of ways to represent the data on a graph besides a simple block graph? If the activity is repeated will the results be the same? Why? Repeat the activity to see.

♟ Dicey data

In pairs, ask the children to take turns to roll a die 30 times and record the number of times they score each number. Then ask them to make a table of the data, and use this to construct a block graph. Introduce the concept of frequency, meaning 'how many times something happens within a set limit'. Ask them to think about which symbols would represent the scores on the graph.

♟ E, i, e, i, o

Pose the question: *"How often do each of the five vowels appear in a paragraph on a page of your reading book?"*. Ask each child to choose a paragraph and find a way to count and record in a table, the number of times each vowel appears. Remind the children about tallying as an efficient way to keep a running score. Compare the results and discuss. Ask: *"If we repeat the activity, will the results be the same? Why?"* Repeat the activity to check.

Plenary

Introduce a survey to find out how children come to school. Ask the children to suggest ways to collect the data. Ask for ways to organise it (table, frequency table, list, graph,) and to interpret it (which questions would we ask?). Then divide the class into three groups of ten and ask three volunteers to conduct the survey on 10 children. Amalgamate the results of the three surveys on the board and ask the children to answer the questions that they suggested earlier. Ask what the most important findings of the survey are and why it is important to have this information. Discuss the differences between this sort of survey and one relating to opinions or favourites and involving voting or choosing. Discuss whether the results would be the same if you asked Year 6, and, who would find this information useful.

Common difficulties

Some children find designing and implementing a survey quite complicated.

Remediation

Work in stages, asking the children to carry out and explain each stage. Show why it is necessary to conduct the survey, for example, ask how we could find out how many children come to school by bus, and also ask why it is important to know.

Homework suggestion

Find out about which flavour crisps the people in your house and your friends at home like best. Then use this to make a chart and think of some questions to ask about the chart.

Key point

Conducting a survey, collecting and recording data in graphs or pictograms, and answering survey questions are all essential skills for future scientific studies.

Related material

Pupil Book
Page 62-63

PCM 30
SCM 30
ECM 30

The yellow robot

31

Comparing and ordering numbers

Materials

- whiteboards
- number cards (0 - 9)
- coins
- coloured strips of paper
- glue
- ordinal cards
- number lines
- task cards

Introduction

In Year 2 the children learned ordering cardinal and ordinal numbers up to 100. These activities focus on ordering numbers up to 1000, recognising the smallest and largest number, and building and comparing three-digit numbers.

Objectives

- To read and begin to write the vocabulary of comparing and ordering numbers, including ordinal numbers to at least 100.

- To compare two given three-digit numbers, say which is more or less, and give a number which lies between them.

Oral and mental starter

 Secret numbers

Each child thinks of a number and gives clues for the others to work it out, for example, my number is even, between 30 and 40, is double 16. How quickly can they find the numbers? What is the fewest number of clues they can give to describe their number?

 Number crunching

Write three numbers (1–9) on the board. Ask the children to use them to make a three-digit number on their whiteboards. Repeat twice more. Now give instructions to rearrange the numbers or change the digits to make the highest/smallest number, or numbers that are 1/10/100 more/less.

Main teaching

Note: Ask the children to show their working out (using apparatus where necessary).

 Three figure deals

The dealer gives three number cards (0–9) to each child so they can each make three-digit numbers. Then they turn over three more cards for a target number. The child who can arrange their digits to make a number closest to the target, wins a point. (Extra points for knowing if it is greater or smaller than the target and by how much!)

Comparisons count

Give each group number cards (0–9). Each child takes two cards to make a two-digit number. They toss a coin, with sides labelled 'H' and 'L', to decide if the winner is the highest or lowest number. Each child presents their number (the order of the digits depends on the winning criterion). Next ask the group to turn over two cards for a target number. The child who makes the number closest to the target wins a point. Then ask them to turn over two more cards to make another target number and whoever can make a number between the two targets wins another point. Repeat the last activity, first using three-digit numbers and then with a mixture of two and three-digit numbers. Why is it easier to compare a two-digit number with a three-digit number? Discuss strategies of comparison.

Paper chains

In pairs, the children make a paper chain with different coloured strips of paper. Then they pick ordinal number cards and use them to ask their partner questions about the chain, for example, in what position is the fifth red link? How do they check each answer?

On the line

Give each child a number line with the first and last two- (or three-) digit numbers written on. They then pick up task cards that ask them to find, for example, all the multiples of five, all the even/odd numbers, or a number which is greater than the start number but with the same unit digit.

Plenary

Write two three-digit numbers on the board. Ask the children to record the greater number. Discuss strategies used to compare the two. Repeat with other pairs of numbers. Ask questions such as, find a number where the tens digit is three and lies between these numbers, or, find the smallest multiple of 10 greater than the starting number. Write five numbers on the board. Ask the children to order them from the smallest to the greatest. Discuss their strategies. Ask for the first number, the last but one, the third etc.

Common difficulties

Some comparisons are difficult, for example, 302 and 320, or 99 and 101. Names of ordinal numbers can be difficult, such as those ending in st, nd and rd

Remediation

Use concrete representations (multibase) to show how the numbers differ. Discuss how 1st, 2nd, and 3rd are written. Then look at 21st, 22nd, and 23rd. Show calendars and sports reviews for real life examples.

Homework suggestion

Draw a pattern of 30 shapes using three different shapes and different colours and think of some questions about the position of different shapes - what shape is the fifth red/what colour is the third square etc.

Key point

Knowledge of place value in numbers is essential for understanding arithmetic and effective problem solving.

Related material

 Pupil Book Page 64-65

 PCM 31 SCM 31 ECM 31

 Ziggy's toy village

It's magic!

Say cheese!

Building blocks

32 Rounding numbers

Key vocabulary

- rounding
- round up (to)
- round down (to)
- nearest 10/100

Materials

- number cards (1-50)
- washing line and pegs
- balance scales
- objects to weigh
- imitation coins
- whiteboards
- strawberry picking results
- two-digit price tags
- squared paper
- a spinner (1-9)
- metre sticks
- Freddy Frog

Introduction

These activities revise rounding numbers to the nearest 10 and introduce rounding numbers to the nearest 100. Rounding plays an important role in showing up errors. For example, 99 + 97 + 98 is close to 100 + 100 + 100, so if the answer is nowhere near 300, the child is alerted to a possible error.

Objectives

- To round any two-digit number to the nearest 10 and any three-digit number to the nearest 100.
- To begin to write the vocabulary of estimation and approximation.

Oral and mental starter

 ### Stand up, sit down

Peg random numbers (1-50) on a washing line. Point to a number and ask the children to stand up if they think the number is rounded up to the nearest 10, or sit down if it is rounded down.

 ### Worth your weight in gold

Prepare a balance scale and a number of different-sized objects, which have masses more than ten 1p coins. Ask the children to estimate on their whiteboards, the number of 1p coins it would take to balance each object (rounded to the nearest 10). Repeat using £1 coins. (For this exercise use real coins).

Main teaching

 ### Strawberry picking

Give each group the results of 10 children's strawberry picking. (A: 367, B: 824, C: 542, D: 356, E: 749, F: 878, G: 333, H: 809, I: 721, J: 384). Ask the group to decide approximately how many strawberries each child collected. Ask each group to present its results. Discuss rounding to the nearest 10 and rounding to the nearest 100 and which should be used. Discuss the different answers and remediate where necessary.

👥 Lucy Locket's pocket

Give the group a set of two-digit price cards (in pence) and purses containing imitation coins in multiples of 10p. Ask the children to match the prices to the purses that hold the nearest multiple of 10 and say if they are rounding up or down each time. How can they check their answers? Repeat with three-digit prices and purses holding multiples of £1.

♟ A rounded arrangement

Ask each child to build a block graph with 11 columns labelled: 0, 10, 20, ... 100. Spin a spinner (1-9) twice for a two-digit number and ask the children to record the number in the correct column by rounding first. Ask where to place numbers that end with a five. Repeat with columns labelled: 0, 100, 200, ... 1000 and spin a three-digit number. Ask about numbers that end with 50.

♟ Rounded targets

Spin a spinner (1-9) three times for a three-digit number. Then choose a multiple of 100 as a target. Ask the children to try to make a three-digit number that is this number when rounded to the nearest 100. See how many different possible answers the children can suggest. Check the answers and repeat with other multiples of 100.

Plenary

Ask volunteers to take turns to move Freddy Frog along a metre stick by throwing a die. Each time he moves, they say which multiple of 10 he lands nearest to. What do they notice about the numbers as they are rounded up or down each time? Discuss the numbers that are halfway. Show a table with distances of different towns from London (up to 1000 km). Ask the children to record the towns which have distances of about 300 km. Repeat with other multiples of 100 km.

Common difficulties

Some children have difficulty rounding, thinking that only the exact number is important.

Remediation

Use a number line to demonstrate the relative physical distance between the numbers. Emphasise how the distance between the number and where it is rounded to is the shorter distance (apart from halfway between, that is solved by rounding up).

Homework suggestion

Find numbers at home, for example, on a shop receipt, and round the numbers up or down to the nearest 10 and if possible to the nearest 100.

Reading scales

Introduction

These activities revise the basic units of mass, the kilogram and introduce the gram. The children apply their knowledge of rounding to read scales to the nearest division.

Objectives

 To read scales to the nearest division.

Oral and mental starter

The long and short of it

Give out paper strips of different lengths. Label different areas of the room: 'less than 5 cm', 'between 5 cm and 10 cm', 'between 10 cm and 15 cm', and 'greater than 15 cm'. Ask the children to measure their strip of paper and go and stand in the right place. They measure each other's strips to check.

Weighty estimates

Pass round a 1 kg object so that the children can feel its mass. Then pass an object round for the children to feel and estimate if its mass is more or less than 1 kg. Weigh the object on an electric scale to check. Repeat with other objects. Next pass round a 100 g weight for the children to feel. Pass round an object and ask the children to decide if its mass is less or more than 100 g. Weigh the object on an electric scale and repeat with other objects.

Main teaching

Can't weight, estimate!

Give each group a set of objects of different masses, some in grams and some in kilograms. Ask the children to feel each object and estimate the mass to the nearest 100 g or whole kg. Ask them to predict the heaviest and the lightest object. Then ask them to weigh the objects, on a gram or kilogram scale where the divisions are labelled, and record the mass of each. See whose estimates and predictions were the closest.

Mass match

Give each group two sets of mass cards. One set has pictures of scales that have divisions marked in multiples of 100 g or whole kg and a pointer (see activity book for examples). The other set has descriptions of different masses in words using vocabulary such as: 'about', 'nearly',' halfway between', and 'almost', for each amount of grams or kilograms. Ask the children to spread the cards out, face down, over the table and play pairs matching the scales with the descriptions.

 ## Masses of bags

Fill some different bags with rice, sand, plastic cubes, counters, or marbles. Ask the children to work in pairs to estimate and record about how many kilograms each bag weighs. They may feel the bags to help them estimate. Ask volunteers to try to put the bags in order from the heaviest to the lightest. Ask if all the children agree on the order referring to their recorded estimates and take a vote if necessary. Then ask other volunteers to weigh the bags to check. Ask who had estimates that were very close.

 ## Make us weight

Ask the children to find an object with a mass of about 500 g or about 300 g. Or, ask them to fill their pencil cases so that they weigh 200 g or 400 g. Discuss the strategies used and the ways of checking.

Plenary

Place an object with a mass of between 2 kg and 3 kg on the scales. Ask the children to read the mass to the nearest division and record it on their whiteboards. Compare and discuss the results and the strategies used. Emphasise reading to the nearest division rather than saying, *"between x and y."* Repeat with objects of other masses. Then repeat with kitchen scales and with masses between 100 g and 1000 g.

Common difficulties

Children may have problems measuring a mass that is not exact. They may not fully understand how to read a scale and how to determine what numbers the mass is between.

Remediation

Prepare a large cardboard picture of scales. Stick a piece of string in the centre of its dial with blu-tac in order to make a moveable indicator. Hang the scales on the board. Ask what the scales read as you move the indicator to different positions.

Homework suggestion

Ask for a set of scales (kitchen or bathroom), practise weighing different objects (to the nearest kg or half kg), and put them in order of weight from heaviest to lightest. Write down the order.

Key point

Estimating and measuring mass introduces children to the world of science and links science to mathematics.

Related material

 Pupil Book
Page 68-69

 PCM 33
SCM 33
ECM 33

 On the scales
A weighty problem

Partitioning and recombining

Key vocabulary

- total
- sum
- multiple
- partition

Materials

- number cards (multiples of 10)
- loop cards
- number cards (11–39)
- dice
- apparatus: number lines, multibase etc.
- two-digit prices
- coins
- price increase cards
- counters
- paper abacuses
- whiteboards

Introduction

Mental calculation strategies enable children to solve simple additions quickly and easily. Partitioning two-digit numbers into tens and units was learned in Year 2. This strategy is now used to calculate the sum of two two-digit numbers, without carrying (except in the case of units adding exactly to 10).

Objectives

 To partition numbers into tens and units, then recombine.

– To use known number facts and place value to add mentally.

Oral and mental starter

 Making a century

Give each child a number card (multiples of 10). They show their cards and find a partner to sit with so that together, their numbers total 100. Repeat with multiples of 100.

Loop the loop

Prepare a set of cards with a number and a tens and units question. Choose any child to start by reading out his or her card. For example, *"I have 21, who has three tens and four units?"* The child with the next card in the series continues with, *"I have 34, who has six tens and seven units?"* Continue until the loop comes back to 21.

Main teaching

 Break up, make up

Give each group a set of number cards (11–39), and a die. The children each take a card. Then they roll the die to find the number of multiples of 10 to add to the number on their card. Ask the child to record the addition sentence they have made and work out the total. How do they do this? Give the group apparatus such as multibase and number lines, to enable them to partition the first number into tens and units. Can they see a way to put them back so that the tens are together? Ask the group to record their working method and the number sentences they make at each stage.

Supermarket sums

Give each group a set of two-digit prices for items in the supermarket, and a set of imitation 10p and 1p coins. Say that the manager has decided to raise the prices. They pick up a card each round to indicate by how much the prices are going up (10p, 20p, 30p or 40p). Ask the children to show and draw the coins for the old and new amounts of each item. How do they add the coins? Are they recording the tens and units separately? Remind the children to record the number sentences at each stage of their working. Extend to price increases of two-digit numbers that are not multiples of 10 making sure the addition does not involve crossing the tens. Emphasise both methods of calculation set out in the activity book.

 Self service additions

Ask each child to write an addition of two two-digit numbers. Tell them that the first term should be a two-digit number and the second a multiple of 10, not exceeding 100. Ask them to place counters (one colour for the tens and another for the units) on a paper abacus to show the value of each digit and add them together to find the total. Then give two two-digit numbers, with sums up to 100 and no carrying. At each stage, ask them to record their methods for adding the tens and the units and how they arrive at a final addition sentence.

 Marvellous methods

Write an addition on the board (constraints as in Self service additions), for example, 34 + 53 and ask them to find at least two different ways to calculate the sum. Discuss the strategies used and their relative advantages. Emphasise 30 + 50 + 4 + 3 or 34 + 50 + 3.

Plenary

Write an addition on the board, involving a two-digit number and a multiple of 10, with a sum up to 100. Ask the children to record the total on their whiteboards. Discuss the answers and the strategies used. Repeat with additions of two two-digit numbers, with no carrying and sums up to 100, discuss the methods and emphasise the two outlined in I2. Then give additions with two two-digit multiples of five and sums up to 100. Remind the children to show their working at every stage. Ask volunteers to show how they performed the calculation, on the board.

Common difficulties

Many children develop incorrect strategies such as, adding the four digits involved, or replacing the multiple of 10 by the corresponding one-digit number.

Remediation

Represent the addition graphically on a number line, or with apparatus such as cubes, counters, or an abacus. Repeat the stages of the calculation and then give similar additions.

Homework suggestion

Roll a dice twice, write down the numbers to make a two-digit number, then use lego bricks to make towers of the tens and units that make up your number. Do this several times.

Related material

 Pupil Book
Page 70-71

 PCM 34
SCM 34
ECM 34

 On the right track

On track

Ziggy's number machine

35

Key vocabulary

- multiple
- sum
- total

Materials

- number cards (0–9)
- target number cards
- whiteboards
- dice labelled 0, 10 .50
- counters
- price list
- coins

Adding more than two numbers

Introduction

The following activities revise the addition of three numbers, showing that more than two numbers can be added together. It is important to discuss the different strategies that can be used and to emphasise that methods may vary but the total is always the same.

Objectives

 To extend understanding that more than two numbers can be added.

 To add three or four single-digit numbers mentally.

 To use known number facts and place value to add/subtract mentally.

Oral and mental starter

 Two-digits down pat

Hold up two number cards from two separate piles of cards (1–9) and ask the children to write on their whiteboards, all the two two-digit numbers that can be made from these cards. Then ask them for the number they need to add to make the next multiple of 10. Repeat, aiming for speed and fluent recall of number facts and place value.

 Totals from three

Give each child a number card (1–9). Ask three volunteers to hold up their cards and ask the rest of the class to write the addition sum and the total on their whiteboards. Check, then repeat several times until all the children have had a turn at holding up their cards. Discuss the strategies used.

Main teaching

 Piling on the tens

Give each group three dice, each labelled: 0, 10, 20, 30, 40 and 50. The children take turns to roll the three dice and find the total each time. They can use apparatus such as multibase, if necessary. What other methods can they use? What do they notice about the numbers they are adding? Extend to four numbers.

Target pontoon

Give each group single-digit number cards and a set of target numbers (multiples of 10). The children each take a single-digit number card and keep taking another card until they either make the target, or 'stick' with a number less than the target. If they go over the target they lose but if they stick below the target they win a counter. Two counters are awarded for making the target exactly. The child has to say the sum obtained to win the counter.

 ### Three for a hit

Give each pair of children a set of number cards (0–9). Ask them to find two sets of three single-digit numbers that add up to 10. Then give a target number and ask the children to find and write on their whiteboards, three numbers that add up to this target. Repeat with other target numbers and extend to finding two different ways to make the total.

Rainy day saving

Display a price list with items priced in multiples of 10p, and ask the children to compile shopping lists of three items that total over £1. For example, 40p + 20p + 50p = £1.10. Ask them to use coins to find the total they need to spend. Extension: Say that now they have decided to spend no more than £1 and save the rest for a rainy day. They need to remove one item from the total and then find the change they will receive from the shopkeeper (for example, £1.10 – 20p = 90p, then £1 – 90p = 10p change).

Plenary

Write the price of three items on the board, and ask the children to calculate their total price (prices in pence, totals up to £1, prices that do not cross the tens when added together). They record the items they are buying and the methods they use to find the total to pay each time. Extend to four items with prices that are all multiples of 10p and have total amounts of over £1. Discuss the methods used each time for working out the totals.

Common difficulties

Even with apparatus and without crossing 10, some children may not be secure enough in their number facts to be able to add three two-digit numbers.

Remediation

Use single-digit numbers that do not cross 10 to help the children with their number facts and to see patterns. Give plenty of practice of addition of three numbers using money, rods, or other concrete apparatus.

Homework suggestion

Roll a die and multiply the number it lands on by 10. Repeat twice more until you have three numbers to add together. Find the total. Write five other addition sums of three multiples of 10 that have the same total.

Related material

 Pupil Book
Page 72-73

 PCM 35
SCM 35
ECM 35

 The automatic food machine

The number pump

Ziggy's tea party

36

Money problems and investigations

Key vocabulary

- total
- change
- how much ... left?

Materials

- whiteboards
- menus
- purses
- money
- word problems
- priced objects
- list of fairground rides

Introduction

These activities require children to apply the six-step strategy for problem solving to two-step problems. The six steps of the strategy are: to read the problem, understand the question, find the relevant data, design a solution strategy, write the answer and check it.

Objectives

 To solve word problems involving numbers in 'real life' and money, using one or more steps.

 To explain how the problem was solved.

Oral and mental starter

All change!

Tell the children that you have a £1 coin and you spend 25p. Ask them to write the change you expect to receive. Repeat with other amounts in multiples of 5p. Extend to starting with £2.

Three coins in the fountain

Say, *"I have three coins in my purse, which make X amount altogether. Which coins could I have?"* Ask the children to write their answers on their whiteboards. Write the different combinations of coins on the board. Then repeat the activity with three notes instead of three coins.

Main teaching

Change café

In groups of four, one child is the waiter in a café and the other three are customers. Give the group a menu with prices and a purse of money to each customer. The waiter works out the bill, takes the money and gives the appropriate change. The customers check the bill before paying, offer an appropriate sum for payment, and check their change. Repeat the activity until all four children have had a turn at being the waiter.

Tackling the two-steps

Give each group a two-step money word problem. For example, Denis has £4. He buys a watch for £1.40 and a small car for £2.50. How much money will he have left? Each group solves the problem and records their strategies and working. Then each group presents its methods and answers to the other groups. Discuss the strategies used. Then repeat with other two-step problems.

Ringing the changes

Hold up an object with a price tag. Ask the children to say which silver coins they could use to pay for the object. Then ask them to work out how much change they would receive from a £1 coin. Ask them to write the number sentence. Provide coins to help with the calculations. Discuss the different ways of paying and working out the change. Then extend to paying with a £2 coin.

Problem makers

Write a price list on the board. Say an amount that the children have to spend. Ask one child to choose two items he or she wants to buy and write the matching word problem on the board in which the question will be either, what change will he or she receive? Or, How much money has he or she left? The children solve the problem and record the method they used. Discuss the methods and ask volunteers to show their working on the board. Repeat with other volunteers, and extend to buying three items.

Plenary

Display a list of six funfair rides and how much they cost (all less than £1 and in multiples of 5p). Spin the spinner (1–6) to choose two rides from the list. Each child buys the appropriate tickets and works out how much change they will have from £1. Discuss the strategies used. Repeat with other combinations of rides and extend to three or four rides with change from a £2 coin. After each transaction, ask a volunteer to show how to check the answers starting from the result.

Common difficulties

Thinking through how to do a two-step problem can be difficult.

Remediation

Discuss the steps, and organise the questions into two distinct parts. Check each part after solving it. Use graphical representations of the problems, and if necessary concrete representation with coins.

Homework suggestion

Find an old reciept at home that shows the following information: a record of how much was spent, how much the person gave the cashier, and how much change they received.

Key point

Two-step word problems introduce the children to 'real' mathematical problems, that involve them in designing and implementing complex solving strategies.

Related material

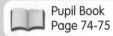
Pupil Book
Page 74-75

PCM 36
SCM 36
ECM 36

At the check-out

Going shopping

mathspace

37

Number operations

Key vocabulary

• operation

Materials

• die marked
  x, x, +, +, -, -

• number sentence
  cards

• multiples of 10
  cards

• measuring
  problem cards

• number cards
  (1–50)

Introduction

Number stories encourage children to find mathematical solutions in contexts broader than the Maths lesson itself. In the following activities they apply their knowledge of the four basic number operations to first define the problem, and then to compute the solution.

Objectives

● To choose and use appropriate operations...and appropriate ways of calculating.

– To make up number stories to reflect statements.

– To say what operation sign a symbol represents.

Oral and mental starter

Operation station

Give the children a target number (up to 20) and ask a volunteer to roll a die marked x, x, +, +, -, -. The children write as many number sentences as they can for the target, using only the operation shown on the die. Write some of the answers on the board and repeat with different target numbers.

Number jumbling

Write three single-digit numbers on the board, for example, 2, 5 and 6. Ask the children to make as many numbers as possible using each number only once and the operations: +, -, and x, for example, 6 – 5 = 1, 5 – 2 = 3, 6 – 2 = 4, 2 + 5 = 7. Discuss the different operations chosen and write some of the results on the board. Repeat with a different set of numbers.

Main teaching

Operating theatre

Give each group a set of number sentence cards with the operation signs missing, for example, 2 * 10 = 12, 12 * 2 = 6, 13 * 5 = 8, 2 * 5 = 10. The children suggest strategies to find the missing signs and then apply them to the cards. Ask them to make up their own number sentences of a similar type for the group. How will they check them? Then ask them to make up stories using suitable vocabulary to match the number sentences.

On you go!

Give each group a shuffled set of multiples of 10 cards. The children line up the cards in a row then work out the operation sign and number needed to move from the last result to the next number. For example, if the numbers were 40, 20, 70 ... then the children would have to give the answers - 20, + 50, and so on. Repeat with multiples of five.

 Near misses

Ask the children to write four single-digit number cards. Say a target number between 20 and 100. The children need to use their numbers only once with +, -, x or ÷ to make a number that is as close as possible to the target number.

 Moving along

The children each choose three cards from a set of number cards (1–20). They show the strategies, calculations and operations they would use to move from one to the next. Repeat with numbers to 50.

Plenary

Write a simple number sentence on the board in which the sign is missing, for example, 3 * 5 = 8. The children need to find the missing sign. Repeat with other number sentences with the signs missing. Then extend to two missing signs with one-digit numbers, for example, 3 * 4 * 2 = 5, or multiples of 10. Discuss the strategies used to find the answers and the methods of checking.

Common difficulties

Some children are not used to finding the sign and sometimes add the three numbers. Some have no idea how to begin.

Remediation

Introduce basic strategies and set questions with very small numbers. For example, 3 * 1 = 2, and explain different strategies such as, try +, then try -. Explain that, if the result is smaller than the first number, it could not be an addition or a multiplication, so try a subtraction.

Homework suggestion

Find at least 5 different ways of making 12 using any of the digits 1-9 once and the signs +, -, x, ÷.

Solutions can include: 9 + 3   6 x 2   3 x 2 + 6

8 + 4   6 + 2 + 4   6 ÷ 3 + 9 + 1

Key point

Solving number operations strengthens mathematical problem solving and reinforces reasoning.

Related material

 Pupil Book Page 76-77

 PCM 37
SCM 37
ECM 37

 Alien maker
In the maths lab

Shapes and patterns

Key vocabulary

- 2-D shape
- 3-D shape
- net

Materials

- 2-D and 3-D shapes
- whiteboards
- tray
- cardboard 3-D shapes
- scissors
- sellotape
- interlocking cubes

Introduction

These activities focus on building compound shapes from basic shapes, building 3-D shapes from pictures of them and visualising the appearance of shapes after a rotation, which all enhance children's spatial vision of 3-D objects. The children also revise classifying shapes according to their properties.

Objectives

- To make and describe shapes and patterns.
- To relate solid shapes to pictures of them.

Oral and mental starter

Screen test

Hold up a shape behind a screen. Describe it to the class in terms of the number of vertices, sides, or faces. Ask the children to guess what shape you are holding and write their answers on their whiteboards. Put the different guesses on the board and ask children to describe these shapes. Then show the shape you were holding and see who was right.

Kim's game

Set out a number of shapes on a tray. Give the children one minute to look at the shapes and then cover the tray. The children write as many of the shapes as they can remember from the tray. Or you can ask for answers and write them on the board.

Main teaching

All in the net!

Each child takes two cardboard 3-D shapes. They cut each one of them to make a net and draw round it, marking in pen where the edges are. They then stick it back together again and make a net for their other shape in a similar fashion. They put all the nets in a hat. Each child pulls out a net and tries to identify the solid that matches it.

One of a kind

Give each child in the group five interlocking cubes. Ask them to join their five cubes together and try to make different models. Ask them to compare models and remind them to look from every angle to make sure they are definitely different. Repeat with four cubes and six cubes. With which number of cubes is it easier to produce different models and why should this be so?

Mothershape to the stars

Give each child access to a set of plastic 2-D shapes to use as templates, including triangles, squares, hexagons, pentagons and octagons. Ask them to use the shapes to create different stars by drawing round the templates. Make a display of the stars. Then ask the children to build different shapes by using triangles only. Make a display and discuss the ways to build each compound shape.

Make a shape

Give each child access to a set of triangles. Ask the children to put two triangles together in different ways and see how many shapes of different numbers of sides, they can design. Repeat with other pairs of 2-D shapes.

Plenary

Show the children a shape made out of cubes like one of those presented in the pupil book. Ask the children to record on their whiteboards how many cubes make up this shape. Discuss the strategies used. Repeat with other compound cube shape pictures.

Show shapes made out of triangles. Ask the children to write on their whiteboards how many triangles they can see. Discuss the strategies used. Repeat with other compound shapes.

Common difficulties

Some children may have difficulty seeing how many basic shapes there are in a compound shape. Some children may only look for obvious triangles and not find the less obvious ones.

Remediation

Rotate a compound shape made of cubes. Discuss the ways to visualise all the cubes even if only some of them are visible. Emphasise the fact that a triangle can be found inside another one, and one should count both.

Homework suggestion

Ask the children to build, or suggest what 3-D shapes they would use to build a robot. For example, a cuboid for its body. Then ask them to say where they could find this shape at home, for example, a cereal box.

Key point

Spatial representation and vision are basic and essential skills in geometry.

Related material

 Pupil Book
Page 78-79

 PCM 38
SCM 38
ECM 38

Right-angled turns

Key vocabulary

- right angle
- degrees
- clockwise
- anti-clockwise

Materials

- squares of paper
- instruction cards
- analogue clock faces
- whiteboards
- washing machine cycle dials RM 2
- paper fasteners

Introduction

Whole turns (360°), half turns (180°) and quarter turns (90°) were introduced in Years 1 and 2. These activities revise these concepts and extend the children's knowledge to include the number of quarter turns and the directions (clockwise and anti-clockwise) involved in rotating given shapes, and ways to estimate if an angle is a right angle.

Objectives

- To make and describe right-angled turns.
- To read and begin to write the vocabulary related to direction.
   - To know 90° equals a right angle.

Oral and mental starter

Right angle angling

Remind children that a right angle equals 90°. Ask each child to make a paper right angle finder (by folding a piece of paper). Ask them to work in pairs to find shapes around the room that have at least one right angle. Ask volunteers to share their findings and ask other children to check the right angles.

Simon spins

Play 'Simon says' with instructions of $\frac{1}{2}$, $\frac{1}{4}$, $\frac{3}{4}$ and whole turns, and a direction clockwise or anti-clockwise.

Main teaching

Clock geometry

Give each group a set of instruction cards with a number of right angles and the direction, for example, two right angles clockwise. Give each child in the group an analogue clock face. One child says an o'clock time and they all set their clocks. Then another child turns over an instruction card and they all move the big hand accordingly. One child reads the new time. Repeat with another o'clock starting time and a different instruction card.

Robotic script

Ask each group to design instructions for a Roamer to make 90° (or right-angled) turns to trace a straight letter of the alphabet. Which letters can they make using only right-angled turns?

 ### Face to face

Appoint one child to be the robot and another four children to stand around him or her in the shape of a cross. The robot faces one of the four children. Then a fifth child gives the robot instructions in the form of a number of right-angled turns, and direction. The rest of the class predicts and then records on their whiteboards, who the robot will end up facing.

 ### In a spin

Give each child a copy of a washing machine cycle dial (RM 2). Using a paper fastener, they fix a pointer onto it. Tell the children the washing cycle starts with the pointer in an upright position. Ask, *"If the pointer moves through three right-angled turns clockwise where would it end up?"*. Repeat as above, but this time ask them to start the pointer at 90° (or 180° or 270°). Finally say where the pointer starts and finishes and ask how many right-angled turns it has turned through. Extension: use the 45° points as starting points.

Plenary

Ask a volunteer to stand up and do a half-turn clockwise. Ask the children to write how many right angles the child turns though. Elicit that two right angles is a half turn, three right angles a three-quarter turn, and four right angles is a whole turn. Extend to turning through five or more right angles and asking how many whole and part turns are made.

Common difficulties

Some children may still have difficulty differentiating between clockwise and anti-clockwise.

Remediation

Explain and show that clockwise is the same direction as a clock turns. Practise with children standing up and turning.

Homework suggestion

Ask the children to draw four different times of day on an analogue clock in which the big hand would have to turn 90° to reach the small hand.

North, South, East and West

Key vocabulary

- North
- East
- South
- West
- compass

Materials

- battleships' grids
- compasses
- treasure maps

Introduction

The relative directions learned so far are right/left turns or clockwise/anti-clockwise. The following activities introduce the absolute directions of North, South, East and West, as seen at the points of a compass. You can integrate this unit plan with a Geography lesson.

Objectives

 To recognise and use the four compass directions, N, S, E, W.

Oral and mental starter

Right angle rondo

Draw a circle on the board and label the cross points, A, B, C and D. Ask the children to copy this diagram. Make a pointer and point it straight up to A. Then ask a volunteer to roll a die and say, *"Imagine your pointer moves x number of right angles, clockwise (or anti-clockwise), show me what letter will it point to."*

Battleships

Set up a battleship grid (A-F, 1-6), hidden behind a screen with different objects on different squares and ask two volunteers to man the grid. Divide the rest of the class into pairs and give each pair of children a blank grid in order to keep a record of the battle. Ask the children to give grid references in terms of A-F, 1-6, and the volunteers tell them if it is a hit or a miss. How long does it take the class to sink all the battleships?

Main teaching

All encompassing

Give each group a compass and teach the rhyme 'Never Eat Sugared Wheat', so that the children know how to read the four points: North, East, South and West. Ask the groups to choose a point in the classroom and position the pointer so that it points to North. Tell them that this is called 'setting the compass'. Ask them to find objects that lie in each of the four compass directions. Repeat from a different standing point. What do they notice about the direction of the compass points each time?

Treasure seekers

Remind the children of the rhyme 'Never Eat Sugared Wheat', so that they can extrapolate the names of all the compass directions from knowing North. Give each group a treasure map on a labelled grid with 'North' clearly labelled. There should be at least eight features or objects marked on the map. One child moves out of earshot while the others decide where the treasure is hidden and write down the co-ordinates. The treasure seeker comes back and tries to work out where the treasure is, using direction questions such as, East of the tree, or, South of the lake. Repeat with a different treasure seeker. How many questions does it take each treasure seeker to discover the treasure?

 ### Weather vanes

Label 'North' in the classroom and ask the children to tell you where East, South, and West should be labelled. Remind the children of the rhyme 'Never Eat Sugared Wheat', so that they can extrapolate the names of all the compass directions from knowing North. Introduce a compass and ask volunteers to check. Remind them that to set the compass, they need to turn it so that the pointer points to the North. Then the children stand in the middle, facing North and give instructions such as, 'Turn one right angle clockwise and say which direction you are facing?'.

 ### Simon orientates

Ask the children to stand facing North and play 'Simon says' in the form of: *"Simon says turn three right angles anti-clockwise."* The children have to say which direction they end up facing. Children who face the wrong direction sit down and the last child still standing is the winner. Play again with a volunteer as Simon.

Plenary

Draw a map with a number of features on the board and draw a compass. Name a starting point on the map with reference to one of the features and say: *"From this feature, I travel North. Write on your whiteboards the name of the first object I will meet."* Repeat with other features and other directions.

Common difficulties

Some children may mix up North and up or, south and down.

Remediation

Repeat the plenary activity with the map on the floor and letting the children use a compass. Rotate the map and repeat the activity.

Homework suggestion

Write directions of how to walk from your front door to the kitchen and then to the lounge. Use instructions such as: North 4, East 3.

Key point

Compass points are common features in everyday life and essential in Geography and orientation.

Related material

 Pupil Book Page 82-83

 PCM 40
SCM 40
ECM 40

 Desert exploration

Find a friend

Key vocabulary

- second/s
- minute/s
- hour/s
- day/s
- week/s
- fortnight

Materials

- digital time cards
- time name cards
- stopwatches or timers
- length of time cards
- activity cards
- time bingo cards
- counters
- dice
- cubes
- whiteboards

Units of time

Introduction

The units of measuring time are different from other measuring units in that they do not use a base of 10. These activities focus on the relationship between hours, minutes and seconds, and drill converting from one time unit to another.

Objectives

- To use units of time and know the relationships between them.
- To suggest suitable units to measure or estimate time.

Oral and mental starter

Time line

Prepare sets of digital time cards that show different 15 minute intervals and make a list of the corresponding times using analogue clock vocabulary. Give each child one card. Call out one of the times from your list and ask the child who has that time to come to the front of the class. The child positions themselves in the line of children already standing, according to the time, so that the times are in order. The children hold their cards in front of them so that the class can check the order.

Here for the duration

Give each child a card from a set saying: second, minute, hour, day, weekend, fortnight, week, month, and year. Ask the children to divide themselves into teams including only one of each card and then line up in order from the shortest time to the longest time. Ask the children to hold up their cards and read them out in order.

Main teaching

Time fillers

Ask all the children to count out a minute while watching the second hand on the clock. Ask each group to make a list of things they think they can do in one minute. Give them a stopwatch or a timer so that they can check their estimates. Then see if they can make a minute timer using sand, and plastic or paper cups. They check its accuracy using a stopwatch. Can they make a two-minute timer? A half-minute? How can they check the number of seconds each time? Finally, give the group two sets of cards. One has selected lengths of time from a minute up to a whole day, including half and quarter hours. The other set of cards has activities. Ask the group to match each card with an activity that could take about that time.

Time converts

Give each group a mixed time such as, 1 hour 50 minutes. Ask the children to make a list of activities lasting about that time. Then ask them to record this time in minutes only. Discuss the strategies used to convert the time from a mixed time to minutes only. Repeat with other lengths of time including seconds, minutes, hours and days.

Cubes of time

Review that 60 minutes equals one hour. Working in pairs, the children take turns to roll a die and collect that number of cubes. Explain that each cube represents five minutes. They keep collecting cubes until they have or pass 60 minutes (12 cubes), and record the number of hours and minutes they have. For example, 15 cubes represent 75 minutes, which is 1 hour 15 minutes. Variation: Use minutes and seconds or hours and days.

Time bingo

Play a bingo matching game with a set of bingo cards showing numbers of hours, minutes and seconds such as, 48 hours, 120 minutes and 30 seconds. Call out times in the form of, two days, two hours, or, half a minute. The children have to cover the matching times with a counter. The first child to cover all their times shouts, "bingo!"

Plenary

Ask how many seconds there are in one minute, how many minutes in one hour and how many hours in one day. Name an activity and ask about how long it takes. Then say how long it took, for example, 1 hour 45 minutes, and ask the children to convert the time to minutes only. Ask them to write their answers on their whiteboards and hold them up. Repeat with other activities and other time conversions from seconds to minutes and from hours to days and vice versa.

Common difficulties

Children may still have difficulty with estimating units of time accurately. They may also be unsure of the units to measure longer periods of time. Children may have problems in converting, multiplying instead of adding, or adding instead of multiplying.

Remediation

Play the 'minute game' whereby the children close their eyes and estimate the length of a minute. Use minutes and seconds, and let the children feel how long this length of time lasts. Extend to checking longer periods of time by setting an alarm clock. Explain that, for example, 1 hour 45 minutes means one hour and 45 minutes, then transform 1 hour into 60 minutes and add the two numbers.

Homework suggestion

Make a time diary in which you note what time you do different activities, for example, eat tea, have a bath, go to bed etc. Draw the analogue and digital clocks to represent the times.

Key point

Knowing units of time and being able to convert from one unit to another are basic life skills. These skills are also used in many scientific domains, especially physics.

Related material

 Pupil Book Page 84-85

 PCM 41 SCM 41 ECM 41

 Running like clockwork

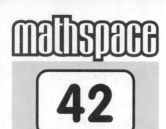
Measuring mass

Key vocabulary

- mass
- kilogram/s
- gram/s
- mixed units

Materials

- weights
- balance scales
- kitchen scales
- objects to weigh
- whiteboards
- sets of different mass objects labelled A to G
- packets of food
- shopping bags

Introduction

In Unit plan 33, grams were introduced and children learned to weigh objects in either kilograms or in grams. In these activities they learn the relationship between these two measuring units, namely that 1 kg is equal to 1000 g.

Objectives

- To measure and compare using the standard units of kilograms and grams.
- To know the relationships between kilograms and grams.

Oral and mental starter

Estimate weights

Pass round a 1 kg weight and ask the children to feel how heavy it is. Then pass round objects of different mass, and ask the children to say if they think each object is more or less than 1 kg. Check the actual mass of each object using balance scales and a kilogram weight. Repeat with 100 g and 500 g.

Combined weights

Prepare a set of objects with different masses that are multiples of 100 g and less than 1 kg, with the mass clearly marked in grams on each one. Display all the objects on your table. Hold up two different objects and ask the children to write what their total mass is. Make sure that the total mass of the pairs of objects you hold up does not exceed 1000 g. Check using weighing scales. Repeat several times with different combinations.

Main teaching

Feeling groovy

Give each group a set of seven objects labelled A to G. Ask the children to order and record the objects from the heaviest to lightest by feeling and estimating. Then ask them to weigh the objects using balance scales, record the real mass of each object in g and kg, and check each other's orders to see how many of them were correct.

👥 Masses of food

Give each group a set of 10 packets of food with their mass crossed out. The children choose one packet and take turns to estimate its mass. Ask them to record their estimates on a chart and compare. Then they weigh the packet and record the actual mass in kilograms and grams, and see whose estimate was the closest. Repeat with the other objects and see if the estimates become more accurate as they progress.

🧍 Kilo-shoppers

Give each pair of children a shopping bag and tell them that they have to buy items that add up to about 1 kg. Ask them to collect things from around the room, weigh them and record their masses in grams, rounding to the nearest 100 g. If they go over 1 kg, they take something out and replace it with an object of about the required mass. When they have about 1 kg in the shopping bag they add up the rounded masses on their list to check.

🧍 Mass making

Prepare sets of mass cards such as 1 kg, $\frac{1}{2}$ kg, almost 1 kg, about 1 kg, less than 1 kg, and more than 1 kg. Divide the class into pairs and give each pair kitchen scales, a set of mass cards and a set of objects that weigh different multiples of 100 g. They turn over a mass card and try to find different combinations of objects that have a combined mass that matches what is written on the card. Ask how many grams equal half a kilogram. If necessary, explain that 500g equals $\frac{1}{2}$ kg and that two objects of 500 g equals 1 kg.

Plenary

Write a cake recipe on the board in which each ingredient weighs a multiple of 100 g. Ask the children to calculate the mass of the cake mixture at each stage of its preparation (as each ingredient is added). As you pass the 1 kg mark, introduce how to write in mixed units using kilograms and grams. After each subsequent 'addition' ask the children to write the new mass in both kilograms and grams, and in grams only.

Common difficulties

Some children may need more practice to develop their awareness of different masses. Some children may have problems in working with, and recording masses of, more than 1 kg using mixed units.

Remediation

Give practice estimating mass in practical contexts. Revise which combinations of multiples of 100 make 1000, using multibase if necessary.

Homework suggestion

Find some packets and tins in the kitchen that have their masses written in grams. Write at least three different combinations of packets and/or tins that total 1 kg.

Key point

Estimating and measuring mass in kilograms, in grams, or both, is a step into the world of science, thus showing the link between Science and Maths.

Related material

Pupil Book
Page 86-87

PCM 42
SCM 42
ECM 42

Load the crates

Weigh the boxes

The strong man

43

Fraction problems

Key vocabulary

- half
- quarter
- three quarters

Materials

- dial scale cards
- grids
- metre sticks
- paper strips
- dice labelled: $\frac{1}{4}$ m, $\frac{1}{2}$ m, 1 m, $1\frac{1}{4}$ m, $1\frac{1}{2}$ m, and $1\frac{3}{4}$ m
- plasticine
- scales
- g/kg recording charts
- word problems
- clocks with seconds hand
- apparatus to facilitate problem solving

Introduction

Fractions were introduced in Unit plans 24 and 25. In the following activities children learn to apply their knowledge to real life problems, especially problems linked to measures. Numbers between one and two are also introduced such as, $1\frac{1}{2}$, and $1\frac{1}{4}$.

Objectives

- To solve word problems using numbers in 'real life', money and measures.
- To solve mathematical problems and puzzles, recognise simple patterns and relationships, generalise and predict. Suggest extentions by asking 'what if...?'

Oral and mental starter

 The whole of it

Ask quick fire questions such as: How many fifths make one whole? Ask the children to write the answer on their whiteboards. Check and remediate. Then write $\frac{5}{5} = 1$ on the board. Repeat with other denominators. Use fraction vocabulary such as numerator and denominator.

 Quartermasters

Give out different size grids of up to 20 squares. Ask the children to colour $\frac{1}{4}$ of their grid and write how many squares that is. Ask: "*What is $\frac{1}{4}$ of 20? Anyone with 20 square grids hold up your answer.*" Ask other questions about different size grids. Repeat with other fractions.

Main teaching

 Measure for measure

Divide the class into groups of three. Give each group a metre stick and three strips of paper measuring 25 cm, 50 cm and 100 cm. Ask the children to use the metre stick and their strips to work out what fractions of a metre their strips are and record their answers. Next give out dice labelled: $\frac{1}{4}$ m, $\frac{1}{2}$ m, 1 m, $1\frac{1}{4}$ m, $1\frac{1}{2}$ m, and $1\frac{3}{4}$ m. Ask each child in turn to throw the die and make the length shown, using the strips of paper.

Weighty matters

Give each group a heavy plasticine ball (or a bag of stones) and scales. Ask the children to weigh out 1 kg and put the rest aside. Then ask them to divide the 1 kg into four equal parts and weigh the parts to check they are all the same. Give each group a chart to fill in to show how much $\frac{1}{2}$ kg, $\frac{1}{4}$ kg, $1\frac{1}{4}$ kg, $1\frac{1}{2}$ kg, and 2 kg are in grams. Next, give each group word problems involving masses, in which they can use the plasticine (or stones) to build a representation of the problem. For example, David ate $\frac{1}{2}$ kg of apricots this morning and 1 kg this afternoon. How many kilograms of apricots did he eat today? How much is this in grams?

Time and again

Divide the class into pairs. Give each pair of children a clock (or watch or stopwatch) with a second hand. Ask the children to work out how many seconds there are in, for example, one minute, $\frac{1}{2}$ minute, $\frac{1}{4}$ minute, and $1\frac{1}{2}$ minutes. Then ask them to try and find an activity for each length of time and make a recording sheet to show their results. Extend to asking the children to work out how many minutes there are in, for example, one hour, $\frac{1}{2}$ an hour, and $\frac{1}{4}$ of an hour, and recording activities for these lengths of time.

Bit problems

Give each child three simple word problems involving fractions, that can be modelled using apparatus. For example, the prices in a shop were: one and a half pounds, three pounds, five and a half pounds and two pounds. In a sale, each price was reduced by half a pound. What are the new prices? Give all the children access to apparatus (in this case coins) and ask them to represent each of their problems, solve them and record the results.

Plenary

Write on the board, a fraction or a simple mixed number measure written in words, for example, an hour and a half or half a kilogram. Ask the children to record the number in figures and then use a different measuring unit to express the same measurement (the hour value in minutes, the kilogram value in grams). Then write a simple word problem involving similar numbers, and ask the children to solve it. Check and if necessary talk through the six steps of problem solving.

Common difficulties

Children find solving word problems involving mixed numbers more difficult than those with only whole numbers.

Remediation

Draw a picture to represent the problem and review the six problem solving steps. If more help is needed, explain how to solve a specific problem, then give the same problem to the children to solve. Finally, give the same type of problem again but with different numbers.

Homework suggestion

Look at a TV guide and find a programme that lasts: $\frac{1}{4}$ hour, $\frac{1}{2}$ hour, 1 hour, $1\frac{1}{2}$ hours.

Related material

 Pupil Book Page 88-89

 PCM 43
SCM 43
ECM 43

 A weighty problem

Reading clock

Quizziggy

Mass and weighing

44

Key vocabulary

- mass
- mixed units
- kilogram/s
- gram/s

Materials

- whiteboards
- sets of small sand bags labelled A-F
- sand/rice/beans
- empty labelled food packets
- six different objects
- kitchen scales
- bathroom scales
- balance scales
- pan balances

Introduction

These activities extend children's knowledge of grams and kilograms. They revise writing masses in mixed units of kilograms and grams and estimating mass, for example, a newborn baby's weight is about 3 kg rather than about 30 kg.

Objectives

- To suggest suitable units and measuring equipment to estimate or measure mass.
- To record estimates and measurements to the nearest whole or half unit, or in mixed units.

Oral and mental starter

Making it up

Ask the children how many grams equal 1 kg. Remind them, if necessary, that 1 kg = 1000 g. Write on the board a mass in grams that is less than 1 kg and a multiple of 100. Ask the children to show you on their whiteboards how many more grams you need to add to make 1 kg. Repeat several times. Then ask them to show you two values that, added to the mass on the board, make 1 kg. Finally, change the target mass, for example, to 800 g.

Puppy weight

Pose the following problem: A puppy weighs 200 g and it grows at a rate of 100 g a week. What will its weight be after three weeks? How many weeks will it take for the puppy to weigh 1 kg? How many weeks until it weighs 2 kg? If necessary, use a number line to explain.

Main teaching

All in order

Give each group a set of six small bags of sand labelled A to F. The sand bags should weigh six different amounts. The whole group guesses the order of the bags if they are arranged from the heaviest to the lightest. Then ask each child to estimate the mass of each bag to the nearest $\frac{1}{2}$ kg. They weigh the bags and see if their order was correct and who was the closest to the right mass for each bag.

Packers' union

Give each group some empty food packets/cartons that show the original mass of their contents in grams and others that have masses in mixed units. Ask the children to fill each packet to its correct weight. They can use sand, rice, or beans. Ask them to then write the values in grams in mixed unit measures, and to write all the masses rounded to the nearest $\frac{1}{2}$ unit.

Weight and see

Weigh four different objects beforehand and label them randomly A–D. Write the four masses on the board, in grams only, and pass the objects round the class. Each child writes which object weighs which mass. Choose four children to come out and weigh the objects on scales. Next, send round two other objects and ask volunteers to estimate their masses. As each volunteer gives their estimate in grams only, the other children stand up if they think the actual mass is higher and stay seated if they think it is lower. Weigh the objects and see who was right. Finally, ask all the children to record all six actual masses in mixed units.

Tools of the trade

Display different apparatus for measuring mass, for example, kitchen scales, bathroom scales, and a pan balance. Ask the children which one they would use to weigh different objects, such as a dog, a pebble, a mug, or a person. Weigh some of the objects and see if they were right. Ask how you could find out the mass of objects that you cannot weigh yourselves, such as an elephant or a space rocket? Discuss ways to check about how much different objects weigh. Suggest looking up information in an encyclopedia or on the internet.

Plenary

Write on the board, the mass of a bag of carrots in grams, for example, 2250 g. First ask the children about how many kilograms it weighs. Then ask the children to record the weight in mixed units: 2 kg 250 g, and in kilograms only: $2\frac{1}{4}$ kg. Repeat with other objects and other masses. Use apparatus to explain how much 250 represents. Show them that if you divide 1000 g (1 kg) into four equal parts each part weighs 250 g, so the mass of each part is $\frac{1}{4}$ kg.

Common difficulties

Some children sometimes find it difficult to convert measurements into mixed units or into mixed numbers or just fractions.

Remediation

Partition a measurement into a kilogram part and a gram part, for example, 2250 = 2000 + 250. Remind the children that 1000 g = 1 kg and ask them how many kilograms 2000 g makes.

Homework suggestion

Using an encyclopaedia or the Internet, find different animals that have the following approximate weights at birth: 1 kg, 3 kg, 5 kg, 8 kg, 10 kg, 20 kg.

Key point

Using mixed units and converting weights and measures from given units to different units is an essential scientific skill.

Related material

Pupil Book
Page 90-91

PCM 44
SCM 44
ECM 44

 Weigh in

Ziggy's televisions

A weighty problem

45

Investigating shapes

Key vocabulary

- prism
- quadrilateral

Materials

- paper shapes
- prisms
- pegboards
- elastic bands
- paper
- scissors

Introduction

Mathematical investigations are a useful tool to promote independent thinking and strategy development. The following activities focus on general statements about familiar shapes that challenge the children to apply the skills and knowledge they have learned.

Objectives

- To investigate general statements about familiar shapes by finding examples that satisfy them.

Oral and mental starter

Crossword puzzle

Write the name of a shape on the board and go round the class asking volunteers to make up different clues for it. Then write a different shape name vertically through the first name as in a crossword puzzle. Again ask for clues for this shape. Keep adding shape names to the crossword and eliciting clues.

Pattern prediction

Stick a three or four-shape pattern sequence on the board. Ask what the twelfth shape will be. Ask other questions about the pattern such as, what the nth shape will be, name the two next shapes, and what will come after/before a given shape.

Main teaching

Are you square?

'All squares are rectangles.' Ask each group to investigate this general statement. Those who think that it is true, must justify their answer and those who think it is not true, need to give at least one counter example (explain the meaning of counter example.) Repeat with the following question statement: All rectangles are squares.

The prism club

Give each group a variety of prisms: triangular, cube, pentagonal, hexagonal, and octagonal. Ask what all these shapes have in common. Ask the children to formulate general statements about prisms. If they do not find any, give them general statements about prisms and ask them to investigate them.

The quad squad

Explain that a quadrilateral is a closed shape with four straight sides. Ask each child to draw a quadrilateral. Compare the results. See if they can draw different ones. They can use pegboards and elastic bands to construct different quadrilaterals and copy them into their notebooks. Then hold up different shapes and ask the children to say whether it is a quadrilateral or not. Ask them to explain their answer, using the general statement: a quadrilateral is a closed shape with four straight sides.

Side by side

Give the children, or ask them to cut out, two identical triangles. Ask them to fit the two identical triangles together along one side, record the resulting shape and say how many sides it has. See how many different shapes they can make. Repeat for other shapes including quadrilaterals, pentagons, hexagons and octagons. What do they notice? Ask the children to make general statements about their results.

Plenary

Write the following general statement: A rectangle always has four right-angled corners. Ask who disagrees. If some children disagree, ask them to find a rectangle with at least one angle that is not a right angle. Repeat with other simple general statements about 2-D and 3-D shapes. Ask the children to make a general statement about various 3-D shapes. Discuss the answers and other possible general statements.

Common difficulties

Children may have difficulty making generalisations, they may make statements that do not hold true for all shapes of that type. Sometimes they think a true statement is incorrect.

Remediation

In cases of making incorrect generalisations, show the children a picture of a counter example and discuss the problem. When a child thinks a true general statement is incorrect ask them to show you a counter example.

Homework suggestion

Make two different types of prisms at home. Record how many faces and corners each one has.

Key point

Children need to develop strategies to check the truth of basic mathematical statements and to be aware that statements can and should be checked. General statements introduce rules in geometry, and serve as introductions to axioms and theorems.

Related material

 Pupil Book
Page 92-93

 PCM 45
SCM 45
ECM 45

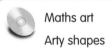 Maths art

Arty shapes

Counting in steps of three, four and five

Key vocabulary

- sequence

Materials

- sets of number cards (1–50)
- squared paper strips
- floor grid (1–50)
- beanbag or counters
- two dice

Introduction

The following activities revise counting on and back, in threes, fours and fives, from different starting numbers.

Objectives

- To count on in steps of 3, 4 or 5 from any small number to at least 50, then back again.
- To describe and extend simple number sequences.

Oral and mental starter

Fizz, buzz or fizzbuzz

Play Fizzbuzz. Count around the class in ones. Explain that if a number is a multiple of two, they say, '*fizz*' instead of the number. When it is a multiple of ten, they say, '*buzz*' and when it is a multiple of 2 and 10 they say, '*fizzbuzz*' . See how long it takes them to realise they will never have to say just '*buzz*' because all multiples of 10 are also multiples of two!

Sequence savers

Say a number sequence that is in steps of twos or tens. Make a mistake, or miss out a number, and ask the children to tell you what they noticed about your sequence. Then chant together how the sequence should go.

Main teaching

Cards in the count

Give each group a set of number cards (1–50). Remove the single-digit numbers and shuffle each part of the pack separately. Ask the children to deal five cards from the two-digit pack to each child. Next they turn over a single-digit card and chant up in threes from that number to 50. If a child is holding a number in the sequence they put it down and win one point. The child with the highest score at the end is the winner. Deal again and repeat the activity this time counting in fours or fives. Variation: Remove number cards (40–50) and count back in steps of three, four or five.

In-betweenies

Each child in the group takes a strip of squared paper and writes a single-digit number in the first square. This is the starting number. He or she then works out what the end number will be if they count up in threes, fours or fives, and writes this number in the last square. They then put all their strips in a bag and give them out so that no one has their original strip. Each child says what number the sequence was counted in on the strip that they are holding. Repeat with a two-digit starting number and counting back.

Making a connection

Ask two volunteers to drop a counter or beanbag onto a floor grid numbered 1–50. One child needs to drop their beanbag between 1 and 10, the other needs to land on any number higher than 10. The class works out whether they can go from one number to the other by counting in threes, fours, or fives, or none of them. Discuss the methods they use to investigate the possibilities.

Chance and chant

Ask a volunteer to roll two dice and add the numbers together to make a starting number. Tell the class that they are going to count in steps of three. The class then chants round the room from the starting number. Put your hand up to stop them as they approach or reach 50. Repeat with counting in steps of fours and then in steps of fives from different starting numbers. Then build a two-digit number with the two numbers shown on a roll of both dice, and count back in steps of threes, fours and then fives.

Plenary

Say a starting number and a rule, such as: count on in threes. Count around the class, then repeat with other starting numbers and other rules (count on/ back in fours/fives). Then give a starting number, a rule and a number of steps (up to four). For example, starting number: 17, rule: 'count on in threes', and three steps. Ask the children to say the end number (in this case: 26).

Common difficulties

Children often encounter difficulties in bridging 10, for example, the next number after 28 when counting on in threes, fours or fives.

Remediation

Use a number line to show the next jump.

Homework suggestion

Give each child a hundred square. Ask them to count up in steps of three and colour every third square yellow. Repeat colouring every fourth square red and every fifth square green. Which squares do you land on with all three numbers?

Key point

Counting in threes, fours and fives continues the exploration of number sequences and patterns and lays the foundation for an easy progression to multiplication.

Related material

 Pupil Book Page 94-95

 PCM 46 SCM 46 ECM 46

 Along the walkway

 On wheels

Round and round the garden

Solving puzzles

Key vocabulary

- product
- total
- difference

Materials

- whiteboards
- dice
- dice labelled 7–12
- instruction cards
- number cards (11–20)

Introduction

Solving puzzles challenges the children to apply their mathematical knowledge in different ways. In these activities, they apply successive operations to a starting number, learn to recognise the rules, and investigate general statements about familiar numbers.

Objectives

 To solve mathematical problems or puzzles, recognise simple patterns and relationships, generalise and predict.

 To investigate a general statement about familiar numbers by finding examples that satisfy it.

Oral and mental starter

True or false

Make a statement that the children can investigate, using basic number facts. For example, 'An odd number plus an odd number always equals an even number.' or, 'Numbers can swap places in an addition sentence'.

Circle sequences

Sit the class in a circle. Make a number pattern around the circle by giving one child a starter number and a simple pattern, for example, +1, +2, +1, +2. Each child in turn quickly says the next number in the sequence. Then ask the children to devise their own patterns on their whiteboards and let some of them try them out around the circle.

Main teaching

Twice is not nice

Ask one child in the group to choose a number between 11 and 100. The group tries to find two numbers that total that number, two numbers that have a difference of that number, and, if possible, two numbers that multiply together to give a product of that number. The constraint is that they may not use the same number twice. Discuss the strategies used.

Number quest

Give a group of children a set of cards with instructions for finding
two numbers that make an addition and a multiplication sentence.
For example, find two numbers that make a total of 8 and have a
product of 15, or, a sum of 5 and a product of 6. Use well-rehearsed
number facts to begin with until the children are familiar with the
exercise. Then see if they can make up their own, more difficult ones,
for example, the sum of 15 and a product of 50.

Totally even

Give each child a die. Ask them to roll it three times and see how
many even totals they can make. They list the number sentences for
the even totals. Can they see a pattern or a rule? Repeat with dice
labelled 7–12.

Oddly enough!

Divide the class into pairs. Give each pair of children a number card
(11–20) and ask them to find different ways to add four odd numbers
to make that total. Discuss the strategies used.

Plenary

Ask a volunteer to choose from a set of instruction cards such as: the
product is 30, a difference of 6, a total of 8 etc. Ask all the children to
find and record as many pairs of numbers as possible that meet the
requirements of the instruction. Discuss the answers and the
strategies used. Extend to finding two even or two odd numbers, if
possible, for the instructions.

Common difficulties

Children sometimes think that finding one solution is finding all the
possible solutions.

Remediation

Ask different children to present their answers, and ask the other
children to check for accuracy.

Homework suggestion

Ask the children to write three single-digit numbers. Then they use
x, +, and = signs to write as many different number sentences as they
can. How many can they answer?

Key point

Solving puzzles
challenges the
children to be flexible
in their mathematical
thinking.

Related material

Pupil Book
Page 96-97

PCM 47
SCM 47
ECM 47

Fact finding
tour

Mental addition and subtraction

Key vocabulary

- multiple

Materials

- four number spinners (1–10), (1–9), (multiples of 10 from 10–90), (multiples of 5–50)
- whiteboards
- price tags with two-digit multiples of 5, up to 95p
- number line (up to 100)
- imitation coins
- target circles (multiples of 5 from 50–100)
- multiples of five cards (up to 100)
- subtraction vocabulary spinner

Introduction

Knowing basic addition and subtraction number facts can help children solve simple number problems and word problems mentally. In these activities, the children practise mental addition and subtraction mainly with multiples of five. Then they apply this knowledge to word problems set in real life situations.

Objectives

- To use known number facts and place value to add / subtract mentally.
- To use knowledge that addition can be done in any order to do mental calculations more efficiently.

Oral and mental starter

Multiplication bingo

Ask the children to write a list of four two-digit multiples of five on their whiteboards. Ask a volunteer to spin a spinner (1–10) and call out the number. The children multiply that number by five and cross off the number if it appears in their list. The first child to cross off all their numbers is the winner. Repeat with multiples of 10, and multiplying a spinner (1–9) by 10. Extend to writing four three-digit multiples of 100 and a spinner marked in multiples of 10, from 10 to 90.

Jumping fives

Display a number line on the board (up to 100) and ask one child to tell you a multiple of five, up to 100, as a starting number. Ask a volunteer to spin a spinner marked with multiples of five, up to 50 to find the end number. The children show, on their whiteboards, how many jumps of five you need to make to move from the starting number to the end number. The jumps may be forwards or backwards. Repeat.

Main teaching

Tagging along

Give each group a set of price tags with prices of two-digit multiples of five up to 95p. Make sure to include numbers ending in 0. The children take turns picking two price tags, finding the total cost each time and then working out their change from £2. They can use imitation coins if necessary.

Target numbers

Give each group a large target circle with a multiple of five (50–100) written in each section, and a set of two-digit number cards that are multiples of five up to 50. The children take turns picking two cards and placing them on the section of the target that represents the total. Ask them to draw or explain how they worked out the totals each time or to demonstrate using apparatus. Does it matter which way round they add the numbers? Next, the children take turns rolling an imitation coin onto the target, turning over one of the cards and finding the difference between the two numbers. The others check. Does it matter which way round they subtract the numbers?

Yo-yoing fives

Place a set of 'multiples of five' cards (up to 100) face down on each table. Each child takes two cards and finds the total. Then they record all the different addition and subtractions they can make using their number sentence. Next, ask them to use all the number cards to find out which pairs of numbers total 100. Ask if it matters which way round they record the numbers.

Take away tango

Ask each child to write two different multiples of five (up to 100) and find the imitation coins to match both amounts. Then spin a spinner marked with subtraction vocabulary such as, find the difference, subtract the greatest from the smallest, and take away. Ask them to find the answers and discuss the different methods used.

Plenary

Write on the board, a list of fairground rides (prices in multiples of 5p) and the amount of money each child has to spend (up to £1). Ask volunteers to choose from the list, two different rides or to have two goes on the same ride. The children work out how much money they need to pay altogether each time, record the coins they will use and calculate the change. Discuss the answers and the methods used. Then ask them to investigate, if they start with £1, how many rides they can go on before they run out of money. How can they show their calculations?

Common difficulties

Some children may need further practice partitioning two-digit numbers to support their addition and subtraction strategies.

Remediation

Give practical experience using multibase equipment. Show how to solve additions and subtractions using a number line.

Homework suggestion

Take ten 5p coins and toss them. Write down the total amount that lands on heads. Then toss the ten coins again and write how much landed on heads again. Write the addition and work out the sum. Repeat several times.

mathspace

49

Understanding addition

Key vocabulary

- total

Materials

- whiteboards
- pizza menus
- imitation coins
- blank number lines
- dice
- toy price list
- multibase
- number cards (1–35)

Introduction

The following activities revise addition of three numbers. Different strategies can be used, and should be discussed. It is important to emphasise that even though the methods may be different, the total remains the same. Some additions involve carrying over. The method of carrying is not formally taught at this stage; the children may find strategies to solve these types of additions and may work with apparatus to find the totals.

Objectives

 To extend understanding that more than two numbers can be added.

 To add three or four two-digit numbers with the help of apparatus or pencil and paper.

Oral and mental starter

Number properties

Divide the class into pairs. Each pair of children writes a number between 20 and 80, on their whiteboards. Say and write a number property such as: a multiple of 10, or, an even number that is a multiple of three. Tell the children that their aim is to produce a number that fits the number property. Then call out a number in the 20 to 80 range and ask the children to add this to their number and write the new total. Then call out a different number for the children to subtract. Continue until a pair of children have an answer that fits the number property given at the beginning. Then repeat with a different number property.

Total partners

Each child writes a two-digit number up to 40 on their whiteboards and then, finds a partner who has the number that is one more or less than theirs. They find the total of their two numbers. Repeat with different numbers and different rules (two, or three more or less) each time.

Main teaching

Addition strategies

Give each group a menu for a pizza parlour with two-digit prices, and imitation coins to use to help with their calculations. Ask the children to choose three items from the menu and work out the total cost. Include some prices that involve crossing the tens. Ask them to show the coins needed and also to explain their working out with pencil and paper. Discuss their own mental methods, jottings, use of writing, what jumps they need to make along a blank number line, counting on in tens first, and bridging through 10, to support their mental strategies.

Towing the line

Give each group a blank number line and two dice. Ask the children to take turns rolling the dice to create a two-digit number and record the number. They do this twice more to produce three different numbers. Then they use a counter to jump along the blank number line writing what jumps it takes to find the total, for example, 25 + 34 + 12: a child might make jumps on the number line 25 -> 55 -> 59 -> 69 -> 71 or might add all the tens first. Look at the different methods and check that they are using their knowledge of place value.

 ### Toys galore

Give each child a list of toys with prices (1p-99p). Each child chooses three toys and works out the total cost. They can use coins to help with the calculations. Discuss the strategies used.

Adding mania

Write three different two-digit numbers on the board. Ask the children to write them down and show how they work out how to add them together. They can use jottings and pencil and paper to support their explanations (if necessary, they can use multibase to help with the calculations). Extend to adding four two-digit numbers.

Plenary

Ask three volunteers to pick a card from a set of number cards (1–35). Ask the children to add up the total for the round, using multibase if necessary. Then ask volunteers to explain the way they worked out the total. Repeat with different numbers and extend to adding four numbers.

Common difficulties

Children using the strategy of addition of the tens digits and addition of the units digits, frequently miss the number carried over.

Remediation

Use towers of 10 cubes and unit cubes. Show how this strategy may fail because you can miss the fact you could build a new tower of 10 cubes.

Homework suggestion

Ask the children to write down their telephone numbers and find three two-digit numbers in it. Add them together using paper and pencil methods.

Understanding subtraction

Key vocabulary

- difference

Materials

- dice
- spinners (1–9)
- coins
- number name cards (for two-digit numbers)
- multibase
- number cards (66–69, 76–79, 86–89, 96–99).
- target number cards
- spinner (5–9)

Introduction

Subtraction has been taught since Reception at different levels. In the following activities, the children learn to subtract two two-digit numbers, without borrowing. Later, when they learn to borrow, the most frequent mistake when a child subtracts tens and units separately is that they always subtract the smaller digit from the larger one (for example, saying that 62 – 15 equals 53, because they work out 6 – 1 = 5 and 5 – 2 = 3). So, it is recommended that in the following activities, the method of subtracting the tens digits then the units digits should be avoided.

Objectives

 To extend understanding of the operation of subtraction.

Oral and mental starter

The shrinking 100

Sit the class in a circle. Starting at 100, the children take turns rolling a die and subtracting the number rolled. How quickly can they pass zero?

Reducing the starter

Write a number between 60 and 99 on the board. Roll a die. Ask the children to multiply the number rolled by 10 and subtract that number from the number on the board. Repeat.

Main teaching

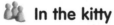 In the kitty

Give each group a spinner (1–9). Each child spins four times and writes down the numbers. They each then make a two-digit number with the two highest numbers, and a two-digit number with the two lowest numbers. They write the numbers as amounts of money, and model the amounts using 10p and 1p coins. Ask them to subtract their smaller amount from their larger amount and put the difference in the 'kitty'. What methods do they use to do the subtraction? How can they record the calculations? They check and discuss methods. Is the correct amount of money in the 'kitty' at the end?

Minus the multibase

Give each group a set of two-digit number name cards. The children take turns to pick a card and record the number in figures. Then they find another number from the rest of the group where both the digits are less than theirs and borrow that card. The lender takes another card. When all the children have two cards, ask them to model their numbers using multibase and subtract the smaller number from the larger number. Then discuss how they could do this without multibase.

With and without

Prepare a set of number cards (66–69, 76–79, 86–89, and 96–99). Shuffle the set of cards and place it face down on your table. Ask a volunteer to pick a card and write its number on the board. Give each child two dice. Each child rolls their dice, makes a two-digit number and then subtracts it from the number on the board first with multibase, and then without. Check, remediate and discuss methods.

Big reductions

Spin a spinner (5–9) twice to make a two-digit number and write it on the board. Tell the children that this is the price of a given toy. Assign them the job of shop assistants who need to calculate the new price after a reduction of 21p. Repeat with other spins and reductions which do not involve borrowing (keep the units digit of the reduction between 0 and 5).

Plenary

Write a subtraction that does not involve borrowing (for example, 87 − 35) and explain that you want to know the number of pages left to read in your 87 page book when you have read 35 pages. Ask the children to work out the answer. Discuss the strategies they used to solve the problem.

Common difficulties

Children could have difficulty understanding what is happening during the subtraction process.

Remediation

Use apparatus to model the question, for example, for 87 − 35, use eight towers of 10, and seven cubes. Show how you first subtract 30 by removing three towers. How many cubes are left? Then take away five cubes. Ask how many cubes are left. The answer is the difference.

Homework suggestion

Give the children the numbers: 98, 23, 55 and 86. For homework they need to write as many different subtractions as they can and find the difference. They can use hundred squares to help them.

Related material

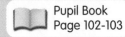 Pupil Book Page 102-103

 PCM 50
SCM 50
ECM 50

 Bingo numbers
Alien maker
Number pump
Splodge guns

Doubling and halving

Key vocabulary

- double
- half
- multiplied by
- times
- divided by

Materials

- number cards (1–20, 30, 40, ..., 100)
- gameboards of multiples of 5
- coins
- counters
- spinners (1p–9p)
- strips of material (multiples of 10cm long)
- glue
- blank price tags

Introduction

Unit plan 20 revised doubling and halving, and the connection between the two operations through 'doubling and halving machines'. These activities extend this knowledge to doubling and halving multiples of five, up to 100, and their corresponding halves. These skills facilitate problem solving and pave the way for the introduction of more complex topics such as fractions and multiplication algorithms.

Objectives

- To derive quickly doubles of multiples of 5 to 100, and all the corresponding halves.
- To use doubling or halving starting from known facts.

Oral and mental starter

Back to back

First say or sing the 2 times-table together. Then ask two volunteers to sit back to back. Ask quick fire questions from the 2 times-table using a variety of vocabulary, such as: '3 times 2' or, '5 multiplied by 2'. The child who says the answer first stays and another challenger takes the place of the loser. Repeat with division questions derived from the 2 times-table.

Human snap

Give each child a number card (1–20, 30, 40, ..., 100). Write a number on the board and say: *"half"* (or *"double"*). Children with the correct number hold up their card and say, *"Snap!"*

Main teaching

Halve or double

Give each group a gameboard with the numbers going up in fives. The children take turns to toss a coin onto the board and see where it lands. If they can halve or double the number correctly they take a counter. Which ones can be doubled? Which ones can be halved? If they can halve their number and then halve it again they take two counters. They can use coins to model their calculations.

Double your money

Give each group a spinner (1p–9p). The children take turns spinning and taking the matching amount with coins. Then ask the children to double their amounts and model the new amount. How many times can they continue doubling? What do they notice as the numbers increase?

Ribbon maths

Divide the class into pairs. Give each pair of children strips of material to make a multicoloured ribbon. The material strips are in lengths that are multiples of 10 cm. Say that the ribbon now has to be half the size that was originally planned. Can they work out the new lengths for each strip of material? What strategies can be used to find the new lengths? At the end the children can use their material to make a ribbon and calculate its total length. Ask them to record a number sentence to represent the ribbon if they had actually made it half the length.

Going cheap!

Ask each child to make price tags for a set of five books with prices that are multiples of 10. Announce that in the end of season sale every book is going to be half price. Ask the children to record the new prices. Discuss the strategies used.

Plenary

Hold up a number card with a multiple of 10 up to 100. Ask the children to first double and then halve the number. Discuss their strategies for doubling: multiplying the tens digit by two and adding a zero to the product, or adding the same number again, and for halving: separating into two sets, working with cube towers, or using multiplication facts. Extend to doubling two-digit numbers ending in five.

Common difficulties

Working with big numbers sometimes leads to 'big' mistakes when rules are misused.

Remediation

Ask the children to estimate the expected result. Use apparatus such as cubes, counters, or coins.

Homework suggestion

At the supermarket, write down six different items that have price labels that are less than 50p and end in five. Ask the children to make one chart showing how much the items would cost if the prices were doubled and a second chart which shows the total price of different pairs of items. Ask them to add an extra column to the second chart in which they write what half these total prices are.

Key point

Linking halving and doubling helps children divide by two and reinforces the links between the two operations.

Related material

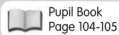 Pupil Book Page 104-105

 PCM 51
SCM 51
ECM 51

 Space painting
Red roofs

The 3 times-table

Key vocabulary

- times
- multiplied by
- times-table
- multiples

Materials

- spinners (1–10)
- die labelled x 2, x 2, x 5, x 5, x 10 and x 10
- whiteboards
- counters
- blank cards
- parts of hundred squares (1–30)
- dice labelled 1, 1, 2, 2, 3, and 3
- number lines (0–30)
- number cards (1–10)
- picture cards

Introduction

Knowing the basic times-tables by heart, is a prerequisite for most arithmetic and algebraic skills. The children have had plenty of practice mastering the 2, 5 and 10 times-table. The following activities focus on the multiplication facts for the 3 times-table.

Objectives

- To begin to know the 3 times-table.

Oral and mental starter

Rolling times

Ask one volunteer to spin a spinner (1–10) and another to roll a die labelled x 2, x 2, x 5, x 5, x 10 and x 10. Then ask all the children to multiply the number spun by the number rolled and show you the new number on their whiteboards.

Who's on 18?

Choose a volunteer to start a count round the circle in threes from zero. Before they start, ask the children to record the name of the child they think will say, for example, 18, on their whiteboards. Chant and see who was right. Repeat with other target numbers.

Main teaching

Spinning threes

Give each group a spinner (1–10). Each child spins it and takes a set of three counters for each unit of the number they spin, for example, if the spinner lands on 4 they take 12 counters. They write the multiplication sentence on a card and place it in its right place among the multiplications already on the table. They continue until the list is complete. Repeat but first mix up the multiplication sentences and ask the children to choose the correct one for each spin of the spinner.

Sees the threes

Give each group part of a hundred square (1–30), with all the multiples of three highlighted in green, as a gameboard. Give each child a different coloured counter. Ask the children to take turns rolling a die, labelled 1, 1, 2, 2, 3 and 3. They move their counters along the gameboard. If they land on a green square, they say the multiplication fact for that product and collect a counter if they say it correctly. The first child to reach or pass 30 is the winner.

Triple jumps

Divide the class into pairs. Give each pair of children a number line (0–30). Ask them to take turns picking a number card (1–10) and, starting at zero, jump that number of steps of three. They record a matching multiplication sentence in their own way, for example 3 x 5 = 15, or 5 x 3 = 15. How quickly can they find all the facts of the 3 times-table?

Problems in triplicate

Give out pictures of a number of children that is a multiple of three. Say a story problem using that number of children, involving the 3 times-table. For example, for a picture of 24 children, say that these children are coming to a tea-party and each table has three chairs. Ask the children to work out how many tables they need. Ask them to write the multiplication representing this problem. Repeat with different numbers of children in multiples of three. Extend by asking the children to make up their own stories for each other using 3 times-tables facts, trying to use different vocabulary.

Plenary

Chant the 3 times-table together. Then go around the class with each child saying the next 3 times-table number fact, i.e. 1 x 3 = 3, 2 x 3 = 6, and so on. Extend to related facts, for example, if 10 x 3 = 30, what is 11 x 3?

Common difficulties

Knowing times-tables by heart takes time and practice. Some children may be able to chant competently in threes but find recalling individual facts hard.

Remediation

Play games like pairs and snap using cards with just the multiplication facts and their answers until the children are competent.

Homework suggestion

Give out copies of the 3 times-table. Ask the children to find a tune for it and practise it a number of times at home. Do a 3 times-table song medley the following day.

Key point

Knowing basic multiplication tables by heart speeds up most mathematical activities.

Related material

Pupil Book
Page 106-107

PCM 52
SCM 52
ECM 52

Ziggy and the beanstalk

In the number lab

Tooty fruity

The 4 times-table

Key vocabulary

- multiplied by
- times
- product
- multiple/s

Materials

- number cards (multiples of five)
- spinners (1–10)
- whiteboards
- materials for miniature tables (e.g. straws, plasticine, matchboxes)
- number lines (1–40)
- dice
- bowls of cubes
- pegs
- pegboards
- toy cars
- number cards (1–10)
- hat
- straws (1 cm – 10 cm)
- ruler

Introduction

Children have already learned the 2, 3, 5 and 10 times-tables in previous unit plans. These activities introduce the 4 times-table.

Objectives

 To begin to know the 4 times-table.

Oral and mental starter

Finding the five

Give each child a number card with a multiple of five. Ask a volunteer to spin a spinner (1–10). Ask all the children to multiply that number by 10 and write the product on their whiteboards. Then ask them to halve the product and write the new number. Tell the children, *"If you think your number card is the answer, stand up."* Check and remediate.

All the fours

Chant round the class starting at zero and counting in steps of four. Then ask each child to write four numbers between four and 40 from that sequence on their whiteboards. Next, say a number from one to 10 and ask the children to double it and double it again. They cross off the number if it appears on their whiteboards. Say different numbers (1-10) until one child has crossed off all their numbers.

Main teaching

Turn the tables time

Give each group materials with which to build miniature tables. Tell the group how many tables they need to build (1-10) and that the tables they build have to have four legs. Ask them to work out how many table legs they need altogether. Discuss the methods used. Repeat with other numbers of tables. Extension: tell the children the number of legs and they calculate the number of table-tops they will need.

Forward to 40

Give each group a number line (1–40), a bowl of cubes and a die. The children take turns rolling the die and moving their counter along the number line. If they land on a multiple of four, they say the multiplication fact and take a cube. When they reach or pass 40 they start again and the child who played the last move takes an extra cube. The child with the most cubes at the end is the winner. Discuss how using the 2 times-table facts can help with the calculations.

 Got that pegged

Give each child a pegboard and pegs. Spin a spinner (1–10) and ask the children to make that many rows of four pegs. They record a matching multiplication sentence using their own vocabulary. How many different ways can they find to express the same multiplication?

 Four wheel drive

Divide the class into pairs. Give each pair 10 toy cars and a hat containing number cards (1–10). One child pulls a number out the hat and the other says the multiplication fact for the total number of wheels. The first child checks by lining up that number of cars and counting the total number of wheels. They swap roles and repeat several times. Finally see if the pairs of children can make up number stories to match one or more of their multiplication facts.

Plenary

Hold up a straw measuring between 1 cm and 10 cm. Ask a volunteer to measure it. Tell the children that this straw represents the length of one side of a fence surrounding a square garden. Ask the children to calculate the total length of the fence. If necessary, draw the fence on the board. How do they work out the answer? How can they check their answer? Repeat with other lengths of straw. Extension: give the total length of the fence and ask the children to calculate the length of one side.

Common difficulties

Some children do not see the connection between the two and four times-tables.

Remediation

Explain with arrays of cubes. First arrange cubes in two rows to show how to build different facts of the 2 times-table. Then show how by repeating the rows again you can deduce the related facts of the 4 times-table.

Homework suggestion

Ask the children to multiply the following numbers by four: 3, 5, 8, 9 and write their answers in a chart. Next they add an extra column, x 2 and multiply each number by two. Do they see a connection between the two columns? Can they find a 'rule'?

Key point

Knowing basic multiplication tables by heart speeds up most mathematical activities.

Related material

 Pupil Book
Page 108-109

 PCM 53
SCM 53
ECM 53

  Ball machine
Ask the robot!

What's for tea?

Understanding division

Key vocabulary

- repeated subtraction
- division
- dividing
- divide by

Materials

- number fans
- die labelled: double, half, x 2, $\frac{1}{2}$, ÷ 2, twice
- bowls
- counters
- paper grids
- scissors
- pegs
- pegboards
- interlocking cubes
- spinner (1–5)

Introduction

Children often find the need for division in everyday life, for example, sharing out objects or sweets with other children. In Year 2, dividing by two was introduced as sharing equally into two equal groups. The following activities explore dividing by 2, 3, 4, 5 and 10, as sharing equally between these numbers. These activities employ various methods, including grouping and repeated subtraction to solve simple concrete division problems.

Objectives

 To understand division as grouping (repeated subtraction) or sharing.

 To recognise that division is the inverse of multiplication.

 To say or write a division statement corresponding to a multiplication statement.

Oral and mental starter

💬 Time to times

Ask the children quick fire questions involving multiplication facts from the 2, 3, 4, 5, and 10 times-tables. Ask them to show the answers on their number fans. Use a variety of vocabulary, such as: What is 3 times 5? or, 8 multiplied by 2? Include some questions that have multiplying by 1 and by 10. Check the answers each time by chanting the whole times-table.

💬 Double or die

Prepare a large die labelled: double, half, x 2, $\frac{1}{2}$, ÷ 2, and twice. Give a starter number and ask a volunteer to roll the die. All the children write the answer on their whiteboards and hold them up. Repeat. Check that they know the ÷ symbol and that $\frac{1}{2}$ means a number divided into two equal parts.

Main teaching

👥 The final countdown

Divide the class into groups of four. Give each group a bowl of 20 counters and ask them to share the counters equally between the children in the group. Discuss the methods used. If no group suggests repeated subtraction, ask them to work out how many counters are left in the bowl when one child has taken his or her counters, two children, etc. Repeat with different numbers of counters that are multiples of four.

👥 Equal cuts

Prepare grids with different numbers of squares (multiples of three, 3 – 30). Ask the children to find a way to cut the grid into sections of threes. Ask them to record each cut as a subtraction sentence and see how many different sections they make. Ask them how many subtraction sentences they need to write to reach a difference of zero. Can they write a division sentence for the whole process? Repeat with grids of multiples of four up to 40 squares and cutting into sections of four.

👤 On the job

Say, *"Five children worked hard together and earned £20. How can they share the amount equally between them? How much does each child receive?"*. Discuss the methods used (repeated subtraction, division as the inverse of multiplication). Repeat with other numbers of children and other amounts.

👤 Describe and record

Divide the class into pairs. Each pair of children sit back to back and one child makes an array of pegs on a pegboard while the other child makes sets of towers of three or four cubes. They take turns to describe their creation to their partner so that the partner can write a matching multiplication sentence and work out the total number of pegs or cubes used by their partner. When they have found the total and checked their answers, each child writes a corresponding division sentence for their partner's pattern of cubes or pegs. What do they notice about the way they record the division sentences? Ask the children to swap apparatus and repeat the activity.

Plenary

Place 30 cubes on the table and spin a spinner (1–5) to find the number of children to share the cubes. Ask the children to calculate how many cubes each child receives. Discuss the methods used. Explain the main division methods. Repeat with different numbers of cubes and spin again.

Common difficulties

Children may find the concept of sharing or grouping into equal parts confusing. They may rightly say that it is possible to share out seven sweets between three people and that all it means is that one person will receive an extra sweet.

Remediation

Use apparatus, and put all questions into real-life contexts so that the children have a sense of sharing fairly, everyone receives the same. Use multiplication to review how multiplication can be seen as repeated addition of the same amount, and show how division can be seen as repeated subtraction of the same amount.

Homework suggestion

Ask the children to count out 24 playing cards and work out how many players from 2 – 5 could play a fair game, i.e. the cards could be shared out equally. Write a multiplication and division for each example.

Key point

In mathematics, dividing means sharing equally, that is, into equal subsets.

Related material

Pupil Book
Page 110-111

PCM 54
SCM 54
ECM 54

Chart planets

Space control

How sweet!

Chugging along

mathspace

55

Word problems

Key vocabulary

- operations

Materials

- lists of fairground attractions and prices
- spinners (1–5)
- number cards (20–50)
- single-digit price cards
- die with 6 replaced with another 5

Introduction

Children are familiar with solving word problems using the six-step strategy: reading and understanding the problem, isolating the question, devising a strategy to solve it (and if necessary, building a graphical representation), applying the strategy, finding the answer, and checking it. The following activities apply the children's knowledge of all four operations, to solving word problems.

Objectives

- To solve word problems involving numbers in 'real life' and money, using one or more steps.

- To choose and use appropriate operations to solve word problems, and appropriate ways of calculating.

Oral and mental starter

 What's the problem?

Give the children a word problem but leave out the question. Ask them to work with a partner and think of a good question to go with the problem. How many different questions can they think of for one problem?

 Co-ops

Write a multiplication sentence on the board and ask the children to say the corresponding division. Then write a division and ask for the corresponding multiplication. Repeat with addition and subtraction sentences.

Main teaching

N.B. Encourage visualisation of problems using drawings where appropriate, and checking calculations with inverse operations.

 The fun of the fair

Give each group a price list of fairground attractions (raffle, pony rides, bouncy castle, goal shoot-out) with prices from 10p to 50p. Each child chooses an activity, and then spins a spinner (1–5) to see how many children can have a go on that activity. They work out how much they have to pay altogether? Ask the groups to present their solutions. Discuss graphical representations, the strategies and the checking methods used. Point out the vocabulary 'altogether' is usually linked to addition. Repeat with basic division problems and emphasise checking using inverse operations. Extend to two-step questions with multiplication and division (or repeated subtraction), for example, say they have £1 to spend, how many pony rides can they have? How much change will they receive?

Problem building

Each group picks two number cards (20–50) and writes the addition sentence. Ask the group to work out the answer using different strategies and discuss the efficiency of each. Then they check their answers using subtraction. Ask them to think of a word problem for their number sentence. They pass their problem to another group to solve.

 Tackling the problem

Divide the class into pairs. Give each pair a multiplication investigation, for example, Samara wants to buy a computer game that costs £27. She saves £3 a month from her pocket money. How many months does she need to save, to buy the game? or, I have 20 sweets and four friends. How can I share the sweets equally with my friends? Guide the children through the six steps of problem solving (see introduction), encouraging them to build a concrete representation of the problem if necessary. Emphasise the importance of checking. Repeat with investigations involving other operations.

Bulk buying

Hold up an item with a single-digit price tag and roll a die with the 6 replaced with another 5 to work out how many of this item you bought. Hold up a second item and say that you also bought one of these items. Ask the children to work out how much you spent. Check their answers and discuss the strategies used. Discuss different ways they could check their answers.

Plenary

Write a simple division word problem on the board, for example, John bought six identical rubbers for 30p. What is the price of each rubber? Ask the children to solve the problem and record their answer. Remind them to check their answer and record the way they checked. Ask volunteers to solve the problem aloud going through each of the six steps of the problem solving strategy. At each step, ask if anyone has a different method.

Common difficulties

Children often need a graphical representation of the problem. Some children have difficulty seeing how to check their answer.

Remediation

Suggest different apparatus to represent a problem, such as, cubes, coins, counters, number lines, or tables. Teach how to check starting from the answer.

Homework suggestion

Tell the children that Natasha receives 20p pocket money a week. Ask them to work out how many weeks it will take her to make £1. Ask them to find out how long it would take if her pocket money was 25p or 50p. Can they see a connection between different amounts, can they explain it?

Key point

Developing good problem-solving habits and learning to work systematically without skipping stages, especially checking the answer, is one of the most important lessons to be learned.

Related material

Pupil Book Page 112-113

PCM 55
SCM 55
ECM 55

 In the maths lab

Cinema problems

Ziggy's space jet

Recognising fractions

Key vocabulary

- half
- halves
- third/s
- quarter/s
- fifth/s
- tenth/s
- numerator
- denominator

Materials

- whiteboards
- fraction cards
- grids
- scissors
- glue
- fraction cards (tenths)
- fraction cards (eighths)
- interlocking cubes (in two colours)
- grid sheets
- spinner (1–10)

Introduction

Fractions were introduced in Unit plans 24 and 25 where children learned about fractions in which the numerator was always one, about fractions as a part of a whole using different shapes, and about fractions as part of a set of objects by grouping the set into subsets. The following activities extend the study of fractions to those with a numerator greater than one, using fractions as part of a whole as well as fractions as part of a set of identical elements.

Objectives

● To begin to recognise simple fractions, that are several parts of a whole.

Oral and mental starter

 Fraction dotty

Write the unit fractions: $\frac{1}{2}$, $\frac{1}{5}$, and $\frac{1}{10}$ on the board. Ask the children to draw 10 dots on their whiteboards and circle the number of dots that represents a $\frac{1}{2}$. They write the number of dots ringed and hold up their whiteboards to show you. Repeat for the other two fractions. Then repeat the activity with 12 dots and the unit fractions: $\frac{1}{4}$, $\frac{1}{2}$, and $\frac{1}{3}$. If time, repeat with other numbers and suitable fractions.

 Twenty answers

Write the numbers 1 to 20 on the board and ask quick fire fraction questions randomly around the class. Questions such as: What is $\frac{1}{2}$ of 18 (or another multiple of two)? Or: what is $\frac{1}{3}$ of 15 (or another multiple of three)? See how many numbers you can cross off the board.

Main teaching

 Fraction pairs

Give each group a set of fraction cards including: fractions written in numerator/denominator notation (numerators can be more than one, denominators up to 10), shapes with fractions shaded, and sets with a ringed subset. The children spread the cards face down over the table and take turns to reveal two cards. If the cards represent the same fraction, the child takes the pair. If not, the cards are turned back over and left in place. The child with the most pairs at the end wins.

Fraction bingo

Give each child in the group, four grids of 10 squares and ask them to colour a different number of squares in each grid. They stick their grids on a four-section bingo card. One child is the caller and draws from a set of fraction cards in tenths. The child who crosses off all their fractions first is the winner. Ask what they notice about $\frac{5}{10}$. Repeat with grids of eight squares and fraction cards in eighths. Ask the children to read each fraction aloud and give assistance when necessary.

 Fraction towers

In pairs the children make towers of cubes of two colours by spinning a spinner (1–10) twice. They make the first number with red cubes and the second with blue. Then they find the total and say the fraction that make up the red cubes and the fraction that make up the blue cubes.

Grid games

Give each child a sheet of twenty 2x5 grids and ask them to see how many different ways they can shade the grids. Ask them to write the fraction in tenths, representing the shaded part, under each grid. They can use the same fraction more than once.

Plenary

Spin two numbers on a spinner (1–10), one for the denominator and one for the numerator, and record the fraction on the board. Ask volunteers to read the fraction and explain its meaning. Then ask each child to draw a representation of the fraction, on their whiteboard. Discuss the solutions proposed. Repeat with other fractions.

Common difficulties

Children often mix up the roles of the numerator and the denominator.

Remediation

Explain that the denominator says into how many equal parts the whole is divided, and the numerator indicates how many of these parts we take.

Homework suggestion

Give the children sheets of squared paper with grids 2x2, 3x3, 2x3, 2x4, 2x5. Then ask them to shade $\frac{3}{8}$ of one of the grids red, $\frac{3}{10}$ of another blue, $\frac{2}{9}$ of a third green.

Related material

Pupil Book
Page 114-115

PCM 56
SCM 56
ECM 56

Ziggy's space jet

Pizza parlour

Ziggy's new creations

Equivalent fractions

Key vocabulary

- equivalent fraction/s
- half
- halves
- third/s
- quarter/s
- sixth/s
- eighth/s
- tenth/s
- numerator
- denominator

Materials

- shape pictures
- number cards (1–10)
- empty grids
- divided cakes
- square paper
- spinners (even numbers to 20)
- spinners (multiples of four to 40)
- pizza sheets
- whiteboards

Introduction

The following activities introduce the concept of equivalent fractions. Understanding that different numbers can represent the same value is quite a sophisticated concept. Concrete representation is encouraged to give a basic understanding of the concept of equivalent fractions.

Objectives

- To begin to recognise simple equivalent fractions.

Oral and mental starter

 Not half!

Show a picture of a shape that is either divided in half or not. Ask the children to show thumbs up if they think the shape is divided in half, thumbs down if not. Then fold the shape to check each time.

 Tenth testers

Draw a large grid with 10 squares on the board. Ask one child to pick a number card (1–10) and shade that number of squares on the grid. The others then say and write down what fraction has been shaded.

Main teaching

 By any other name

Give each group two 4x2 grids. Ask them to colour half of one of the grids and write the matching fraction. Then ask if the same picture can be represented with a different fraction. If no group finds a solution, give some hints (how many squares is the grid divided into?). Repeat with $\frac{1}{4}$. Then repeat with 3x4 grids and ask the children to colour $\frac{1}{6}$, $\frac{1}{4}$, $\frac{1}{3}$, and $\frac{1}{2}$.

👥 Piece of cake

Give each group a set of 'cakes' divided into an even number of equal parts and with different numbers of sections shaded. Ask one child to turn over a fraction card and all the children decide which cakes have that fraction shaded. Ask them if they can describe the shaded area with a different fraction. Repeat with grids instead of cakes.

♟ Spin a grid

Pass round several spinners (even numbers to 20) and square paper. Each child spins a spinner and cuts out a grid with that number of squares. They shade half of their grid. Then they compare their grid with a friend's. What do they notice? Discuss the equivalent fractions. Repeat using spinners with multiples of four to 40 and ask the children to shade $\frac{1}{4}$ of their grids.

♟ Slices of pie

Give each child a sheet with five 'pizzas' divided into two, four, six, eight, and ten equal parts respectively. Write $\frac{1}{4}$, $\frac{2}{4}$, $\frac{3}{6}$, $\frac{4}{8}$, and $\frac{5}{10}$ on the board. The children look at each denominator and choose the appropriate pie. Then they look at the numerator and shade that number of slices of the pie. Ask them to write the fraction under each drawing. What do they notice about the amount of pie shaded each time? What conclusions can they come to about these fractions? Can they find a way to explain this?

Plenary

Draw a 4x6 grid on the board and ask the children to copy it onto their whiteboards. Then ask them to colour half of the grid and write as many equivalent fractions as they can to represent this amount. Give hints if necessary, for example, how many rows are there and how many are shaded? And, how many squares are there and how many are shaded? Repeat with other grids and other fractions.

Common difficulties

For many children, different numbers cannot represent the same value. Some children have difficulty seeing the same fraction of a shape coloured in different ways.

Remediation

Use many concrete representations including different shapes and elements of a set. Show that taking $\frac{1}{2}$ of a pizza, gives the same quantity as taking $\frac{2}{4}$ of a pizza, and so on.

Homework suggestion:

Design a fraction wall by giving the children a squared piece of paper (12 x 12). Ask them to colour different horizontal strips to show halves, quarters, thirds, sixths. Ask them to write as many equivalent fractions as they can using the fraction wall.

Key point

Equivalent fractions introduce the concept of writing the same number in different ways. This is an extension of knowing that the same number can be represented by different number sentences.

Related material

Pupil Book Page 116-117

PCM 57
SCM 57
ECM 57

Railway signals

Comparing familiar fractions

Key vocabulary

- one whole
- (numerator)
- (denominator)

Materials

- number cards (1–40)
- grids
- drawings of shapes and sets
- strips of square paper
- cubes or pegboards and pegs
- plasticine
- spinner (even numbers to 20)
- large blank fraction cards

Introduction

The focus of the following activities is to show that a whole can always be split into a sum of fractions that have the same denominator. The children implicitly learn that to add fractions with the same denominator, you only add the numerators.

Objectives

 To compare familiar fractions.

 To begin to recognise simple fractions which are several parts of a whole.

Oral and mental starter

Quartermasters

Show a set of number cards (4–40) and ask the children to decide which ones can be divided into quarters and which ones cannot. Discuss the methods they use to work out the answers.

Equal partners

Give each child a grid shaded in halves, thirds, quarters or tenths. Ask them to find a partner who has the equivalent fraction shaded. Ask each pair to make a statement about their equivalent fractions, such as, 'four eighths is equivalent to five tenths.' Repeat with shapes and ringed elements of a set.

Main teaching

Fraction folding

Give each group strips of squared paper and ask the children to investigate the fractions that make up the whole of each strip. For example, with a strip of four squares, first they fold one square over and see what fraction they have folded. What fraction is left? How many quarters make a whole? How do they know? Ask them to record the fractions and the matching addition, for example, e.g. ? + ? = 1. Then ask them to fold over two squares. What is left? Repeat with strips of six, (folding $\frac{1}{3}$ and then $\frac{2}{3}$), eight, and 10 (folding $\frac{1}{2}$ and $\frac{1}{5}$) squares.

Following orders

Give each child in the group, a set of cubes, or pegs and a pegboard, and a set of instruction cards such as: make $\frac{1}{2}$ red, then $\frac{1}{4}$ blue and the rest green, or, make $\frac{1}{2}$ red, $\frac{1}{5}$ blue and the rest yellow. One child turns over an instruction card and they all use their apparatus to match the instruction. What fraction is the 'rest'? What do they notice? Ask the children to record the matching addition of fractions to show what equals one whole.

 ### Splat!

Give each child a lump of plasticine or dough. Ask a volunteer to spin a spinner with even numbers up to 20 and ask the children to make that many balls of plasticine. Then ask them to squash some of the balls, for example, five and record the fraction they have squashed and the fraction that is left. Ask them to write an addition sentence to represent the two fractions and their relation to the whole. Repeat.

Giant fraction action

Prepare sets of number cards (1–9). Divide the class into pairs and give each pair a set of cards and a blank fraction card. The children take turns to pick two cards and place the smaller number above the larger number on the blank fraction card to represent the top number and bottom number (the words numerator and denominator are not presented till Year 5 but can be used here with more able children). They then cut out a strip of squares to represent the bottom number (denominator) and colour squares to match the top number (numerator). Finally, they identify the remaining fraction to make a whole and record the matching addition of fractions.

Plenary

Draw a 3x2 grid, and colour $\frac{1}{3}$ of it blue and $\frac{2}{3}$ red. Ask the children to write the 'blue fraction', then the 'red fraction'. Ask what the sum of the two fractions is. Record the matching addition sentence and show how it equals one whole. Then repeat with other grids. Finally, extend to using three colours to split the grid into three fractions.

Common difficulties

A very frequent mistake is to write: $\frac{1}{3} + \frac{2}{3} = \frac{3}{6}$, adding both the numerators and the denominators.

Remediation

Show on grids, how two fractions $\frac{1}{3}$ and $\frac{2}{3}$ add up to one whole.

Homework suggestion

Ask the children to write 10 different fraction addition sentences that total one whole.

Bar charts

Key vocabulary

- bar chart
- tallies
- data

Materials

- spinner (1–9)
- food tally chart
- bags of small shapes
- squared paper
- coloured dice
- tuck shop tally charts
- Key point

Introduction

Bar charts are used for classifying and organising information. The ability to read and fill in a bar chart accurately, is an essential skill in Maths as well as in daily life. These activities revise tallying and bar charts, and extends their knowledge to reading bar charts that have intervals labelled in twos. The two basic rules of bar charts are that one has to fill them in from bottom to top, and that the same units have to be used in all the columns.

Objectives

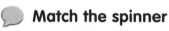
To solve a given problem by organising and interpreting numerical data in simple lists, tables and graphs.

Oral and mental starter

Match the spinner

Write the numbers 5, 6, 7, 8, and 9 on the board and spin a spinner (1–9). Ask the children to combine at least three numbers by using either or both addition and subtraction to make the number indicated on the spinner. Extend to writing 1, 2, 3, 4, and 5 on the board and spinning the spinner twice to make a two-digit number.

Food, glorious food

Give each child a tally chart with information about favourite foods. In turn each child says which food he or she prefers, and all the children have to update their tally chart. At different stages, check the status of the tally charts.

Main teaching

Bar shapes

Give each group a bag of 40 small shapes. Ask the children to record the number of each type of shape. Discuss the different methods of recording. Ask them to represent the data in a graphical way. Discuss the solutions proposed, and emphasise the use of a bar chart. Remind the children about labelling the axes correctly and numbering the vertical axis. Then ask questions about the information displayed in the bar chart, for example, how many circles were there in the bag? Which shape are there the most of? Can they ask each other questions about the data based on the graph? Can they think of a way to keep all the data on the page? (Change the scale to two units for one – what about odd numbers?) How might the table change if more shapes were in the bag?

👥 Roll up to the bar

Give each group a coloured die (red, red, red, green, blue, and yellow). Ask the children to roll the die 30 times, collect the data and make a bar chart on squared paper. Ask what they notice about the frequency of the colours and other questions about the differences between the bars. Ask how they can show the totals if there are not enough squares on the paper. Suggest a scale of two for one. Ask the group to make a bar chart using the new scale. Then give them a different die (blue, blue, red, green, yellow and yellow). Can they predict the results this time? Ask the children to roll as before, collect the data and see the results.

♟ Tuck shop news

Divide the class into pairs. Give each pair a tally chart showing the number of children who go to the tuck shop each day for a week in the winter. Ask them to design a bar chart to show the information and ask them questions about the data: how many children visit each day? Which day is most/least popular? Then ask the children to add information to the chart. Show them how to change the scale on the vertical axis if there are not enough squares. Then ask if the chart would be different for a week in the summer.

♟ Star of the show

Elicit a list of well-liked bands or singers or TV shows and write them on the board. Ask the children to predict which they think is the most popular. How can they find out? Ask the class to vote on their list and ask a volunteer to keep a tally. Ask them to make a bar chart on squared paper and see if they were right. Ask questions about the data. Can they add data about other children in their year? Can they make a scale to show the data when there are more children? Would it be the same if they asked children in Year 6?

Plenary

Conduct a survey of what the children like to eat with five given dishes. Discuss how to display the results on a bar chart and draw it on the board. Ask questions about the information in the bar chart such as: How many more children preferred dish A to dish B? Ask the children to explain how they worked out their answers. Let the children ask other questions that can be answered from the bar chart. Triple the results and discuss how to label the intervals on the vertical axis in twos.

Common difficulties

Some children may not record their data starting from the base line of the chart. Others may have difficulty reading the bar chart.

Remediation

Count the number of objects again and check they match the number in the bar chart. Provide coloured squares, each colour representing one criterion and each square, one object. Sort and place the squares on a large squared paper graph, inside clearly defined columns. Ask questions about different parts of the graph.

Homework suggestion

Ask how many pairs of socks each member of your household has. Make a bar chart to represent the results, with the intervals on the vertical axis going up in twos.

Key point

The ability to read and fill in bar charts accurately is a useful tool for displaying information.

Related material

Pupil Book Page 120-121

PCM 59
SCM 59
ECM 59

Ziggy's survey
Super survey

Pictograms

Key vocabulary

- pictogram
- tally chart
- frequency
- data

Materials

- weather charts
- squared paper
- playing cards

Introduction

The following activities revise basic pictograms. The children use pictograms in which two units are represented by one symbol, and continue to interpret data and answer questions by reading the data from pictograms and other basic charts.

Objectives

● To solve a given problem by organising and interpreting data in simple lists, tables and graphs.

Oral and mental starter

 Picto-favourites

Quickly generate data from the class about favourite football teams, colours, or sports. Ask the children to suggest a symbol to represent each category. Draw a pictogram on the board to show the information and then ask questions about the data.

 Commuter survey

Ask each child to say how they came to school in the morning and make a tally chart on the board. Draw a class bar chart labelled in twos and revise the different parts of the graph. Ensure that some of the bars show odd numbers by adding your own journey, if necessary. Ask questions about the data such as: How many more children come on foot than by car? And, 'what if' questions such as: what if it were a rainy/sunny day?

Main teaching

 Whatever the weather

Use a weather chart that has been kept by the class for two weeks prior to the lesson. Make a tally chart for the different types of weather and from that create a frequency chart. Then ask the children to discuss how best to represent the data on a graph. Suggest the use of symbols. Give each group squared paper on which to design a pictogram and think of appropriate symbols to represent the data. Restrict the size of the paper so that they need to work out how to represent two units with one symbol and how to show the odd numbers. Ask them to write a key stating the scale of one symbol for two units. Then ask questions about the data.

👥 Early to bed, early to rise

Do a sleep survey to see how many hours of sleep the children had last night. Ask each group to design a pictogram and think of appropriate symbols to represent the data. How can they show the data if there is not enough room for one symbol to represent each shape? Suggest pictograms with a key saying one symbol represents two units. What happens to odd numbers? Do they think it would be different if they asked children in Year 6 the same question?

♟ Suitable cards

Divide the class into pairs. Give each pair of children 20 random playing cards (no royal cards). Ask them to design a pictogram showing how many cards of each suit they have. How can they show the data if there is not enough room for one symbol to represent each shape? Suggest pictograms with a key that shows one symbol for every two units. What about odd numbers? Elicit suggestions. Ask questions about the distribution of the suits. Give each pair five more cards and ask them to add the new data, or, ask what would happen if they had, for example, three more hearts.

♟ Heavy traffic

Take the children (or set the task as homework) to conduct a survey of the traffic that passes a particular spot over a ten-minute period. Ask different children to count different categories for example types of vehicle, colours of vehicles etc. Ask the children to design a pictogram for the survey data and think of which symbols to use. Suggest pictograms with a key that shows one symbol for every two units. Ask questions about their data or see if they can think of their own to ask other children. Ask if the data would be the same on a Saturday or Sunday?

Plenary

Say you want to check which TV programmes children watched yesterday. Ask the children how to conduct the survey and record the steps on the board. Ask them how to record the data. Use a pictogram and explain you want each symbol to represent two children. Ask the children to explain why this is useful. Then ask them to conduct the survey and one child records the data on the board. The other children check for accuracy. Then let the children ask, and answer, questions with answers relating to the information on the pictogram.

Common difficulties

Some children always interpret each symbol as representing one item or unit, even when a key states otherwise.

Remediation

Ask about the TV programmes again and show, each time, that the number of children does not match the number of symbols on the pictogram.

Homework suggestion

Ask the children to look out of a window at home and make a pictogram to show how many of each type of thing they can see. Use a scale of one symbol to represent two items.

Key point

Pictograms with symbols representing more than one unit are more frequent than those with one symbol for one unit and children need to know how to record and interpret them.

Related material

Pupil Book
Page 122-123

PCM 60
SCM 60
ECM 60

Off the beaten track
Waiter, waiter!

Comparing and ordering three-digit numbers

Key vocabulary

- greatest
- smallest
- greater than
- less than
- between

Materials

- whiteboards
- washing line
- pegs
- number cards (0–100)
- counters
- spinners (0–9)
- blank cards
- number lines
- three-digit number cards

Introduction

Unit plan 31 introduced comparing two three-digit numbers. These activities teach how to order more than two three-digit numbers. Problems occur when the tens digit is a zero, and special attention is given to this and reinforcing the understanding of place value.

Objectives

 To compare two given three-digit numbers, say which is more or less, and give a number which lies between them.

 To order whole numbers to at least 1000, and position them on a number line.

Oral and mental starter

Close calls

Choose a two-digit number and tell the children they have to guess what it is. Ask the children to write their guesses on their whiteboards. Give clues for the number you are thinking of, using comparative vocabulary (more than, less than, between). The child whose number is closest wins the round. Repeat with different numbers.

Numbers out to dry

Peg a set of numbers (1–100) on a washing line. The numbers should be in order but not consecutive. Ask the children to think of numbers that lie between pairs of numbers and write them on cards. Ask volunteers to come out and peg their number in the correct place.

Main teaching

N.B. Review the strategies of comparison and ordering such as comparing the hundreds first, then the tens, and finally, the units. Alternatively, use a number line or apparatus.

Order for counters

Give each group a set of number cards (0–9). Ask each child to take three cards to create a three-digit number. Then ask all the children to order their three-digit numbers from the smallest to the greatest. The child with the highest number wins a counter. Repeat with different winning criteria such as, the smallest number, any number greater than 500, or, numbers between 400 and 600.

Spin to order

Give each group a spinner (0–9) and ask each child to spin it three times to create a three-digit number. Then they record all their numbers on blank cards and place them in order on a number line. Ask one child to shuffle the cards and see if they can put them back in the right order. Make sure they understand numbers in which one or more of the digits are zero.

Orderly triplets

Give each child a three-digit number card and ask the children to sit with two other children in a group of three. Ask them to order themselves from the smallest to the greatest. Ask volunteers to explain how they ordered their numbers. Discuss the strategies.

But why?

Divide the class into pairs and give each pair a set of number cards (0–9). Ask them to pick three cards. How many different three-digit numbers can they make? Ask them to order their numbers. How did they do this? Can they explain why 261 is greater than 216?

Plenary

Place five three-digit numbers on a line. Ask the children to record them on their whiteboards, ordering them from the smallest to the greatest. Ask volunteers to explain the strategy they used for ordering the numbers. Discuss the strategies. Ask them to write on their whiteboards the greater of two numbers in which the tens and units digits are swapped, and one of these digits is zero, for example, 306 and 360, or 408 and 480. Ask volunteers to explain why one is greater than the other.

Common difficulties

Children sometimes have difficulty with numbers that contain one or more zero digits.

Remediation

Use different representations, and, if necessary, use concrete representation to show the value of the numbers in each column. Use multibase to show that in 405, there are four 100-squares and five unit cubes but no tens. Use a number line to show that 405 is after 400 since there are 4 hundreds, and before 410, since it has only 5 units and no tens.

Homework suggestion

Ask the children to write eight cars' registration numbers. Ask them to order the registration numbers from smallest to greatest using the three-digit numbers they contain.

Related material

 Pupil Book
Page 124-125

 PCM 61
SCM 61
ECM 61

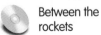 Between the rockets

Sheep crossing

Building blocks

Estimating and approximating

Key vocabulary

- estimate/s
- approximately

Materials

- jars of marbles
- two-digit quantity cards
- whiteboards
- three-digit number cards (up to 500)
- small pieces of paper
- number lines (up to 500)
- small post-its
- three-digit number mass cards

Introduction

A sensible estimate shows an understanding of a number as a representation of a quantity. The following activities extend rounding and estimating the position on a number line to three-digit numbers, and applying the knowledge of ordering three-digit numbers acquired in previous unit plans.

Objectives

 To read and begin to write the vocabulary of estimation and approximation.

Oral and mental starter

 Marvellous marbles

Prepare several jars containing different numbers of marbles. Pass one round the class asking the children to guess approximately how many marbles there are in the jar. Repeat with the other jars. Discuss the strategies they used to estimate the number each time.

 Round amounts

Prepare a set of cards with two-digit quantities of different measures, for example, 32 g, 26p, and 54 cm. Ask the children to write the quantities on their whiteboards, rounding the amount up or down, to the nearest 10. Repeat with different quantities and then with three-digit amounts.

Main teaching

 Take your places

Give each group a set of random three-digit number cards (101–499). Ask each child to take one card and put it in its approximate place on a number line marked in 50s from 100 to 500. Ask them to discuss the positions of the numbers until the whole group agrees. Then ask them to round the numbers to the nearest 100, and then to the nearest 10.

Personal positions

Give each group a scale or number line from 100 to 500 with divisions marked in 50s. Ask each child to think of a number, record it on a small piece of paper, and place an arrow on the line at its approximate place. Each child then asks the group to estimate the position of their arrow. Ask them to explain how they decide what the number is. Extend to a number line with divisions marked in 100s.

 ### Post-it position-it

Working in pairs, each child writes a three-digit number on the back of a small post-it and sticks it, number side down, on a number line (300–600 marked in 50s). The other child says what the number could be. They check and see the difference between the number and their estimate. Repeat and see if they can reduce the difference.

Mass positioning

Each child picks a mass card from a set of three-digit masses. Ask them to record on the card, the mass to the nearest 100 and to the nearest 10, and place it on a number line. Ask the children to look at all the cards and check them for positioning and correctly rounded numbers.

Plenary

Write a three-digit number on the board. Ask which hundred this number is greater than and which hundred it is smaller than. Ask which hundred the children would round it to. Repeat with other three-digit numbers. Then place an arrow on a number line (0–500 marked in 50s with only the 100s labelled) and ask the children to round this unspecified number to the nearest 100. Ask them to guess which number it could be. Repeat with other arrows.

Common difficulties

Children sometimes make wild guesses instead of sensible estimates.

Remediation

Break the amounts down into smaller quantities to estimate then build them back up again to the original total.

Homework suggestion

Ask the children to estimate different distances, for example, from the bedroom to the bathroom, from the door to the window, from the television to the sofa etc. Make a chart to show their estimates. Then ask them to measure the actual distances and show these in an extra column on their chart. (The actual distances will only be approximate as they will probably only have a ruler to use.)

Related material

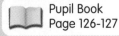 Pupil Book Page 126-127

 PCM 62
SCM 62
ECM 62

 Sorting out the warehouse

63

Describing and extending number sequences

Introduction

In previous unit plans the children explored number sequences where the rule was counting on or back in given steps (see Unit plan 46). The following activities revise number sequences and introduce new strategies for finding the rule of a sequence, and applying it to fill in the missing numbers.

Objectives

- To describe and extend number sequences.

Oral and mental starter

Table turns

Give out cards with multiplication facts of the 2, 3, 4, 5, and 10 times-tables. Say: *'I have 1 x 2 = 2, who has 2 x 2?'* Ask the children to stand up in turn and read out their multiplication sentence. When all the twos are standing, chant the 2 times-table together. Then ask the 2 times-table to sit down and repeat with the 3 times-table etc.

Target counting

Count round the class randomly by pointing at different children, on or back in ones from a two-digit or three-digit starting number to a target number. Repeat, counting in tens.

Main teaching

Going by the rules

Give each group a set of number sequence cards with the first three numbers from a sequence of three-digit numbers. The group copies the numbers from each card and write the next two numbers in the sequence. Ask them to discuss their strategy. Do they have to find the rule first? Does it help to find the difference between the numbers? Ask them to say the rule for each card, for example, *"The rule is add three,"* or, *"The rule is subtract 10."*

👥 Peter pointers

Appoint one child in each group to be the 'pointer'. The pointer stands to one side, out of earshot, while the rest of the group decide on a three-digit starting number and what rule their sequence is going to follow, for example, counting in steps of five. Each child writes what their number in the sequence is on their whiteboard. The children stand in a row in order keeping their whiteboards hidden. The 'pointer' returns and is told the starting number. He or she then points to one of the other children who reveals their number. From this information the child works out what each of the other children's numbers is. Repeat with different children acting as the pointer, choosing different sequences and starting numbers. Counting back sequences may also be used.

🔹 Making up the rules

Working in pairs, ask each child to decide on a number sequence and write the first three numbers. They pass their sequence to their partner to continue with the next three numbers. Ask them to check each other's work and explain to each other how they found the rule.

🔹 Sequence strips

Ask the children to choose a rule for their own number sequence for example, going up in steps of 2, 3, 4 etc. The children roll three dice, one for the hundreds, one for the tens and one for the units to produce a start number. Then ask them to make their own sequence strips on card and draw divisions on their strips so that they mark their chosen sequence and write in the end number. They pass the strip to their neighbour who works out the scale and fills in the numbers in the sequence. They can make their numbers count forwards or backwards.

Plenary

Choose a starting three-digit number and a rule, and write the first three numbers of the sequence on the board. Ask the children to record the next two numbers of the sequence on their whiteboards. Discuss the strategies used. Repeat with other numbers. Repeat with counting back sequences.

Common difficulties

Finding the rule is sometimes hard and some children continue all sequences as if the rule is 'add one'.

Remediation

Use apparatus to show a concrete representation of the sequence or place the first three numbers on a number line. Guide the children towards finding the rule, and then calculating the next numbers.

Homework suggestion

Ask the children when it would be useful to count in twos, threes, fours, fives or tens. What suggestions can you think of?

Add and subtract near multiples of 10

Key vocabulary

- near multiple

Materials

- spinners (0–9)
- die labelled +9, - 9, -9, +11, -11, -11
- whiteboards
- hat
- number cards (101–199)
- near multiples of 10 cards
- gameboards (1–300)
- counters
- 100 squares

Introduction

Unit plan 7 revised adding and subtracting 9 and 11 using the mental strategy of adding or subtracting 10 and adjusting by 1. It also introduced bridging through a multiple of 10 and adjusting, and adding a one-digit number to a two-digit number using this strategy. These activities review all the above skills and extend to applying addition and subtraction strategies to three-digit numbers.

Objectives

- To add and subtract mentally 'a near multiple of 10' to or from a two-digit number.

- To use patterns of similar calculations.

Oral and mental starter

The adjustable one

Ask a volunteer to spin a spinner (0–9) twice and write the two-digit number on the board. Ask another volunteer to roll a large die labelled, +9, - 9, -9, +11, -11, -11. Ask the children to add or subtract accordingly and write the answer on their whiteboards.

Class subtraction

Ask the children to write on their whiteboards a subtraction of two close two-digit numbers. Then ask the whole class to stand in a circle. One child shows it to the person to their left who says the answer. If the answer is correct the child holding up the whiteboard sits down and turn passes to the other child. How far round the circle can the class go before a mistake is made? Make sure some questions include crossing a multiple of 10, for example, 52-48. Next write a three-digit question on the board and discuss how to solve it, for example, 433 – 429.

Main teaching

Nearly there

In groups of four, the children turn over a starting number card (101–199). One child says the number plus 10, plus 20 and plus 30. The next child says the starting number plus 9, plus 19 and plus 29, and the third child gives the starting number plus 11, plus 21 and plus 31. The fourth child checks and awards a point for each correct answer. Discuss the strategies and remind them of the strategy of 'adding 10 and adjusting by 1' and explain how it can be extended for higher multiples of 10. The children then swap roles and repeat the exercise several times. Then repeat the activity this time subtracting the numbers.

Snake aways and adders

Give each group several sets of near multiples of 10 cards (19, 21, 29, 31, 39, and 41), a gameboard (1–300), and a spinner (1–9). Each child spins the spinner to find their starting square. The children take turns turning over a card and adding it to their starting number. They move round the board and the others check that the moves are correct. The first to reach or pass 300 is the winner. Repeat with subtraction, starting on numbers 291 to 299 and descending to 1.

Strategy analysis

Ask the children to add 37 and 49. Discuss the strategies used. If necessary, ask which multiple of ten they can use to work out the answer. Discuss the method and present other questions for the children to work out.

Three coins in the fountain

Working in pairs, give each child three counters of a certain colour and each pair, a 100 square. Ask them to put their counters anywhere on the square. Write a two-digit number on the board and then hold up a near multiple of 10. The children add or subtract the near multiple from the number on the board and see if any of their counters are on the answer. If it is, they reclaim their counter. The first child to reclaim all three counters is the winner. Discuss the strategies used.

Plenary

Give each child a 100 square. Write an addition of a near multiple of 10 on the board using two-digit numbers, for example, 50 + 21. Ask how to work it out and discuss the possible strategies. Tell the children to colour the starting square and the final square (or put a counter on each). Do several more subtractions, and additions. What do they notice? Repeat without the 100 square. Discuss the methods used. Extend to adding and subtracting a two-digit near multiple of 10, from a three-digit number.

Common difficulties

Some children may still count up or back and not use the methods above. Some children may still need concrete representation.

Remediation

Start by doing quick fire drills of number facts of 10. Then give extra practice of adding a single-digit number without crossing a multiple of 10. Explain the methods in this unit plan again using a number line with the children drawing each step. Practise adding and subtracting multiples of 10 to a given number.

Homework suggestion

Give each child a table grid and ask them to write down five consecutive two-digit numbers along the top and the same ones down the left column. Ask them to add the pairs of numbers to fill in the squares in the table. What do they notice? Did they fill in some entries without actually doing the calculation?

Related material

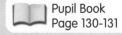 Pupil Book Page 130-131

 PCM 64
SCM 64
ECM 64

 The billboard
In the maths lab
Name that number!

mathspace

65

Mental calculations

Key vocabulary

- number facts
- place value

Materials

- whiteboards
- place value cards
- dice
- multibase cubes
- three-digit number cards
- beanbags
- targets
- spinner (1–9)

Introduction

One of the basic steps towards adding two three-digit numbers is adding a multiple of 100 to a three-digit number. The following activities focus on this type of mental calculation and its application to problem solving.

Objectives

 To use known number facts and place value to add / subtract mentally.

– To add a multiple of 100 to a two-digit or three-digit number.

Oral and mental starter

 Maths hangman

Divide the class into two teams. Play hangman on the board using addition and subtraction vocabulary. Include words such as: difference, sum, total, equals, add, plus, subtract, more and altogether. The teams take turns to suggest letters and may guess the whole word only after their letter has been accepted.

Stick 'em up!

Say a three-digit multiple of 10. Ask the children to write the number in figures on their whiteboards and hold them up. How fast can the whole class hold up the correct number?

Main teaching

 Place the value

Prepare sets of place value cards by making hundreds cards. Label the cards 'hundreds' on one side and put a digit (1-9) on the other. Make tens and units cards in a similar fashion. The children create a three-digit number (less than 400) using the cards. Then they roll a die to find how many hundreds they should add to it. Ask them to find the hundreds card to make the new number and place it on top.

⚖ Hundred differences

Give each group multibase hundreds, and three-digit number cards. They spread the number cards face down on the table and play 'pairs' matching numbers where the tens and units are the same. When each child has at least one pair, they find the difference between the two numbers in each of their pairs and show, with multibase, how many hundreds they had to add or subtract each time.

♟ Full of beans

Choose five volunteers and give each one a three-digit starting number (less than 400). Ask one of them to throw a beanbag at a target with multiples of 100 up to 600. The whole class adds their score to their starting number to find their final score and writes it down beside their name. Repeat for the other four volunteers. Who made the highest number? Change the volunteers and repeat with numbers from 600 to 999 and subtracting to make the lowest score.

♟ Leaping hundreds

Working in pairs, each child writes a two-digit number on their whiteboards. They then take turns to roll a die and add that number of hundreds on to their starting number. The first one to pass 1000 is the winner. Discuss how they calculate the additions. Repeat with a number in the 900s and subtract from it in hundreds until they pass zero. Discuss the methods used for subtracting whole hundreds.

Plenary

Write a two-digit number on the board and ask a volunteer to spin a spinner (1–9) to see how many hundreds to add. Ask the children to record the total on their whiteboards. What methods did they use? Repeat with a three-digit number (900–999) and subtract the hundreds. Then write a three-digit number on the board and ask the children to add a multiple of 100 (keep totals to less than 1000).

Common difficulties

Some children sometimes add the multiple of 100 as if it were a multiple of 10.

Remediation

Use multibase, number lines and hundreds-tens-units representation to show the calculations.

Homework suggestion

Ask the children to write their names. Ask them to give the first letter a value, either a two-digit or a three-digit number and assign 100 for each of the rest of the letters in their name. What is the final total? Write the number sentence in the form a + b = c (not as a list of a +100 +100 ...). Think of a really long name and a really short name and find their totals?

Key point

Adding multiples of 100 to a two-digit or a three-digit number is a pre-requisite to understanding addition calculations.

Related material

Pupil Book
Page 132-133

PCM 65
SCM 65
ECM 65

In the games room

The strong man

Working with three-digit numbers

Key vocabulary

- multiple

Materials

- multibase
- spinners (multiples of 100 to 900)
- paper targets
- beanbags
- two-digit multiples of 10 cards
- number cards (1-9)
- toy poster

Introduction

Unit plan 65 introduced mentally adding and subtracting multiples of 100 to or from a two-digit or three-digit number. These activities extend this knowledge to mentally solving more complex additions and subtractions, such as adding or subtracting a multiple of 10 to or from a three-digit number or another multiple of 10 greater than 100, and adding or subtracting two multiples of 100, crossing the 1000 boundary.

Objectives

- To use known number facts and place value to add or subtract a pair of numbers mentally.

Oral and mental starter

 ### Not single anymore

Write three single-digit numbers on the board. Ask the children to write as many two-digit numbers as they can, using these three single digits, and using each digit only once in each number. Check and remediate. Write the final list on the board. Then ask the children to add or subtract a near multiple of 10 from each number. Check and remediate each question before going on to the next.

 ### Grand stand

Give out multiples of 100 cards and then say another multiple of 100. Ask the children to stand up if their number added to your number, makes 1000.

Main teaching

 ### Going for the grand

Give each group a set of multibase to use if necessary, and a spinner (multiples of 100 up to 900). One child spins the spinner twice and all the children add the two numbers together. If the total is greater than 1000 and he or she says it correctly, the spinner wins five points. If the total is less than 1000, the spinner spins again and adds the next number to the total. If the total is greater than 1000 this time, the spinner wins four points. If not, the spinner continues deducting a potential point each time. Repeat with subtraction with the aim being to reach or pass zero with a similar scoring system.

👥 Increasing the stakes

Put a paper target (1-9) on the ground and give the group two beanbags. The children take turns to throw the beanbags onto the target and make a two-digit number. Each child multiplies by 10 and says the corresponding three-digit number for their original number. They then say what they need to score to make the next 100.

♟ Show of the century

Give each child a multiples of 10 card (10-90). Make two piles of number cards (1-9) on your table, call one the hundreds pile and the other the tens pile, and place a zero for the units. Ask a volunteer to pick one card from each pile and write the three-digit number, ending in zero, on the board. Ask the children to hold up their number if it makes the next hundred, when added to the number on the board. Discuss possible methods of working it out.

♟ Century bingo

Ask each child to write down a list of four different multiples of 100. Then spin a spinner (with multiples of 100 on it) twice and write the two numbers on the board. If the sum or the difference of these two numbers is equal to one of the numbers in a child's list, they cross it out and record the matching number sentence. Continue until a child has crossed out all their numbers and shouts, 'bingo!'The winner stands up and reads out their number sentences. Discuss the methods used. Repeat with other numbers.

Plenary

Display a poster with the masses of different toys written in grams (multiples of 100, from 100 to 900). Ask a volunteer to choose two toys. Ask all the children to calculate the total mass and record the matching number sentence. Discuss the methods used. Repeat with other pairs of toys.

Common difficulties

Some children may find it difficult to follow place value.

Remediation

Let the children use multibase or other apparatus to model the different questions to find the answers.

Homework suggestion

Ask the children to look at an old receipt of at least four different prices. For each price work out how much you need to add to make the next pound. Then work out which whole pounds you would use to buy each item and work out how much change you would get.

mathspace

67

More mental calculations

Key vocabulary

- multiple
- two-digit number
- three-digit number

Materials

- multiples of 10 number cards (up to 100)
- labelled die: 0, 10, ...,50
- labelled die: 40, 50, ..., 90
- imitation coins
- multiples of 10p cards (up to £1)
- snakes and ladders boards
- counters
- dice
- instruction cards
- number cards (11–99)
- multiples of 10 spinner (10–100)
- three-digit start and finish number cards
- large 1–200 number square

Introduction

The following activities continue teaching mental strategies for calculating additions and subtractions. The next level of difficulty involves crossing the hundreds while adding or subtracting a multiple of 10 to a two-digit or three-digit number.

Objectives

● To use known number facts and place value to add/subtract mentally.

Oral and mental starter

On the cards

Give each child two multiples of 10 number cards (10, 20, ,.100). Prepare two large dice labelled 0 to 50 in multiples of 10. Ask two volunteers to roll a die each and ask all the children to calculate the total. Children with the number card showing the total, hand in their cards. The first child to hand in both their cards is the winner. Repeat with subtraction using dice labelled 40 to 90 and finding the difference using number cards (0 to 50).

Random round

Count on or back around the class, to or from a three-digit number. First count in ones, then tens, and then hundreds, choosing children at random to say the numbers in sequence.

Main teaching

Price hikes

Give each group a bag of 1p, 2p, 5p and 10p imitation coins. Each child takes a handful of coins and works out their total. Then the group turns over a card showing a multiple of 10p to see how much the amounts are increased or reduced. They each estimate and record how much they think they will have after the increase or reduction. Then they work out the actual amount. Each child in the group shows their working and explains how they estimated and then calculated the answer. The group uses the coins to check each answer. Discuss the methods used. Repeat using imitation pound coins.

Snakes and ladders

Give each group a snakes and ladders board and a set of instruction cards to add or subtract multiples of 10 (up to 200). The children play snakes and ladders but with the variation that they take a card each time they land on the bottom of a ladder or the head of a snake. If they can apply the instruction to the number of the square they are on, they may go up the ladder or avoid sliding down the snake. If they cannot subtract because they are on a number smaller than the number on the card, they say, "impossible," and it is counted as a correct answer. If they answer incorrectly, they either cannot climb the ladder or have to slide down the snake, depending where they are on the board.

Current accounts

Give each child a number card (11–99) and access to imitation coins up to £2. Ask them to take the sum of pennies indicated by their card. Ask a volunteer to spin a multiple of 10 spinner (up to 100), representing the money they earned this week. The children calculate how much money they have altogether and show the amount in coins. Discuss the methods used. Repeat with other numbers.

From start to finish

Prepare cards with two three-digit numbers, where the second number is a multiple of 10 more than the first one, for example, 346 and 396. Ask them to write the start number and an instruction on the back of the card, so that another child can work out what the end number is. They can use multibase or number lines to help them. They swap cards with a partner and see if they can follow the instruction on their new card. Then they turn over the card to check.

Plenary

Display a 1–200 number square and a 'multiples of 10' spinner. Write a two-digit number on the board and ask a volunteer to spin a two-digit multiple of 10. Ask all the children to work out the total. Discuss the strategies used. Ask for examples of apparatus that might be used to represent the calculations. Repeat with other pairs of numbers. Repeat with subtraction. Extend to three-digit numbers.

Common difficulties

Place value becomes more difficult as the numbers increase.

Remediation

Use different apparatus to model the different questions and show the children how to work out the answers.

Homework suggestion

Ask the children to roll two dice and make a two-digit number. They write down the number as a price in pence. Then they toss ten 10p coins and write down the total amount that lands on heads. Ask them to add the amount of 10ps that land on their heads to the original price and write down the whole number sentence. Repeat several times.

Related material

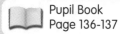
Pupil Book
Page 136–137

PCM 67
SCM 67
ECM 67

In Ziggy's shop

Addition pencil and paper methods 1

Key vocabulary

- informal pencil and paper method

Materials

- dice
- whiteboards
- number lines
- price lists

Introduction

The following activities of addition using a number line and partitioning the second number and adding the most (or least) significant digits first (see reference page at the back of this book), help children learn how to show their informal addition methods and keep track of larger numbers in addition. The advantage of the formal method of vertical addition is automation, so that problems can be solved without having to invent calculating strategies each time. The main drawbacks are, misapplication (using vertical addition in improper contexts), and accepting the result without checking its plausibility.

Objectives

- To use informal pencil and paper methods to support, record or explain HTU + TU, HTU + HTU.

Oral and mental starter

Breaking the barrier

Ask a volunteer to roll two dice and use the numbers to write a two-digit number. Ask the children to add or subtract a single digit that crosses the next multiple of 10 and hold up their answers on their whiteboards. Check and remediate.

Target the tens

Write a two-digit number on the board. Ask the children how much you need to add to reach the next multiple of 10. Repeat several times. Then ask questions with three-digit numbers that contain a whole numbers of tens.

Main teaching

Pick your own

Give each group two three-digit numbers which, when added together do not cross a tens. Say that these numbers are the number of raspberries picked by children on two consecutive days. Ask them to calculate the total. Discuss the strategies used. Show the method of using a number line and partitioning the second number, for example, $213 + 325 = 213 + 300 + 20 + 5$. Then introduce adding the most significant digit first, outlined on the reference page at the back of this book. Ask the group to add other pairs of three-digit numbers that do not involve crossing the tens, using a pencil and paper method.

General electric

Give each group a price list of electrical items with prices from £101 to £444, in which the digits are all between 0 and 4. Ask them to choose two items and calculate the total price. Discuss the methods used. Ask all the groups to use the method of using a number line and partitioning the second number. Then ask them to use the informal vertical addition method outlined on the reference page at the back of this book.

Robert's ramble

Tell the class that Robert walked 325 metres before stopping for lunch, and then 473 metres after lunch. Ask the children to calculate the total distance Robert walked. Discuss the methods used. Show the method of using the number line and partitioning the second number. Then introduce the informal vertical addition method outlined on the reference page at the back of this book. Ask the children to use this method to solve other similar stories involving addition of two three-digit numbers that do not cross the tens.

Vertical values

Write two three-digit numbers that do not cross the tens when added. Ask the children to work out the sum. Discuss the methods used. Did anyone partition the numbers into tens and units and add? Then show how to set out the numbers vertically and how to add the most significant digit first.

Plenary

Write a horizontal addition of two three-digit numbers that do not cross the tens. Ask the children to find the total. Discuss the methods used. Then ask them to find the total using a number line and partitioning the second number. Finally, ask them to use the informal vertical addition method. Repeat with other pairs of numbers.

Common difficulties

The informal vertical addition method can be meaningless for some children, who will misuse it.

Remediation

Use multibase or similar apparatus to work through the addition. Then use the number line and explain the informal vertical addition method, working in parallel with the apparatus.

Homework suggestion

Ask the children to roll a die three times and form a three-digit number where the first digit is between 1 and 4. Repeat. Add the two numbers together. What is the highest total they could make with the dice? What is the lowest?

Related material

 Pupil Book Page 138-139

 PCM 68
SCM 68
ECM 68

 Switch on addition

69

Key vocabulary

- informal pencil and paper method

Materials

- whiteboards
- number lines
- spinners (1–4, 1–9)
- maps (optional)

Addition pencil and paper methods 2

Introduction

These activities extend using the paper and pencil method from Unit plan 68 to numbers that cross the tens barrier.

Objectives

- To use informal pencil and paper methods to support, record or explain HTU + TU, HTU + HTU.

Oral and mental starter

 ### Who's it going to be?

Sit the class in a circle. Tell the children that that they are going to count round the circle in tens. Give a starting number to one specific child and ask the children to predict and write the name on their whiteboards, of the child who is going to say a certain number. Chant round the class and check. Then ask how much more needs to be added to reach the next hundred. Check and remediate.

 ### Putting pen to paper

Write two three-digit numbers, that do not cross the tens, on the board and ask the children to work out the sum, first using any method, then using a pencil and paper method learned in Unit plan 68. Repeat with other similar pairs of numbers.

Main teaching

 ### Strawberry fields forever

Give each group pairs of three-digit numbers that when they are added together will cross the tens but not the hundreds or thousands. Say that these numbers are the number of strawberries picked on two consecutive days. Ask the groups to calculate the total. Discuss the strategies used. Emphasise using the number line and partitioning the second number, and then the informal vertical addition method adding the most (or least) significant digits first (see reference page at the back of this book). Then ask them to add other pairs of three-digit numbers that cross the tens and the hundreds, using the informal vertical addition method.

🐾 Spinning numbers

Give each group two spinners (1–4, and 1–9). One child spins the 1–4 spinner four times, to find the hundreds and tens digits of two three-digit numbers. Another child spins the 1–9 spinner twice to find the two units digits. Then they each build two three-digit numbers and add them together, trying to make the largest total possible. The child with the largest total that has been calculated correctly is the winner. Discuss the methods used, then, if necessary show them how to apply pencil and paper methods to this example. Repeat. Extend to using the 1–9 spinner for the tens digits as well.

🐾 High as you can

Write five single digits on the board. Ask the children to use these numbers to make one two-digit number and one three-digit number. Tell them that their challenge is that when the numbers are added together they will make the highest number possible. Ask them to find the sum using a pencil and paper method and then to compare their method and answer with a partner. Repeat with six single digits and making two three-digit numbers.

🐾 Route masters

Give each child a simple map, or list some distances on the board (two-digit and three-digit numbers of km, less than 500 km). Ask the children to work out the distance from A to B, and from B to C etc. Check, remediate, and discuss pencil and paper methods of addition. Extension: say a total distance and ask the children to work out which route to take.

Plenary

Tell the children that a snail went on a two-day hike! He covered 467 cm on the first day and 295 cm on the second. Ask them to calculate the total distance covered by the snail. Discuss the methods used. Emphasise the use of a number line and of the informal vertical addition method. Repeat with other distances involving crossing tens and hundred (but not thousands) and ask the children to work out the sums using pencil and paper methods.

Common difficulties

Some children find pencil and paper methods difficult to use, as their mental strategies are not strong enough. For example, in the question 467 + 295, they may have difficulty because the method asks them to work out 400 + 200 = 600, 60 + 90 = 150 and 7 + 5 = 12 and then find the total of these three answers.

Remediation

Practise addition of multiples of 10 crossing 100, and addition of units with totals up to 20. Use concrete representation.

Homework suggestion

Give out photocopies from a chart at the back of a map, atlas or train schedule etc. Give a list of routes you want them to take from one city to another via a third, for example, from London to Glasgow via Newcastle/Tyne. Ask the children to use pencil and paper to calculate the total distance.

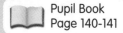

Number problems and puzzles

Key vocabulary

• number problems

Materials

• playing cards
• question cards
• dice

Introduction

The children have acquired many mathematical tools and used them to solve straightforward calculations. The following activities provide a deeper understanding of the concepts and skills by applying them to solve mathematical problems and puzzles.

Objectives

 To solve mathematical problems and puzzles, recognise simple patterns and relationships, generalise and predict. Suggest extentions by asking, 'what if...?'

Oral and mental starter

 Class vs. teacher

Make statements describing a 2-D shape by its properties. How fast can the children recognise the shape? If they guess correctly after one statement, they score three points, two points after two statements, and one point if it takes them three statements. If they do not guess correctly after three, the teacher scores five points!

💬 **What more can I add?**

Write four different two-digit numbers on the board. Working with a partner, the children choose two of the numbers, record them as an addition or subtraction and work out the answer. Then they read out their sentences, using a variety of addition and subtraction vocabulary, and explain their methods. Extend to three-digit numbers.

Main teaching

 Card lark

Give each group a set of playing cards with the picture cards removed, and a set of question cards such as: find two cards with a difference of six / a product of 40 / a total of more/less than 10. Extend to questions with three cards. How many different ways can they find to answer each question?

👥 Many ways to arrive

Give each group a target number and ask them to find different ways to combine two numbers to make it. Can they find at least 10 different ways, using each of the four operations at least once?

👤 Treble chance

Using three dice, ask the children to see how many odd totals they can make. Ask them to record their numbers and see how many dice showed even numbers and odd numbers each time. What is the most frequent sum?

👤 Four for the century

Ask the children to explore different ways to add four multiples of 10 to make 100. Discuss the methods used and the different solutions.

Plenary

Ask the children to use the digits: 2, 3, 4 and 5, and the signs: +, -, x and ÷, to make three different numbers between 100 and 200. Show them examples such as, 50 x 2 + 32 = 132. Ask volunteers to show their solutions and ask the others if they can make the same total in a different way.

Common difficulties

Children sometimes do not know where to start in puzzle solving.

Remediation

Show how to solve a number puzzle, presenting different methods for the same puzzle.

Homework suggestion

Ask the children to make all the numbers from 0 to 10 using the numbers 2 and 3 and the signs +, -, x and ÷ (as many times as they like). Can you make the numbers 11 to 20 as well?

Key point

Mathematical problems and puzzles provide children opportunities to think about and explore mathematical ideas.

Related material

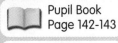
Pupil Book
Page 142-143

PCM 70
SCM 70
ECM 70

Capacity

Key vocabulary

- capacity
- litre/s
- millilitre/s

Materials

- containers
- water
- container picture card (with three-digit litre measurements)
- different-sized measuring jugs
- marker pens
- capacity cards
- envelopes
- hat

Introduction

The basic concepts of capacity and volume were introduced in Years 1 and 2. These activities revise the standard unit of one litre, and reading scales to the nearest unit. They also introduce the millilitre. Children practise addition of hundreds, and learn how to convert from millilitres to litres, and from litres to millilitres.

Objectives

 To know the relationship between litres and millilitres.

 To read scales to the nearest labelled and unlabelled division.

Oral and mental starter

💬 Loads of litres

Prepare different-shaped containers that hold 1 litre, $1\frac{1}{2}$ litres and $\frac{1}{2}$ litre of water, labelled A, B, C, etc. Ask the children to say which holds the most and to order them from most to least. Use vocabulary such as, 'full', 'empty', and 'half full'. Revise the concept of litre and ask the children to estimate if a container holds more than, about or less than one litre.

💬 Rounded litres

Give each child a card with a picture of a container holding a three-digit amount of litres. Ask the children to find another child whose number rounds to the same 100 litres as theirs. Shuffle the cards and deal again. This time they need to find a child whose number rounds to the same nearest 10 litres.

Main teaching

Up to the brim

Give each group a 1 litre measuring jug and other measuring containers such as, a 100 ml cup, and a 200 ml teacup or plastic cup. Ask them to see how many ways they can fill the jug using different containers and record the different amounts they use. Ask them to estimate how many millilitres there are in a litre (check for accurate filling). Repeat with a half litre jug and ask the children to estimate how many millilitres there are in a half a litre.

👥 Making your mark

Give each group a set of different-sized but standard shaped containers (1 l, 2 l, or $1\frac{1}{2}$ l) and marker pens. Ask the children to calibrate their containers (in 100 ml increments) using a 100 ml measuring jug. Then give them an assortment of different-sized and shaped containers and ask them to use their 'measuring containers' to find the capacity of each one. They should use language such as more than, less than, and exactly.

🧍 Shared liquid assets

Give each pair of children a 1 l container, and a set of 100 ml, 200 ml and 300 ml measuring jugs. Ask them to find different ways to fill the 1 l container using these jugs and record their results. What combinations equal one litre? How much is one litre in millilitres? Repeat for a $\frac{1}{2}$ l container.

🧍 Liquid orders

Prepare containers of different capacities, labelled A, B, C, etc., and envelopes labelled A, B, C, etc., with a record of each container's capacity sealed inside. One child chooses three envelopes out of a hat and writes the letter names on the board. All the class then writes the letter names in order of capacity. Choose three volunteers to come out and measure the capacity using a measuring jug. Who had written the correct order? Open the sealed envelopes to check the capacities had been measured correctly.

Plenary

Ask how many millilitres there are in one litre. Review the answers and write 1 l = 1000 ml, on the board. Repeat with 500 ml. Then write a multiple of 100 ml on the board. Ask the children to record the number of 100 ml needed to fill this quantity. Repeat with two multiples of 100 ml (with sums up to 1800 ml). Ask the children to record the total in litres and millilitres.

Common difficulties

Some children may not realise that the calculations in the plenary are linked to real life situations.

Remediation

Ask the children to test their answers with real containers and liquid.

Homework suggestion

Look in the cupboard or the fridge for containers that have their capacities written in millilitres. Find two labels in millilitres that add up to more than a litre and write their total, and two labels that have a total capacity of less than a litre and write their total.

Key point

Knowing the relationship between litres and millilitres is important in other subjects such as Science.

Related material

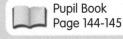
Pupil Book
Page 144-145

PCM 71
SCM 71
ECM 71

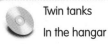
Twin tanks
In the hangar

Measuring capacity

Key vocabulary

- litre/s
- millilitre/s
- capacity

Materials

- containers
- half-litre measuring jug
- two-litre plastic bottles
- container picture cards
- whiteboards
- measuring cylinders
- capacity cards

Introduction

The following activities focus on estimating capacities and rounding measurements to the nearest whole or half unit. Children learn to measure using mixed units and suggest suitable units to measure a given capacity. Piaget's famous tests show that children encounter inherent difficulties in estimating capacity, so it is important to be aware of the basic misconceptions.

Objectives

 To record estimates and measurements to the nearest whole or half unit, or in mixed units.

To suggest suitable units and measuring equipment to estimate or measure capacity.

Oral and mental starter

 Halfway houses

Write two numbers on the board (either two non-consecutive numbers on up to 20, or two multiples of 10, or two multiples of 100). Ask for the number halfway between the two. Repeat several times. Then write two consecutive single-digit numbers on a number line and ask what the division halfway between them represents. Repeat with different consecutive digits and extend to two-digit numbers.

Less than litres

Ask questions about half-litres such as: How much is half a litre? What could we fill with half a litre of liquid? What type of containers would overflow and which would not be filled? Line up a set of different containers, labelled A to E, and ask the children to predict the outcome of pouring half a litre into each, in terms of: not enough water, too much, or exactly right. Ask for a show of hands for each option. Repeat with other containers and ask about different 100 ml amounts.

Main teaching

 Fill it up!

Ask the children to fill one measuring container and measure its capacity using the scale. Next, give the group six different containers, labelled A to F, and a measuring jug. Ask each of the children to use their knowledge of the demonstration container to write estimates of the capacity of each of the six containers in litres and millilitres. Then ask the group to fill each container and find its capacity. Check the actual capacity against their estimates. Ask them to convert all the values to millilitres.

👥 Made to measure

Give each group a two-litre plastic bottle and a measuring jug. Ask the children to pour 500 ml of water into the bottle at a time, and mark the graduations as $\frac{1}{2}$ l, 1 l, $1\frac{1}{2}$ l, and 2 l. Then they use their 'measuring bottle' to measure the capacity of different containers to the nearest half litre.

♟ Capacity conundrums

Hold up different items such as a spoon, a bucket, a cup, and pictures of a bathtub (the capacity is about 120 l), a small vase, etc. Ask the children if they would measure the capacity of the items in litres or millilitres? Then write the capacities of the different containers (including mixed units and the $\frac{1}{2}$ notation) and ask the children to say which capacity matches each item. Ask volunteers to measure to check the answers.

♟ Quite contained

Show a variety of different containers. Ask the children to write down which container they think has the largest capacity and which has the smallest. Ask two volunteers to measure the capacities using a measuring cylinder that has divisions of 100 ml. Then ask two other volunteers to measure using mixed units.

Plenary

Ask one child to pour 100 ml of liquid into a container so that all the children see where the liquid level comes to. Then ask the children to record on their whiteboards, their estimate of the capacity of the whole container. Discuss the estimates and then ask a volunteer to check the actual capacity by measuring. Repeat with different containers.

Common difficulties

Capacity is not a tangible quantity. Misconceptions are frequent at this stage for a number of reasons: you cannot hold a measurable capacity, different-shaped objects have different capacities, and it is not easy to compare capacities. Millilitres are not a common everyday measurement.

Remediation

Let the children pour the same quantity of liquid from one container to another, different-shaped, container, and see the different levels of the liquid. Ask them to estimate and mark 100 ml on the side of different containers and then check by measuring.

Homework suggestion

What things around the house have a capacity between 200 ml and 500 ml? Give the children a list of different measurement bands and ask them to find objects that have capacities between the pairs of measurements.

73

Symmetry and mirror lines

Key vocabulary

- symmetry
- line/s of symmetry
- reflection

Materials

- grids
- mirrors
- scissors
- cut-out shapes
- paper
- drawn circles

Introduction

Children see symmetry in their everyday lives as reflections in mirrors, and other shiny surfaces. The concept of symmetry was first introduced in Year 1. The following activities introduce lines of symmetry. They show that a 2-D shape may have more than one line of symmetry and that there are some that have no line of symmetry. The children learn to sketch the reflection of a simple image.

Objectives

 To identify and sketch lines of symmetry in simple shapes, and recognise shapes with no lines of symmetry.

 To sketch the reflection of a simple shape in a mirror line along one edge.

Oral and mental starter

Percussion sequences

Make a percussion sound and go around the room asking each child to repeat the sounds in the sequence so far, and then add one of their own. How long can they keep the sequence going before they need to start a new sequence?

Alphabet symmetry

Ask the class who has a symmetrical letter in their name. Ask the children to each write a symmetrical letter, swap with a partner's and check. Ask a volunteer to write their name in capitals on the board. Ask how many symmetrical letters are in the name and which ones they are. Write SYMMETRICAL on the board and ask how many letters in the word SYMMETRICAL are symmetrical.

Main teaching

Mirror, mirror

Give each group 6x4 grids. Ask them to colour in squares to make a symmetrical shape. Then they cut them in half along the line of symmetry. Ask each child to take a half picture and, using a mirror, colour a blank 6x4 grid to recreate the original. Extension: Draw paths instead of colouring squares.

Symmetry on-line

Give each group a selection of cut-out shapes, including some with no lines of symmetry. Ask the children to look for lines of symmetry by folding or using a mirror. Ask them to draw around each shape and draw the lines of symmetry, if any. Ask them to record underneath, the number of lines of symmetry they found for each shape.

Origami symmetry

Take a piece of paper, fold it in half and then cut out a shape from the folded edge. Ask how many lines of symmetry the resulting paper has. (Depending on the shape, it can have more than one line of symmetry even at this stage.) Fold another piece of paper in half twice, cut out a shape, and ask how many lines of symmetry there are now. Give the children paper and scissors and ask them to make shapes with one and two lines of symmetry. How many lines of symmetry would they get if they folded the paper in half a third time?

Symmetrical art

Ask the children to draw a shape with no lines of symmetry, one line of symmetry, and two lines of symmetry. Ask them to compare their shapes with a partner to check each other's lines of symmetry using a mirror or by folding. Give each pair three circles. Ask them to colour them so that one circle has no line of symmetry, one has one line, and one has two lines of symmetry. Compare and discuss the results.

Plenary

Go through the alphabet (or letters in a name or word) and identify which letters have no line of symmetry, one line of symmetry, two lines of symmetry, or more. Discuss the strategies used for finding the lines of symmetry. Then draw half a shape with one dotted edge. Ask the children to copy it on squared paper and complete the other half using the dotted edge as the line of symmetry. They can check using a mirror or by folding.

Common difficulties

Instead of drawing the reflection, some children draw the same thing again the same way round.

Remediation

Take a half-shape and show how it looks in the mirror to make the new symmetrical shape. Put the mirror against the incorrectly drawn shape and show that it does not show what is drawn.

Homework suggestion

Find different pictures or sketch pictures of objects in your room that have no, one or two lines of symmetry.

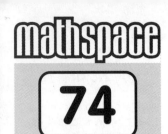

Position and direction

74

Key vocabulary

- co-ordinates

Materials

- blindfold
- photographs
- squared paper
- grids
- instruction cards

Introduction

Unit plan 40 introduced absolute directions: North, South, East, and West. These activities focus on grids and co-ordinates. Co-ordinates are pre-requisites to function representation. At this stage co-ordinates will not refer to intersections of lines and columns but to the squares themselves. This knowledge gives the children the tools to work with position, direction and movement.

Objectives

- To read and begin to write the vocabulary related to position, direction and movement.

Oral and mental starter

Blind man's turn

The children take turns to wear a blindfold. The others give instructions for turning through a number of right angles. Limit the number to three until the children gain confidence. The blindfolded child says which way they think they are facing after the moves.

Photo op

Take photographs of objects in the playground. Explain which direction is North and show the pictures. Ask the children to say the direction of each one from a given vantage point.

Main teaching

Co-ordinated rescue

Give each group a grid marked on large squared paper. Draw a boat on one square and tell the children that it is sinking. Explain that they need to tell the coastguards the location of the boat. Ask the groups to suggest solutions. Explain the basic convention of labelling columns: A, B, C, etc., and rows: 1, 2, 3, etc. Show how a square is described by giving first the column letter, then the row number.

Co-ordinate shopping

Give each group a labelled grid (columns A, B, C, etc., rows 1, 2, 3, etc.) of squared paper with some supermarket areas (frozen food, meat, tins, bread,...) drawn on it. Ask each child in the group to think of one supermarket object or area to add to the grid. Ask them to take turns to describe where they want their item to be placed and describe its position for the others to draw in the correct square on the grid. Extend by asking them to design a route for a shopper to find their way round, listing the objects as a shopping list with their co-ordinates. Remind them to use the letter-number convention and to describe the directions, for example, South 2.

Along the way

Give each child a labelled grid with objects in different squares and a set of instruction cards such as, move from A 2 to E 3, then from E 3 to C 4. The children trace their path with horizontal and/or vertical moves, giving the direction and number of squares moved (for example, North 4) as well as recording the objects they can collect along the way. Ask volunteers to show how they collected each of their items. Repeat with other instructions.

Show the way

Give each child a labelled grid. Say two co-ordinates and ask the children to write a set of instructions for a partner to move from one square to the other, for example, East 3. Ask them to see who has produced the quickest route. Extension: Ask each child to work out their route secretly, then say, for example, *"I can go from A 5 to D 1 in three moves. What could they be?"* Their partner has to work out a possible route.

Plenary

Display an 8x8 grid on the board and label the columns A, B, C, etc. and rows 1, 2, 3, etc. Draw different objects in some squares. Ask the children to record on their whiteboards, the position of a given object. Repeat with other objects. Then write a list of co-ordinates on the board and ask the children to record all the objects they would land on and to describe the route they would take in terms of direction and number of steps from one object to the next.

Common difficulties

Some children may still not fully understand the convention of co-ordinates. The most frequent error is reversing the letter and the number, an error which is crucial to avoid when moving to the mathematical number-number notation.

Remediation

Teach simple ideas to remember the convention, such as: *'column begins with C and row with R, and C always comes before R'* or *'along the corridor and up the stairs!*

Homework suggestion

Give each child a 10x10 grid and ask them to write a letter of the alphabet that has mainly straight lines. Ask them to write a 'program' using co-ordinates and directions to describe how to draw their letter.

Right angles

Key vocabulary

- right angle
- degrees

Materials

- compass direction labels
- clock faces
- time cards
- shapes
- paper
- geo-strips
- angles cards
- shape sheets

Introduction

The children revised right angles and learned how to decide if an angle was a right angle in Unit plan 39. The following activities focus on comparing angles with a right angle. The children also learn that a straight line is equivalent to two right angles. They will use these skills in many contexts in geometry, for example, there cannot be more than one right angle or obtuse angle in a triangle.

Objectives

 To recognise that a straight line is equivalent to two right angles.

 To compare angles with a right angle.

Oral and mental starter

💬 From every angle

Draw a polygon on the board containing at least one right angle and label its angles A, B, C, etc. Ask the children to write on their whiteboards the letter names of all the angles that are right angles. Check, remediate then repeat with a different polygon.

💬 I spy right angles

Label the four compass points on the walls. Say, for example, *"I spy with my little eye, something that has one/two/four right angles, between North and East."*

Main teaching

Right on time

Give each group a clock face, and a set of time cards. Ask one child to turn over a card and set the clock. Ask the group to discuss and decide whether the angle between the hands is greater, less than, or exactly, a right angle.

Right angle I.D.

Give each group a set of different shapes, each with its angles labelled with a different letter of the alphabet. Ask the children to fill in recording charts saying which angles are greater than a right angle, which angles are smaller than a right angle, and which are right angles. Discuss the strategies used and show them how to check using the corner of a square or piece of paper.

Folded finders

Working in pairs, ask the children to fold a piece of paper to make a right angle finder. Give each pair a geo-strip and ask them to open it to make a right angle, using the right angle finder. Ask the children to draw angles that are smaller than a right angle, using their geo strips to help, and cut them out. Then give each pair a random angle card and ask them if their angle is greater or smaller than a right angle. Discus the strategies used. Draw an angle on the board. Ask the children to say whether it greater or smaller than a right angle and ask a volunteer to come up and check.

About turn

Give the children the following instructions. *"Draw a line in blue, then put a pencil along it. Turn the pencil clockwise through a right angle and draw a line in green. Then start your pencil on the green line and turn clockwise through another right angle and draw where the pencil is in red. What do you notice about the red and blue lines? What do two right angles make?"*

Plenary

Give each child a sheet with different triangles and quadrilaterals, some with right angles, and all the angles labelled with a letter. Include a 180°angle. Ask the children to mark the angles that are less than a right angle in blue, the angles that are more than a right angle in red, and the right angles in green. Discuss the answers shape by shape. Discuss the strategies used for measuring right angles. Discuss the 180°angle, and ask the children to estimate if it is more, less, or equal to two right angles.

Common difficulties

Some children think that a right angle must have a horizontal edge and a vertical one and may miss right angles that are not 'standing straight'.

Remediation

Ask the children to check their comparisons using a right angle finder or any other concrete tool.

Homework suggestion

Ask the children to draw three triangles: where the angles of one triangle are all less than 90°, the second contains one angle of 90°, and the last has one angle of more than 90° Can they find any triangles like these around the house? Write or cut out examples of each one.

Key point

Comparing an angle to a right angle is essential for many geometric activities.

Related material

Pupil Book
Page 152-153

PCM 75
SCM 75
ECM 75

 Tangled angles

Recognising multiples

Key vocabulary

- multiples

Materials

- multiplication question cards
- pointing stick
- flip chart cut into three columns
- number cards (0–9)
- spinners (10, 50, and 100)
- gameboards
- dice
- counters

Introduction

In Year 2, the children learned to recognise, two-digit multiples of two, five, and 10, without counting. The following activities extend this knowledge to three-digit numbers and recognising multiples of 50 and 100. Knowledge of multiples is useful for simplifying fractions and for discovering rules in number sequences.

Objectives

 To recognise two-digit and three-digit multiples of two, five or 10, and three-digit multiples of 50 and 100.

Oral and mental starter

Table testers

Chant the 2, 5 and 10 times-tables together with the class. Give out multiplication question cards from these times-tables. Hold up different product cards and say: *"Hold up your card if it equals mine"*.

Flip chants

Prepare a flip chart made of three separate columns representing H, T and U. Tell the children that they are going to count in hundreds, tens and units when you point to the relevant column. Ask a volunteer to work the correct column in the flip chart as they count. Repeat starting from different starting numbers. Extend to chanting up in 50s from any multiple of 100.

Main teaching

Marvellous multiples

Give each group two sets of number cards (0–9) shuffled together. They take turns taking five cards and making as many three-digit multiples of two as they can. One child records the numbers. The children score one point for every multiple of two and lose one point if they suggest an odd number. They score extra points if they can identify any of their numbers that are also multiples of 10, 50 or 100. Then, ask them to compare their lists and write the highest and the lowest numbers. One child spins a spinner (labelled 10, 50, and 100) and the children write all the numbers that are multiples of that number, between the two three-digit numbers. Repeat with multiples of five and 10.

🏙 Boardroom bonuses

Give each group a gameboard numbered with random two- and three-digit numbers, of which many of them are multiples of two, five, 10, 50, and 100. The children take turns rolling a die and moving their counter along. If they land on a number that is a multiple of two, five, and/or 10, 50 or 100 they score a point if they correctly identify what the number is a multiple of. Remind the children that some numbers are multiples of more than one of the numbers so they can pick up bonus points.

♟ Half hundred multiples

Elicit some three-digit numbers that are multiples of 10, and ask how the children identified them. Then ask if any of them are multiples of 100, or multiples of 50. How do they know? What's the rule? Ask the children to write the next multiple of 50 and the next multiple of 100.

♟ Need to know basis

Write a long number on the board, keeping it hidden with a large piece of paper. Reveal one number from the right and ask whether it is a multiple of two, five, 10, 50, or 100. Ask which ones they can identify and which require further information. Ask what they need to know for the others.

Plenary

Write a three-digit number on the board and ask the children to round it to the nearest 10. Then ask them what this number is a multiple of. What do they notice? Elicit that multiples of 10 are always multiples of two and five, and sometimes multiples of 50 and/or 100. Then, ask for the next multiple of five after 60. How do they know? How do they work it out? Ask about the next multiple of 50 and 100.

Common difficulties

Some children do not know their times-tables well enough and learn the rules of 'what is a multiple of x?', by rote rather than understanding them.

Remediation

Give plenty of practice at chanting the times-tables and quick fire questions. Ask questions about which small numbers are multiples of x and gradually build up to larger ones. Practise the rules (for example, a multiple of two is always even, a multiple of 10 ends in zero) using the times-tables to find examples that follow the rules.

Homework suggestion

Ask the children to look for two-digit prices of different items. Make a list of the items and their prices. Which prices are multiples of two, three, four, five, 10? Why do you think shopkeepers try to avoid multiples of 10p?

Key point

Recognising multiples of numbers is a basic mathematical skill and the foundations of arithmetic.

Related material

Pupil Book Page 154-155

PCM 76
SCM 76
ECM 76

Lucky numbers

Spacey horses

mathspace

77

Investigating general statements

Key vocabulary

- strategy

Materials

- 'multiples of four' cards
- parts of 100 squares
- right angle finders

Introduction

These activities focus on investigating general statements about multiples, and the properties of shapes (including right angles). Solving puzzles involves the application of mathematical knowledge in ways that are not always straightforward. It is a valuable tool for ensuring full and thorough understanding of the concepts.

Objectives

 To investigate a general statement about familiar numbers or shapes by finding examples that satisfy it.

 To solve mathematical problems or puzzles.

Oral and mental starter

Reverse 'rithmetic

Ask the children to write a two-digit number, using two digits from one to four, and then reverse the digits to form a second two-digit number. Ask them to add the two numbers together and see what they notice.

Multiples in the middle

Ask the children to write numbers that lie between 30 and 50 but are not multiples of two, five, 10, or 50. How many different numbers can they find? Ask them to write a multiple of each of the following: two, five, 10, 50 and 100, that lie between 331 and 675. Ask for suggestions and see how many examples they can find. Repeat with other numbers.

Main teaching

Dividing by 2 and 2 again, is the same as dividing by 4

Divide the class into groups of three. Give each group a set of 'multiples of four' cards (4–40). They turn over a card and each take a task. One child divides the multiple by four, another divides the same number by two and passes it to the third child who divides it by two again. Ask them to discuss the results relating to the statement. Can they model these divisions by dividing counters into equal sets? Can they find higher numbers that also follow this statement? Ask them to use counters to check.

Not all quadrilaterals have a line of symmetry

Ask the group to think of a way to test this statement. If necessary, suggest trying to draw some quadrilaterals that prove the statement. Then discuss if it is possible and, consequently, whether the statement is true or false.

 Ten times a multiple of five is always a multiple of 50

Give each child a different part of a 100 square and ask them to colour in all the multiples of five. Discuss how they identified them. Then ask each child to choose four of the multiples and multiply them by 10. Are they multiples of 50? Then ask the children to repeat the multiplication with a number that is not a multiple of five. Variation: Ask the children to investigate if 10 times a multiple of 10 is always a multiple of 100. Ask volunteers to explain their methods of investigation.

 All triangles have at least two angles that are less than 90°

Ask the children to draw a triangle and check the angles with their set squares or right angle finders (or just by looking). Ask them to record the number of angles that are less than 90°. Ask them to try and draw a triangle that has two angles that are 90° or more. What about a triangle that has three angles less than 90°, does this follow the general statement?

Plenary

If the total of two numbers is even, the difference between the two numbers must also be even. Discuss ways of checking this statement and implement the suggestions. Then ask the children to investigate the inverse statement about odd numbers. Discuss the strategies used and check that the investigations were thorough, covering all possible combinations of odd and even numbers, more than once.

Common difficulties

Some children find investigating general statements difficult. They can see that the statement is true or false, and can identify from a given list, the numbers or shapes to prove it, but they have difficulty finding more examples.

Remediation

Give one solution to begin with and see if the children can find others that are similar. Discuss ways of finding further examples.

Homework suggestion

Investigate, using the internet or the library, the statement 'If the last two digits of a year is a multiple of four, then the year is a leap year.' Ask the children to try and find an exception to this general statement (Explain, on the following day that the rule for years ending in double 00 is that they have to be divisible by 400 to be leap years, for example, 1600 and 2000).

Related material

 Pupil Book Page 156-157

 PCM 77
SCM 77
ECM 77

 The number screen

Doubles and halves of multiples of 50

Key vocabulary

- multiples

Materials

- addition question cards
- price tags
- multibase
- 'multiples of 50' cards
- boxes
- whiteboards
- 1000 squares
- counters
- spinners
- number lines
- price lists

Introduction

In Unit plan 51, the children learned doubling and halving multiples of five and 10, and the connection between these two operations through 'doubling and halving machines'. The following activities extend this knowledge to doubling multiples of 50 to 500, and their corresponding halves. These skills facilitate problem solving as well as more complex topics, such as fractions and multiplication calculations.

Objectives

 To derive quickly, doubles of multiples of 50 to 500, and all corresponding halves.

Oral and mental starter

Dabbling in doubles

Hold up different addition questions that require knowledge of doubling to solve, for example, 80 + ? = 160, and 60 + 60 = ? Use doubles of one to 20 and multiples of five up to 100.

Double your money

Show an item with a price tag (1p–20p and multiples of 5p up to 50p). Ask the children to show you double the price in pence. Ask them which coins they could use to pay.

Main teaching

Chinese whispers

Give each group sets of multibase and 'muliples of 50' cards (up to 500). One child takes a number card, reads it to him or herself, and uses multibase to double the number. They put the multibase in an open box and record the number on their whiteboard. The box is passed on to the next child. The next child looks at the multibase, works out the half, and records that number on their whiteboard. He or she models the answer with multibase and passes it on. The third child doubles the number again and records it, and the fourth halves it again and records the result. They check the results by looking at the original card and checking that alternate children have the same number. Repeat several times, then ask the children to devise a way to multiply or divide by two without using the multibase. Discuss the methods used.

👥 'Rithmetic roulette

Give each group a grid (marked 100, 200, 1000), a spinner (multiples of 50 up to 500), and 10 counters per child. Appoint one child to be the banker. The other children place counters on the square they think the double is going to be. One child spins the spinner, and anyone who thinks their counter is on a number square that is double the number the spinner landed on, asks the banker to pay them. Only if the child is correct do they receive an extra counter. If the child is incorrect they forfeit an extra counter. Repeat several times to see who is the overall winner, then appoint another child as the banker and start again. Repeat for halves, with the grid marked in fifties up to 500, using a spinner in whole hundreds up to 1000.

👤 Line dancing

Give each child a number line marked in fifties up to 1000. Ask them to double 250. Ask volunteers to explain how they used the number line to do this. Discuss the methods used. Did anyone use a method that uses their previous knowledge of doubling multiples of five up to 50? Repeat with other multiples of 50 to 500. Repeat with different questions such as half of 700.

👤 Stocking up

Give each child a price list of items, priced in multiples of £50 up to £500. Ask them to buy two of the same item and find the price. Check and remediate. Then announce a half-price sale and ask them to find the price of one item from the list. Check and remediate again, and discuss the methods used.

Plenary

Write a multiple of 50 in which the first digit is even, for example, 400 and ask the children to halve it. Then write a multiple of 100 beginning with an odd number, for example 300 and ask them to halve this number. Write a multiple of 50 that ends in 50 (up to 500), for example, 350, on the board. Ask the children to double it and elicit the different methods used. Repeat with other multiples of 50. See if they can find a rule for doubling multiples of 50. Show how to write doubles and halves as x 2 and ÷ 2.

Common difficulties

Children are often more wary of working with large numbers as they think they are very complicated.

Remediation

Show them how to build on known facts. Emphasise the connection between facts of 10, 100 and 1000. Use multibase and other apparatus for concrete representation.

Homework suggestion

Roll two dice and if they land on numbers 1 to 5, multiply the total by 50 (if you roll a 6 roll again). Double the answer and record the results. Repeat five times. Then roll four dice (roll again if you roll a 6) and multiply the total by 50. Halve your answer and record the result. Repeat five times.

Key point

Linking halving and doubling helps children divide by two and strengthens the links between these two operations.

Related material

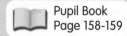
Pupil Book
Page 158-159

PCM 78
SCM 78
ECM 78

Red roofs

3 and 4 times-tables

Key vocabulary

- multiple

Materials

- 'multiples of three' cards
- 'multiples of four' cards
- number stick
- picture of a ladybird (RM 3)
- spinners (1–10)
- target wheels (1–10)
- beanbags
- spinners (multiples of three)
- spinners (multiples of four)
- apple
- price tags: 3p and 4p
- number lines (1–50)
- multiplication question cards

Introduction

The 3 and 4 times-tables were introduced in Unit plans 52 and 53. The following activities focus on mastering the facts of these times-tables, and starting to learn the corresponding division facts.

Objectives

 To begin to know the 3 and 4 times-tables.

 To say or write a division statement corresponding to a given multiplication statement.

 To recognise that multiplication is the inverse of division.

Oral and mental starter

 Missing multiples

Stick 'multiples of three' cards (up to 30) on a number stick. Chant the numbers together. Then remove some of the cards and ask the children to identify the missing numbers. Repeat with multiples of four.

 Rounds of applause

Count round the circle in ones. The children say *"fizz"*, for every multiple of three, and *"buzz"*, for every multiple of four. The children who say, *"fizzbuzz"* receive a round of applause!

Main teaching

 Build a ladybird

Give each child in the group a copy of the ladybird (RM 3). The children take turns spinning a spinner (1-10) and saying the multiplication facts from the 3 time-table according to where the spinner lands. If the multiplication fact they say is the same as one of the numbers by the ladybird's legs then they colour it in. They miss a turn if they spin a number they have already coloured. The winner is the first to colour all the legs.

It's on the cards

Give each group a target wheel with sections marked 1 to 10, and a beanbag. Each child throws the beanbag onto the target and mentally multiplies their score by four. They then find the corresponding 'multiples of four' card and the rest of the group checks that the correct card has been chosen. If the card is not available the child waits for their next turn. After all 10 cards have been taken, the child with the most cards is the winner. Repeat with a set of 'multiples of three' cards and multiplying by three. At the end, ask the children to say the multiplication and corresponding division for each of their cards.

Apples and pears

Show an apple or a pear with a price tag of 3p (or 4p). Ask a volunteer to spin a spinner (1–10) to find how many apples to buy. Ask the children to work out the total price. Repeat with spinners marked with multiples of three (or four) and ask the children to work out how many apples can be bought with the amount shown on the spinner.

Down the line

Give each pair of children a number line (1–50). Say a simple number story that uses a given multiplication or division fact from the 3 or 4 times-tables. The children work out the number sentence, and demonstrate it on their number line, jumping forwards or backwards as appropriate. Ask them to work out the inverse number sentence and use it, on the number line, to check their answers.

Plenary

Use multiplication and division vocabulary to ask quick fire questions. For example: *"How many threes make 12? How many fours in 12? What is three multiplied by three?"* etc. Use number sentences printed on cards as well as oral questions.

Common difficulties

Children may 'see' the obvious corresponding divisions but may not understand that multiplication is the inverse of division.

Remediation

Use interlocking cubes to make concrete representations of the multiplications. Put them together and then re-divide them, recording each stage as a number sentence.

Homework suggestion

Give the children a number code sheet (a = 28, c = 4, d = 30, e = 21, h = 12, i = 40, k = 3, l = 27, m = 16, n = 24, o = 15, p = 8, r = 36, s = 18, t = 32, u = 9, w = 6, y = 20). Ask the children to work out this word '4 x 4   7 x 4   8 x 4   4 x 3   6 x 3 2 x 4 7 x 4 1 x 4 7 x 3'. Then ask them to make up three secret words using the multiplication code.

mathspace

80

Key vocabulary

- partition

Materials

- number cards (1–50)
- number cards (multiples of 10)
- 'multiples of 10' grids
- spinners (2, 3, 4, 5 and 10)
- number lines
- multibase
- dice labelled 2, 3, 4, 5 and 10
- hats
- whiteboards

Mental multiplication and division

Introduction

Now that children have learned some basic multiplication tables, and have begun to learn to derive the corresponding division facts, they are in a position to apply and extend this knowledge to mental calculations including, multiplying and dividing two-digit numbers by two, three, four and five, and to dividing a three-digit multiple of 100, by 10 or 100. Practising this type of mental calculation builds an important base for multiplication and division algorithms, and facilitates problem solving.

Objectives

 To use known number facts and place value to carry out mentally simple multiplication and divisions.

Oral and mental starter

Triple gridlock

First chant the three times-table together. Draw a 2x5 grid on the board and write random multiples of three (up to 30) in the squares. Ask quick fire questions using a variety of multiplication vocabulary. Ask volunteers to come and circle the correct answers.

Tens in training

Give out number cards (1–10, and multiples of 10 up to 100). Ask the children to find a partner to make a multiplication sentence in the 10 times-table. Ask them to say the multiplication (and the corresponding division facts) for their numbers. Repeat with multiples of 100 and discuss the patterns and rules.

Main teaching

All in a spin

Give each group a grid with two-digit multiples of 10 randomly placed, and a picture stuck over each number. Each child lifts a picture to reveal the number and spins a spinner (2, 3, 4, 5 and 10). They multiply the two numbers using a number line or multibase to help. They record their scores and add up their total points at the end of the activity.

Maths to die for

Give each group a set of multibase blocks, a die labelled 2, 3, 4, 5 and 10, and a set of number cards (10, 20, ..., 50). Each child takes a card and makes that number with the multibase. Then they roll the die and multiply their card number by the number rolled, making a note of the answer. Ask them to use the multibase to help them do the multiplication. Can they see a pattern in their calculations? Discuss how to use place value and number facts to multiply two-digit numbers, and how partitioning into tens and units and multiplying separately makes the multiplication simpler.

Mad hatters

Tell the children they are selling hats and give them the orders from three customers, for example, 'One customer orders four hats, the second orders 10 hats, and the third orders 40 hats'. Hold up a hat with a single-digit price in pounds. Ask the children to calculate the cost of the order for this type of hat. Repeat with hats of different prices. Repeat with different orders such as: three hats, 10 hats, and 30 hats, or five hats, 10 hats, and 50 hats.

Divide and conquer

Write a multiple of 100 (100-900) on the board. Ask the children to divide the multiple by 10 and then by 100. What do they notice? Discuss. Then ask each child to write a similar division sentence of a multiple of 100 divided by 10 or 100, and the answer. Divide the class into pairs. Each child shows their partner their sentence with one of the numbers covered. The partner needs to work out what the missing number is.

Plenary

Write a term from the 3 times-table on the board, for example, 2 x 3, ask the children to calculate similar multiplications, (2 x 30 and 2 x 300). Discuss the strategies used. Encourage the use of known number facts. Repeat with other pairs of numbers, not crossing the 1000 boundary. Finally pose different division questions about dividing a three-digit multiple of 100 by 10 or 100, for example 600 ÷ 10.

Common difficulties

Even when they find the correct answers, some children may not understand the calculation. Large numbers may have no significance for children. Children, who have not mastered basic multiplication number facts, may find this type of mental calculation rather difficult.

Remediation

Use apparatus (multibase or money) to model the calculations. Drill and practise times-tables.

Homework suggestion

Work out how much your first name is worth if each letter is worth 5p, if each letter is worth 20p and if each letter is worth 50p. What happens if each letter is worth £1, what is that in pence? Can you write the multiplication each time?

Key point

Basic times-tables number facts are necessary for more complex calculations.

Related material

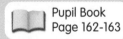 Pupil Book
Page 162-163

 PCM 80
SCM 80
ECM 80

 Flying school
Red roofs

81

Remainders

Key vocabulary

- remainder/s

Materials

- number cards (2–40)
- counters
- spinners labelled 2, 3, 4, 5, 10
- product number cards
- cubes
- number lines
- whiteboards

Introduction

Division is a complex operation, involving multiplication and subtraction. These activities introduce the concept of a remainder. Through learning how to do simple divisions with a remainder, children also realise that the remainder has to be smaller than the quotient.

Objectives

 To begin to find remainders after simple division.

 To round up or down after division, depending on the context.

Oral and mental starter

Tables lottery

Give each child a number card (2, 3, 4, 5 or 10). Hold up a number that is a multiple of one or more of the numbers on the cards. Ask the children to hold up their card if they think it divides your number exactly. Elicit the division and the corresponding multiplication.

Rounding thumbs

Ask quick fire rounding questions to the nearest 10 (or 100). Say a two-digit or three-digit number and ask the children to show thumbs up if they think the number should be rounded up, and thumbs down if it should be rounded down.

Main teaching

Share and be aware

Give each group of four children, a set of number cards (13–39). Each child takes a card and collects that number of counters. Do they think their number of counters can be divided equally between the group? Ask them each to share their counters and see if they were right and how many, if any, are left over each time. Introduce the term 'remainder'. Repeat a few times until all the cards have been used.

Overflow boats

Give each group a spinner (2, 3, 4, 5 and 10) and a set of number cards (11-40). Tell the children that there will be a class boat trip and they need to take a number card to find out how many children are going. Then ask them to spin the spinner to find out how many can sit in each boat. Their challenge is to find out how many boats are needed. Each child spins the spinner and takes a number card. Ask them to record (or draw) the number of full boats, and to record (or draw) how many children are in the not full boat (if there is one). Tell them the number of children in the not full boat is called the remainder. Can they explain their situation and their results?

🎲 Dividing the cards

Prepare products cards for each of the 2, 3, 4, 5 and 10 times-tables, for example, '2, 4, 6, ..., 20' for the 2 times-table etc. Hold up a product card and ask the children to divide it by a one-digit number that will involve them finding a remainder, for example, 18 ÷ 5. Ask if they can divide it equally or not. What number is the answer? How many are left over? How do they work it out? Which tables do they use each time?

🎲 Make the connection

Divide the class into pairs. Give each pair a set of counters (representing apples). Tell the children that they are in an apple-packing factory and their job is to find out how many packets of three they can make. How many will be left over? Repeat with making 'packets' of four, five and 10. Ask how many 'packets' would they need if they wanted to pack all the apples each time.

Plenary

Give division word problems involving decisions about rounding up or down. Ask the children to work out the answers using cubes or a number line, then say and write the division sentence with the remainder. For example, 'There are 30 children in the class. How many tables of four are needed to seat them all?' (rounding up) or alternatively, 'How many children will be left standing?' (rounding down). Or, 'There are 38 cakes. How many boxes can you fill if each box holds four cakes?' (rounding down), or, 'How many boxes are needed to hold them all?' (rounding up).

Common difficulties

Some children may not know their tables well enough, leading them to find a remainder that is more than the quotient, for example, when dividing by 5, they may find a remainder of 7. Some children do not understand the meaning of sharing equally (if one group has one more it is still sharing).

Remediation

Give more practice of times-tables facts. Show how to check their answer by checking whether they can make one more set (or group). Explain that all the sets must contain an equal number of items.

Homework suggestion

Ask the children to find a deck of playing cards and remove the jokers. Ask them: *"If you were to share the cards between each member of your household, how many would each person receive? How many would be leftover? What is the remainder? What would happen if you removed the royal cards? Would the cards share evenly? Would the remainder stay the same? Why or why not?"*.

Key point

Division is the most complex of the four basic operations. Understanding the idea of remainder is pre-requisite to paper and pencil division methods.

Related material

Pupil Book
Page 164-165

PCM 81
SCM 81
ECM 81

At the sweetshop

Space control

Painting buildings

Key vocabulary

- double
- half
- partition

Materials

- spinners (0–10, 1–4, 1–9)
- whiteboards
- multibase
- number lines
- two-digit price lists
- imitation coins
- number cards (11–30, even numbers 50–100)

Mental multiplication and division strategies

Introduction

Unit plans 51 and 78 focused on doubling and halving multiples of five and 10. Children learned the connection between the two operations through 'doubling and halving machines', and they also learned the doubles of multiples of 50 to 500 and their corresponding halves. The following activities extend this knowledge to doubling any two-digit number, and halving even two-digit and simple three-digit numbers, using known facts.

Objectives

- To use doubling or halving, starting from known facts.
- To use known number facts and place value to carry out mentally simple multiplications and divisions.

Oral and mental starter

MATHS

Ask the children to write the word M A T H S at the top of five columns on their whiteboards and to stand up. Ask a volunteer to spin one spinner (0–10), and a second spinner (0, 1, 2, 3, 4, 5, 10). Ask all the children to multiply the two numbers and write the answer under the letter M. Check the answers. If correct they win a point. If not, they sit down. Continue through the letters. However, if a 1 is spun on either of the spinners, they lose all the points in that column. If a 0 is spun, they lose all their points gained so far. They may decide to sit down at any time and protect the points already won. Ask questions until no children are left standing. Then they all add up their total points to find the winner.

Division face-off

Choose two volunteers to sit at the front of the class. Say a division fact based on one of the known times-tables. The first child to answer correctly stays sitting and a new challenger takes the loser's place.

Main teaching

N.B. *Supply multibase and number lines to support these activities and encourage jottings.*

Double purchase

Give each group a two-digit price list of items in a shop, and coins. Ask the children to buy two of one item, write an appropriate number sentence and discuss the ways to find the total amount to pay. Extend to more complex multiplications by giving the group a spinner (2, 3, 4, 5, 10) to find how many of each item to buy. Discuss the strategies used. Explain that, for sramaple, 42p x 4 can be written as (40p x 4) + (2p x 4).

🎎 Again and again

Give each group a set of number cards (11–30). Ask the children to each take a card then work together to see how high they can double, recording as they go. Then give the group larger even numbers (50–100) and ask them to find a quarter of the number by halving and halving again. Discuss the strategies used. Explain the strategies presented in the pupil book.

🧍 Smaller and smaller

Say: *"Four"* and ask the children to halve it and halve it again. Write the answer on the board. What number sentences represent this operation? Now ask them to do the same with 8, 12, and all the other multiples of four up to 40. What do they notice?

🧍 Method madness

Write a multiplication such as 35 x 2 on the board. Ask the children to work out the answer using jottings to help them. Emphasise the method of partitioning the numbers and multiplying the tens and units separately, then combining, for example, double 30 (30 x 2) plus double 5 (5 x 2). Look for alternative methods such as: 40 x 2 minus 5 x 2. Then pose a different multiplication and ask the children to use similar methods with different number facts. Repeat with halving even two-digit numbers. Extend to simple even three-digit numbers.

Plenary

Ask two volunteers to spin two spinners, a 'tens' spinner (1–4) and a 'units' spinner (1–9) to make a two-digit number (11–49). Say that this number represents the number of pairs of gloves in the cloakroom. Ask: *"How many single gloves are there?"* Ask the children to present the way they solved the problem. Discuss the different strategies. If necessary, review the method of partitioning the numbers and multiplying the tens and units separately, then combining. Repeat with other two-digit numbers. Then write a multiple of four on the board, representing the number of wheels on cars in a car park. Ask the children to calculate the number of front wheels, and then the number of cars. Discuss the strategies used. Repeat with horses in the field and front and back legs.

Common difficulties

Mental calculation involves abstract thinking. Some children may produce the wrong answer, using their own incorrect made-up methods.

Remediation

Encourage the children to use apparatus such as ten-cube towers and unit cubes. Ask them to estimate the expected answer before starting the question.

Homework suggestion

Think of ten people you know who are different ages. Double their ages. For anyone whose age is an even number, find half of it. Make a chart to show all your results.

Key point

Using known number facts and place value to carry out simple mental multiplications and divisions allows children to work out mentally more difficult calculations.

Related material

Pupil Book
Page 166-167

PCM 82
SCM 82
ECM 82

Multiplication and division word problems

Materials

- bowls of counters
- two-digit number cards
- dice (one and six covered)
- two-digit price tags
- imitation coins

Introduction

Word problems play a central role in Maths. In these activities the children use their new multiplication skills (multiplying two-digit numbers by single-digit numbers) and division skills (halving, and finding remainders) to solve word problems. Simple proportion problems are also introduced. It is recommended to encourage children to use the six-step strategy for problem solving: reading and understanding the problem, isolating the question, devising a strategy to solve it (and if necessary, building a graphical representation), applying the strategy, finding the answer, and checking it.

Objectives

- To choose and use appropriate operations to solve word problems and appropriate ways of calculating.

Oral and mental starter

Any leftovers?

Give the children access to bowls of counters. Ask a volunteer to choose a two-digit number card (10-50). Ask another to roll a die with the 1 and 6 covered. Then ask all the children to work out how many equal groups can be made and find the remainder if there is one. How do they check their answers?

Maths in chains

Ask one child to say a single-digit number and start a doubling chain round the class. How long can they continue the chain without breaking it? When it breaks, ask the next child to start again with a single-digit number. Repeat, starting with an even two-digit number and halving. What can they tell you about the final number? What happens when you start with a multiple of 10?

Main teaching

N.B. Review and encourage the recommended problem-solving strategy; the use of jottings, drawing and visualising; checking with the inverse calculation.

Price hike

Give each group a set of two-digit price tags, a die (with the 1 and 6 covered), and a set of imitation coins. The children each take a tag, and one child rolls the die. Tell the children that the prices must be multiplied by the number on the die. The children work out the new prices and show the coins needed to buy each item. Ask them to record their methods and calculations.

Doughnut dilemma

Give each group the following word problem: David eats three doughnuts every day. How many doughnuts does he eat in seven days? Ask the groups to present their solutions. Discuss how to draw the situation, and the strategies and the checking methods used. Repeat with other simple proportion problems (giving the situation for one unit, and asking them to find the outcome for n units). Emphasise checking by using the inverse operation, and discuss the meaning of it in the context of each problem.

Working on the web

Say:"*A spider has eight legs.*" Then ask the children to work in pairs to find how many legs there are on two, three, four, five and 10 spiders respectively. Ask them to draw the problem, then show how they work out the answer each time. What strategies do they use to help them calculate more efficiently?

Football crazy

Say: "*A bag of 10 footballs costs £30. If I receive £2 pocket money a week, how many weeks will it take me to buy the bag? How can I check?*" Discuss the strategies used.

Plenary

Write the following problem on the board: A box of popcorn costs 12p. Jerry wants to buy five boxes. How much must he pay? Ask the children to solve the problem and record their answers. Remind them to check their answers and record their checking methods. Then ask six volunteers to present each stage of the six-step problem-solving strategy for solving this problem.

Common difficulties

Proportion is one of the most difficult topics in Primary school.

Remediation

Provide apparatus to model the problem such as money, cubes, counters, and coins. Begin with very simple one-step proportion problems.

Homework suggestion

Set a word problem such as: Deepak is doing a sponsored swim. His grandfather sponsors him 50p a length. How much does he raise if he swims eight lengths? How many lengths does he have to swim to raise £6.50?

Key point

Understanding and using proportion is one of the main skills in arithmetic.

Related material

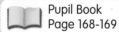 Pupil Book Page 168-169

 PCM 83
SCM 83
ECM 83

 The law of the jungle

Fractions

Key vocabulary

- half
- halves
- third/s
- quarter/s
- tenth/s
- one whole

Materials

- 20 square pictures
- interlocking cubes
- paper pizzas
- unit fraction cards
- unlabelled number lines
- fraction cards
- 60 cm strips of paper
- laminated number lines
- whiteboards

Introduction

The following activities focus on comparing fractions. A basic problem is that two is smaller than four, but $\frac{1}{2}$ is greater than $\frac{1}{4}$. Concrete representation, drill and practice help overcome this problem. The children also learn to position fractions on a number line, creating a mental link between one whole (one unit), and the segment between zero and one.

Objectives

 To compare familiar fractions.

Oral and mental starter

A fraction shady

Draw or display a shape of 20 squares on squared paper, of which $\frac{3}{4}$ is shaded. Ask the children to say what fraction is, and is not shaded. Repeat with different square pictures and different fractions.

Unfrazzled fractions

Give the children access to cubes and ask them to make towers, if necessary, to help them answer simple fraction questions such as: what is $\frac{1}{3}$ of 12, $\frac{1}{4}$ of 20, and $\frac{1}{10}$ of 30.

Main teaching

Pizza party

Divide the class into groups of five. Give each child a paper circle to represent a pizza. Ask each child to decide on a different fraction (halves, quarters, thirds, fifths, or tenths) and cut their pizza into that number of equal slices. Ask them to write the matching fraction on each section. Then ask the children to each contribute one slice of their pizza to a pizza line-up. The group places the slices in order of size. Ask them what they notice about the size of the pizza slices compared to the name of the fraction. Then give each group a set of unit fraction cards. The children shuffle them and lay them out face down. They each take one card and the child with the largest fraction wins the round. They can use the pizza line-up to check.

Between the wholes

Give each group an unlabelled number line, folded and marked with five divisions (for 0, $\frac{1}{2}$, $\frac{1}{4}$, $\frac{3}{4}$, and 1). Tell the children the line represents one whole and ask them to decide how to place number cards (0, 1, $\frac{3}{4}$, $\frac{1}{4}$, and $\frac{1}{2}$) in the correct positions on the line. Check and remediate. Then attach a second strip to the first one, divided into sections up to two whole units and ask them how the continuation of the line should be labelled.

♟ Wall of fractions

Give each child five 60 cm strips of paper. Ask them to take one strip and colour it in two equal parts, recording $\frac{1}{2}$ on each. Then, using the remaining strips, tell them to colour and record fractions so that one is coloured in three equal parts, one in four, one in five and one in ten. Discuss which strategies they used to split the strips into equal parts. Ask the children to build a fraction wall with their strips. Ask questions about fractions such as: Which is larger, $\frac{1}{4}$ or $\frac{1}{2}$? How many quarters in a half? How many thirds make a whole? Ask them to use the wall to find and show you their answers.

♟ Placing the parts

Prepare laminated number lines marked 0 and 1 at each end, and with three equal divisions between the two numbers. Divide the class into pairs. Give each pair a laminated number line and two fraction cards from $\frac{1}{4}$, $\frac{1}{2}$, and $\frac{3}{4}$. Ask them to place the cards on the line in their correct positions. Extend by giving the pair a number line with end points marked 0 and 2 with seven equal divisions between the two numbers. Discuss the positions of the different numbers, for example, $1\frac{1}{2}$ is halfway between 1 and 2.

Plenary

Give each child a laminated number line marked 0 and 1 at either end. Ask a volunteer to spin a spinner: more than half, less than three-quarters, greater than a quarter, between a half and one whole, etc. Ask the children to make a dot on the line according to the instruction. Check and remediate. Then ask the children to erase their dot and repeat with a new spin. Next give out 20 cm laminated number lines marked (0–5), with all the $\frac{1}{2}$ and $\frac{1}{4}$ divisions marked on, but not numbered. Prepare fraction cards such as: $4\frac{1}{2}$, halfway between 3 and 4, between $2\frac{1}{2}$ and 3. Ask a volunteer to pick a card, and the rest of the class to use their number lines to say where the fraction or mixed number lies. Then ask the children to label the whole of their number lines. Finally, ask fraction-related questions, such as: Which is larger: $1\frac{1}{2}$ or $1\frac{3}{4}$? Write a number between 4 and 5.

Common difficulties

Children may not understand that $\frac{1}{2}$ is greater than $\frac{1}{4}$ because two is smaller than four.

Remediation

Use pizza slices, with the fraction recorded on each slice, to show the size of different fractions.

Homework suggestion

Ask the children to draw a line that is 32 cm long. Tell the children that a flea jumps backwards half as much everyday. If the first jump is 32 cm, how many jumps does it take until it jumps $\frac{1}{4}$ cm?

Key point

Comparing fractions, and mixed numbers with simple fractions is a first step towards general number comparison.

Related material

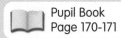
Pupil Book
Page 170-171

PCM 84
SCM 84
ECM 84

Estimating fractions

Key vocabulary

- half
- third
- quarter
- fifth

Materials

- number lines
- grids
- paper circles
- containers
- marbles
- circle segments
- clock faces
- card 'pieces of cake'
- pizza fractions

Introduction

The following activities focus on estimating a simple fraction.

Objectives

 To estimate a simple fraction

Oral and mental starter

Quarter to, quarter from.

First chant together to and from five, in quarters. Display a number line with the quarter divisions marked but without numbering every division. Ask the children fraction-related questions such as: name a number between $2\frac{1}{2}$ and 3.

Whole mates

Give each child a grid with different fractions coloured in. Ask them to find a partner whose fraction together with theirs, makes one whole.

Main teaching

What about...?

Give each group divided paper circles with a little bit more or less than exact fractions coloured. Ask, for each circle, *"About what fraction is coloured?"*. Repeat with circles without the divisions. Can the children still estimate the fractions coloured?

Unfulfilled

Give each group a number of different-sized containers such as
yoghurt pots and small plastic containers. One child part-fills (half or
quarter) a container with marbles and the others estimate the fraction
of the container that is filled and the number of marbles. Then they
estimate and see how many marbles the full jar or container would
contain. Extend to a full jar and pour out about half then a quarter.
Discuss the strategies used and the ways to estimate and check the
estimate.

Slice of the pie

Divide the class into pairs. Give each pair an identical set of pieces of
'pie' (about $\frac{1}{4}$, about $\frac{1}{3}$, about $\frac{1}{2}$, about $\frac{2}{3}$, about $\frac{3}{4}$). The children record
on each segment, the fraction they estimate it is of a whole 'pie'.
Discuss the strategies used and the ways to check.

A fraction of time

Show a clock face with the hands showing a time and ask the
children to write the fraction of the clock face they estimate lies
between the two hands (about $\frac{1}{2}$, $\frac{1}{4}$, or $\frac{3}{4}$, $\frac{1}{3}$ or $\frac{2}{3}$). Extend by asking the
children to show their own times and ask their partner to estimate
the fraction.

Plenary

Display a card piece of cake. Ask the children to record the fraction of
the cake they think it is. Discuss the ways to estimate. Show $\frac{1}{4}$, $\frac{1}{3}$, $\frac{1}{2}$, $\frac{2}{3}$,
and $\frac{3}{4}$ of a pizza (with the fraction recorded on each) and ask if it is
more or less than the slice of cake. Repeat with other slices of pizza
and pieces of cake.

Common difficulties

Children may make wild guesses when estimating fractions.

Remediation

Show a half pizza or half full jar, and ask what fraction it is. Then ask if
the part shown is more or less than $\frac{1}{2}$. Then show $\frac{1}{4}$ or $\frac{3}{4}$ of a pizza, and
ask if it is less than $\frac{1}{4}$, more than $\frac{1}{4}$, or between $\frac{1}{4}$ and $\frac{1}{2}$.

Homework suggestion

Ask the children to find different times of day where the space
between the hands of the clock is about $\frac{1}{4}$ and say what you do at
that time. Repeat for 'about $\frac{1}{2}$' and 'about $\frac{3}{4}$'. Challenge the children
not to use o'clock, half past, quarter to or quarter past times.

86

Partition into 'five and a bit'

Key vocabulary

- method

Materials

- 'multiples of 10 and 5' cards
- die labelled 0, 0, 0, 5, 5, 5
- number cards
- price tables
- dice labelled 1, 2, 3, 3, 4, 4
- spinners (6–9)
- addition cards
- 10x5 grids, and 2x5 grids

Introduction

These activities introduce another adding technique, namely, partitioning into 'five and a bit'. This procedure involves recombining as well as partitioning, and using the fact that addition is associative.

Objectives

 To partition into 'five and a bit' when adding 6, 7, 8, or 9.

Oral and mental starter

Totting up

Hold up a 'multiple of five' card. Go round the class asking each child to say two different numbers that add up to this number. When a child repeats or makes a mistake, set a new target number.

Fives in a frenzy

One child picks a number card (1-4) and writes the number on the board. Another child rolls a large die (0, 0, 0, 5, 5, 5) and writes their number on the board to form a two-digit multiple of five. Choose two more volunteers to create a second two-digit multiple of five in a similar way. Then ask the class to work out all the addition and subtraction sentences they can make with these numbers.

Main teaching

Market mark-up

Give each group a price table where the first column shows prices in multiples of five, and the second column shows the increase in price, by 6p, 7p, 8p or 9p, of each item. Ask the children to write the new price list and record the method they used to perform the calculation. Discuss the methods used and introduce the partitioning into 'five and a bit' and recombining method. For example, 35p + 8p = 35p + 5p + 3p = 43 p.

Biting the bit

Give each group a die (labelled 1, 2, 3, 3, 4, 4) and a spinner labelled 6, 7, 8, 9. Ask one child to roll the die to find the tens digit and another child to spin the spinner for the units digit, of a two-digit number. Repeat to find a second two-digit number. Ask them to add the numbers together to find the total. Discuss the methods used, emphasising the partitioning into 'five and a bit' then recombining method.

A bit of a challenge

Prepare addition cards consisting of a two-digit number with a unit digit above five added to a single-digit (6-9). Divide the class into pairs and give each pair an addition card and two grids (10x5, and 2x5). The children colour the grids to represent the addition colouring in row by row. They colour the squares in the incomplete row in a different colour. They can now rewrite both their numbers as a multiple of five and *n* left over. Then they add all the numbers together. For example, 38 + 7 becomes 35 + 3 + 5 + 2. Extend to addition of two two-digit numbers.

Two-digit two-method additions

Give each pair of children a two-digit addition with both unit digits above five. Ask the children to find their own ways to work it out using two different methods. Look for partitioning into tens and units and, if necessary, suggest the method of adding using partitioning into 'five and a bit.'

Plenary

Ask a volunteer to pick two number cards (6, 7, 8 and 9). Ask all the children to find the total by partitioning both numbers into 'five and a bit' and recombining, first the fives and then the left over units. Repeat with other numbers and extend to adding single digits above five, to a teens number (16–19), and then to any two-digit number up to 90. Finally ask questions in which they add two two-digit numbers where the total does not cross 100.

Common difficulties

Some children use calculation 'rules' without fully understanding them.

Remediation

Use concrete representations of the additions. Allow children to use other strategies that they understand to check their additions.

Homework suggestion

Ask the children to find an old receipt, or look up some prices in a catalogue and add the prices up using the 'partition into five and a bit' method. Is this method useful for all combination of prices?

Key point

Mastering various calculation methods gives children more tools to help them solve calculations.

Related material

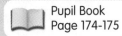
Pupil Book
Page 174-175

PCM 86
SCM 86
ECM 86

The billboard

mathspace

87

Subtraction pencil and paper methods

Key vocabulary

- pencil and paper methods

Materials

- priced fruits and vegetables
- subtraction cards
- blank number lines
- multibase
- three-digit money cards

Introduction

The main focus of these activities and those in the following Unit plan, is to use informal pencil and paper methods to solve subtractions (see reference page at the back of this book for detailed explanations of each of the methods). When mental subtraction becomes more difficult, different pencil and paper methods need to be introduced. It is important to choose methods that help the children form a solid foundation before moving on to formal column subtraction. This unit concentrates on showing children how to use a number line and partitioning the number being subtracted $84 - 61 = 84 - 60 = 24 - 1 = 23$. The children also learn to use decomposition.

Objectives

- To use informal pencil and paper methods to support, record or explain HTU – TU, HTU – HTU.

Oral and mental starter

Have I got a bargain!

Show the class fruit or vegetables with a two-digit price. Say that the price has been reduced by a near multiple of 10p, for example, 39p, and ask the children to write the new price. Then ask them to pretend to be market traders announcing the new, bargain price.

Head take away head

Prepare subtraction cards (TU – TU, not crossing the tens boundary). Divide the class into two teams. Each child in turn goes head to head with the child opposite working out the answer mentally. The child who says the correct answer first, wins a point for their team.

Main teaching

Note: The complementary addition, decomposition and compensation methods of subtraction are all explained in detail in a reference page at the back of this book.

Take away tactics

Give each group a subtraction sentence (TU – TU, not crossing the tens boundary) and a blank number line. Ask them to think of ways to subtract, such as counting back from the larger number in two logical steps, or counting up from the smaller number in three logical steps (complementary addition). Ask them to show their methods with jottings. Extend to HTU – TU and HTU – HTU. Discuss the decomposition method.

Column counting

Give each group subtraction sentences (HTU – TU, not crossing the ten boundary) and ask them to use multibase to help find the answers. Ask them to discuss the different possible methods. Suggest the decomposition method. Extend to questions that involve HTU – HTU without the need for borrowing.

Give and take

Write an example of an HTU – TU on the board. What methods can the children suggest to efficiently solve this subtraction? Look for methods involving rounding up the smaller number first then subtracting that rounded number (i.e. taking off too much) and then adding back as in the compensation method. Ask volunteers to show this method on a number line. Extend to HTU – HTU. Discuss other pencil and paper methods such as: complementary addition and decomposition as explained in the group activities.

Spend and record

Give each child a three-digit money card in £.p notation (where all the digits are between 5 and 9). Write a price list on the board, with three-digit prices (£1.01 – £4.44, where all the tens and units are less than 5). Ask each child to choose an item, and calculate the change they expect to receive. Discuss the methods used. Emphasise the use of a number line with the counting back method presented in the activity book or the complementary addition method or the compensation method. Then show how to write the subtraction using the decomposition method.

Plenary

Tell the following story: John scored 859 points during a two-day competition. On the first day, he scored 532 points. How many points did he score on the second day? Discuss the methods used. Emphasise the use of a number line for complementary addition, and the compensation method and work through the decomposition method.

Common difficulties

Informal pencil and paper methods can prove to be very difficult for some children.

Remediation

Use concrete representation with multibase, tens towers, or money. Begin with problems involving two-digit numbers only, then HTU - TU and build up to HTU – HTU.

Homework suggestion

Write the following subtractions on the board and ask the children to copy them and work them out for homework using a pencil and paper method. Ask them to check with addition.

1. 67 – 41   2. 95 – 54   3. 488 – 356   4. 687 – 45   5. 935 – 814

Key point

Using informal pencil and paper methods to solve subtractions is an important stage before the subtraction algorithm.

Related material

Pupil Book
Page 176-177

PCM 87
SCM 87
ECM 87

 Points make prizes

Tea time

More pencil and paper methods for subtraction

Introduction

These activities extend informal pencil and paper methods to solve subtractions that cross the tens boundary.

Objectives

 To use informal paper and pencil methods to support, record or explain HTU – TU, HTU – HTU

Oral and mental starter

 Diving to the hundred

Give a three-digit starting number. Go round the class, asking each child to subtract a single-digit number until they reach the previous multiple of 100. Then repeat with a new three-digit number.

 Reductions reviewed

Write an example of a subtraction (TU – TU, not crossing the tens boundary) on the board. Ask the children to choose a pencil and paper method and solve it. Review the methods.

Main teaching

Note: The complementary addition, decomposition and compensation methods of subtraction are all explained in detail in a reference page at the back of this book.

 Subtraction detectives

Give each group a set of four two-digit numbers, and ask them to find how to take one away from the other in order to make the largest difference. Then ask them to choose and use a pencil and paper method from the previous lesson, to work out the answers. Discuss the calculation methods used. Emphasise the counting up, (complementary addition) and compensation method using a number line, and decomposition.

 Subtract from a hat

Give each group two dice (1–6, and 7, 8, 9, 7, 8, 9). Ask each child to roll the regular die three times to make a three-digit number, then roll the second die twice for a two-digit number to subtract from the first number. They each record their subtraction using paper and pencil methods and hide the result from the rest of the group. Ask them to place all the workings and results in a hat, pick out one at a time, and discuss the methods used.

👤 Decline to nine

Ask each child to write a two-digit number, then reverse the digits to create a second number. Then ask them to use pencil and paper methods to subtract the smaller number from the larger number. What do they notice about the digits in the answer? (They will always add up to nine.)

👤 Money methods

Prepare menu cards with two-digit prices in pence, and money cards with two-digit amounts in pence. Ask the children to choose an item to order, take a money card and the matching imitation coins for their kitty. Then ask them to work out the change they will receive. How will they set out their method? If they use partitioning, see how they partition the money into tens and units. Ask what they should do if they don't have enough pence, or, ask: *"How can you subtract a larger amount of pence from a smaller amount?"* Teach changing one 10p into units - decomposition with carrying. For example, 81p – 46p

$$\begin{array}{rcl} 80 + 1 & = & 70 + 11 \\ - 40 + 6 & & - 40 + 6 \\ \hline & & 30 + 5 = 35 \end{array}$$

Extend to the difference between two three-digit amounts, for example, the total earned in £s today compared to the total earned in £s yesterday.

Plenary

Write the following problem on the board: Melanie scored 452 points in a two-level computer game. She scored 127 of them in the first level. How many points did she score in the second level? Discuss the methods used. Emphasise the methods that use a number line and show how to solve the problem using the decomposition method.

Common difficulties

Even informal pencil and paper methods can prove quite difficult for some children. A common mistake is to subtract the smaller number from the larger one regardless, for example, 452 – 127 = 335, a child could make the mistake of subtracting 4 – 1 = 3, 5 – 2 = 3, 7 – 2 = 5).

Remediation

Use concrete representation with multibase, tens towers, and money. Begin with problems involving two-digit numbers only and crossing the tens only, and build up to HTU – HTU. Ask the children to estimate the expected answer. Encourage them to use number lines.

Homework suggestion

Ask the children to use the following numbers to make as many different three-digit numbers as they can 2, 6, 3. Then subtract all the numbers from the highest number in the list.

Key point

Using informal pencil and paper methods to solve subtractions is an important stage before introducing the subtraction algorithm.

Related material

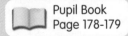
Pupil Book
Page 178-179

PCM 88
SCM 88
ECM 88

Using a calendar

Key vocabulary

- January …
  December
- first … thirty-first
- day
- week
- month
- year
- calendar

Materials

- various calendars
- month cards
- number cards
  (1–12)
- calendar
  vocabulary signs
- calendar pages
- spinners (days of
  the week)
- a class calendar
- list of events

Introduction

Calendars are basic everyday tools that have particular social importance. Using the calendar practises time perception, positioning of events, and time management. Many mathematical concepts are involved including ordering (previous, following), tables, and ordinal numbers.

Objectives

● To use a calendar.

Oral and mental starter

 ### Names and numbers

Sit the children in a circle. Shuffle month cards and number cards (1–12) and place them in the centre of the circle. Ask volunteers to pick a number card then find the corresponding month in the order of months in the year. Give extra points if they can name the month before and the month after the selected one. When all the months have been selected, re-shuffle the cards and repeat until all the children have had a turn.

 ### Signs of the times

Prepare a set of time vocabulary signs (minute, hour, day, week, month and year). Ask questions about the appropriate units of time to measure different events (the length of playtime, time in bed, the time spent in school every week, the summer holidays, your age). Ask the children to discuss with a partner, then choose volunteers to come out and hold up the appropriate sign. Then ask how many hours there are in a day, days in a school week, months in the winter, and so on.

Main teaching

 ### Calendar analysis

Give each group a few different kinds of calendars and ask them to discuss the features of each one (include diaries, day by day calendars, yearly planners and monthly calendars). What features are common to all the calendars? Which features are necessary and which are 'extras'? Ask the groups to make a list of the different ways a calendar can be used. Ask each group to report their findings to the class.

Maths of the month

Give each group a page from a calendar showing one month, and a spinner (days of the week). Ask the children to spin the spinner and find all the possible dates for that day in that month. Ask them to think of two questions each about the days and dates, to ask the rest of the group. For example, which day of the week does the 1ˢᵗ fall on? If the first Monday in the month is the 2ⁿᵈ, what will the next Monday's date be? How many days will occur four times in this month, and how many will occur five times? Explain why.

Birthday brainers

Give each child a calendar. Ask the children to write their own birthday date, including the date, month and year, and discuss all the different ways they can record it. Ask them to write their name on this day on a class calendar. Ask them to compare the years they were born. Can they put their birthdays in order? What do they notice? Who is the oldest/youngest?

The big 365

Give each pair a different month from a calendar. Ask them to write questions for their partner about the number of days or weeks from one date to another. Then look at all the months together. Discuss the number of days in each month (use the knuckle test to check, i.e. when you hold your fists out together, on the knuckle represents a month with 31 days. Note: July and August are both 'knuckle' months) and how to work out how many days there are in a year.

Plenary

Display, or draw on the board, a month from a calendar and a list of school and social events. Ask the children to each write one event on one day in that month. Then ask questions about information on the calendar, such as, how long from one event to the next? How many Sundays involve a celebration? How many times each week are parents invited to the school for an event? On which days and dates do certain events fall?

Common difficulties

Intervals of time can cause problems. A holiday from May 5ᵗʰ to May 7ᵗʰ, is three days long but $7 - 5 = 2$ so often, children will say that it is a two-day holiday.

Remediation

Ask the children to count the days of holiday one by one.

Homework suggestion

Ask the children to use a calendar at home to answer the following type of questions: What day of the week does the 31ˢᵗ December fall on? What is the date of the first Monday in June? What day of the week does your birthday fall on this year? What is the date of midsummer's day. Ask them to use the calendar to find out how many weeks and days there are between 1ˢᵗ January and midsummer's day.

Key point

Calendars are basic everyday devices involving many mathematical concepts.

Related material

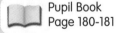 Pupil Book Page 180-181

 PCM 89 SCM 89 ECM 89

 That's a date

Venn and Carroll diagrams

Key vocabulary

- Venn diagram
- Carroll diagram
- data
- tally

Materials

- number cards (1–50)
- spinner (2, 3, 4, 5 and 10)
- whiteboards
- hoops
- flags
- post-its
- 3-D objects
- shapes
- blank Carroll diagrams
- chalk

Introduction

The children have already learned how to describe properties of different things and how to classify according to certain criteria. Venn and Carroll diagrams are powerful tools with which to analyse sets and properties of elements. They integrate many mathematical skills, and facilitate in-depth organisation and interpretation of data as data analysis.

Objectives

- To solve a given problem by organizing and interpreting numerical data in simple lists, tables and diagrams.

    – To classify objects, shapes or numbers according to one, then two criteria and display on Venn and Carroll diagrams.

Oral and mental starter

Bunches of cherries

Prepare number cards (1–10) and a spinner (2, 3, 4, 5 and 10). Ask a volunteer to spin the spinner to find how many bunches of cherries there are, and turn over a number card to say how many cherries in each bunch. Ask how many cherries there are altogether. Ask the children to show the multiplication sentence on their whiteboards. Repeat.

Dicey tally

Review tallying. Pass a pair of dice round the class. Each child rolls the dice and works out the sum for their roll. Build a tally chart for dice totals 2–12. Continue passing the dice around the class until you have collected sufficient data. Chant up the tally marks in fives. Discuss the results.

Main teaching

N.B. For each activity, ensure that the children understand the method of classifying, and ask questions they can answer using the information.

Red flag, green flag

Give each group two hoops and ask them to arrange them so that they overlap. Give the group about 20 different country flags. Ask them to label the hoops: 'flags with green', and 'flags with red'. Discuss where flags that have both green and red should be placed and where those that have neither colour should be placed. Then ask the children to take turns to place a flag in the right place and give their reasons each time. Ask them to ask each other questions about their diagram and see what information the diagram can give them.

👥 Carroll shapes

Give each group a set of shapes and ask them to decide two criteria for sorting them. Give them a blank Carroll diagram and ask them to discuss how to label it and where to put each shape. Then they compare their results with another group and write four differences.

👤 Venn you make sets

Place two overlapping hoops on the floor. Give each child a 3-D object, and tell them that the first hoop is for objects that roll, and the second for those that slide. Ask them to put their shape in the right place in the 'Venn diagram'. Discuss the meaning of each of the possible four areas. Remind the children, if necessary, that there is an outside area where you put the objects that do not slide or roll.

👤 Quite a hairy situation

Draw a top row of a Carroll diagram on the board with one column labelled, 'brown hair', and the other, 'not brown hair'. Label the row, 'children'. Then ask the children to write their names on post-it notes and place them in the correct boxes. Next, add a second row and change the 'children' label to 'boys' and label the second row 'girls'. Ask those children who now have to change the position of their post-its to come up and do so. Then chalk a large Carroll diagram on the floor (columns labelled 'boy'/'not a boy', rows labelled 'more than'/'less than five letters in my first name') and ask the children to stand in the appropriate sections. Ask them to explain how they decided where to stand.

Plenary

Lay out two overlapping hoops, labelled with two criteria, for example, 'in the 5 times-table'/ 'in the 2 times-table'. Give each child a number card (1–50). Each child, in turn holds up their card and the class decides where each number should be placed. Where do they put numbers that occur in one/both/neither hoop? What are the properties of the numbers in each of the four possible areas? Then, give out the same set of numbers again. Display a large Carroll diagram (in which the columns are labelled: 'one-digit numbers'/ 'two-digit numbers', and the rows labelled: 'multiples of five'/ 'not multiples of five') and ask the children to write their number in the correct place. Discuss the benefits of each type of diagram.

Common difficulties

Distinguishing between the elements belonging to one set and those belonging to both is sometimes difficult.

Remediation

Use easier examples, involving colours, shapes, and properties in everyday life (sweet/salty food, relations/friends). Ask the children to decide where to put each object in the Venn diagram and ask them to check that it does not belong in any of the other three areas.

Homework suggestion

Ask the children to make a Venn diagram showing two different properties (characteristics) of animals. Tell them that they need to find at least four examples of different animals that appear in each section of the Venn diagram.

Related material

Pupil Book
Page 182-183

PCM 90
SCM 90
ECM 90

The loading bay

Venn diagram

Assessment - Teacher's notes

The assessment resources in Year 3 are written in test format similar to that of the National Tests. The assessments are designed to be carried out at the end of each half term, but may be used whenever a teacher feels confident that they have covered all the topics. The aural assessment should last about 30 minutes and the written paper about 40 minutes. Each assessment has remediation resource references indicating the unit plan numbers and the associated CD activities. The teacher can use the activities in the unit plan to re-teach when necessary and use the activities to reinforce the skills learned.

The assessment section includes:

1. Aural assessment information for teachers: presented in table format, containing the NNS objectives, the questions, answers and suggested remediation resources.

2. Aural assessment answer sheets for pupils: simple-to-use answer sheet for pupils.

3. Written assessment information for teachers: charts containing the NNS objectives, answers, and suggested remediation resources.

4. Written assessment answer sheets for pupils: a 40 minute written test for each half term.

5. Record keeping charts so that each child can be plotted against each objective and the teacher has an 'at-a-glance' overview of the levels of their class.

Children will need the following equipment:

- ◆ a pencil
- ◆ a centimetre ruler with which they are familiar
- ◆ a rubber
- ◆ spare paper (optional)
- ◆ access to coins and counters to facilitate working out (optional)

Aural assessment: Teacher's notes

OBJECTIVES	WHAT TO SAY	ANSWERS	MARK	REMEDIATION UNIT	REMEDIATION CD ACTIVITY
Read and write whole numbers to at least 1000 in figures and words	1. Write in box 1, the number seven hundred and forty-five.	745	1	1	In Ziggy's garden The counting machine Payday
Know what each digit represents	2. Write in box 2, the tens digit of the number 403.	0	1	1	At the crossroads Lottery numbers Sew it up
Say the number that is 1, 10, or 100 more or less than any given two- or three-digit number	3. Write in box 3, the number that is 10 more than 38.	48	1	2	In the games room Name that number!
	4. Write in box 4, the number that is 100 less than 250.	150	1	2	On wheels
Know by heart addition facts for each number to 20	5. Write in box 5, the number you need to add to 7 to make 20.	13	1	5	Blast off! Ziggy's solar system Splodge guns
Identify near doubles using doubles already known	6. Write in box 6, the answer to 30 add 31.	61	1	6	The billboard On the right track Bingo numbers
Bridge through a multiple of 10, then adjust	7. Write in box 7, the answer to 46 add 9.	55	1	7	The billboard Points make prizes
Add and subtract mentally a 'near multiple of 10' to or from a two or three-digit number	8. Write in box 8, the answer to 60 take away 11.	49	1	7	Name that number!
Understand and use £.p notation	9. In box 9 write 205p as pounds and pence.	£2.05	1	9	Going shopping Changing money At the check-out
Choose and use appropriate operations to solve word problems Find totals and give change	10. Write the answer to this problem in box 10. Lynn has £4.50. She buys a CD for £3. How much money does she have left?	£1.50	1	10	In Ziggy's shop
Know the relationships between kilometres and metres, metres and centimetres	11. Write in box 11, how many centimetres there are in one metre and 20 centimetres.	120cm	1	12	Quiz time
Classify and describe 3-D and 2-D shapes	12. Write in box 12, two features of a triangle.	3 sides 3 corners 3 angles straight sides	1	14	At the amphitheatre Arty shapes

Name: _____ Date: _____

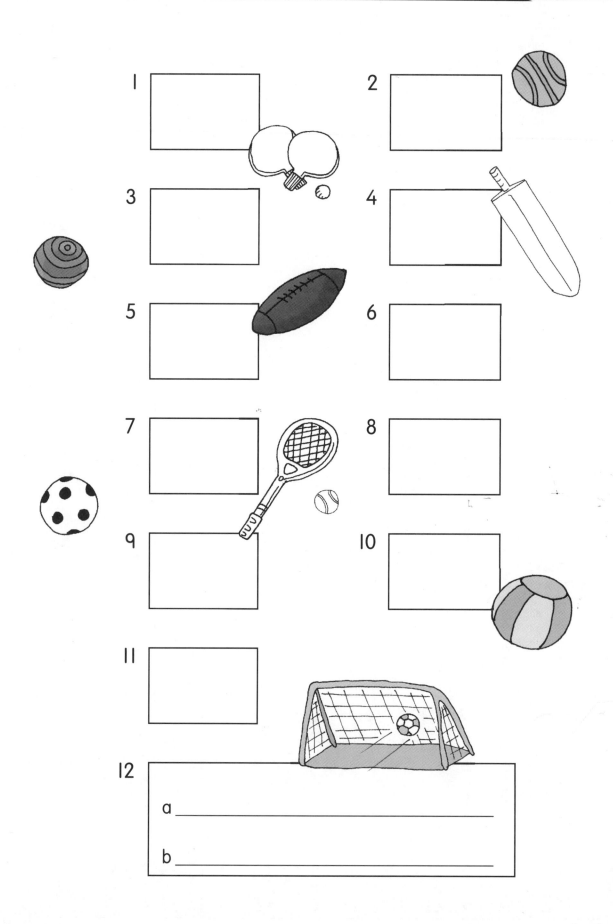

1 ☐

2 ☐

3 ☐

4 ☐

5 ☐

6 ☐

7 ☐

8 ☐

9 ☐

10 ☐

11 ☐

12
   a _____

   b _____

Written assessment: Teacher's notes

AUTUMN TERM
FIRST HALF

QUESTIONS	OBJECTIVES	ANSWERS	MARK	REMEDIATION UNIT	CD ACTIVITY
1a	Read and write whole numbers to at least 1000 in figures and words	617	1	1	The counting machine Payday
1b	Know what each digit represents	1	1	1	At the crossroads Lottery numbers Sew it up
2	Say the number that is 1, 10, or 100 more or less than any given two- or three-digit number	a. 290 300 b. 572 472 c. 524 514	2 2 2	2	In the games room Name that number! On wheels
3 and 4	Estimate up to 100 objects	3. 30 4. Any number from 70 to 90	1 1	3	Show time Butterflies
5	Read scales to the nearest labelled division	6 cm	1	4	Made to measure
6	Know by heart addition facts for each number to 20	a. 20 b. 8 c. 6 d. 9	1 1 1 1	5	Blast off! Ziggy's solar system Splodge guns
7	Identify near doubles using doubles already known	a. 79 b. 31 c. 17 d. 179	1 1 1 1	6	The billboard On the right track Bingo numbers
8	Add and subtract mentally a 'near multiple of 10' to or from a two or three-digit number	a. 73 b. 9 c. 44	1 1 1	7 7	The billboard Points make prizes Name that number!
9	Extend understanding of the operations of addition and subtraction	a. 35p b. 66p c. 34p	1 1 1	8	At the check-out
10	Understand and use £.p notation	a. £4.20 b. £8.46 c. £2.05	1 1 1	9	Going shopping Changing money At the check-out
11	Solve word problems involving money	Show working £3.50	1 1	9	In Ziggy's shop

Written assessment: Teacher's notes

QUESTIONS	OBJECTIVES	ANSWERS	MARK	REMEDIATION UNIT	REMEDIATION CD ACTIVITY
12	Choose and use appropriate operations to solve word problems Find totals and give change	a. £1.20 + £1.30 = £2.50 b. £10 - £2.50 = £7.50	2 2	10	In Ziggy's shop
13	Use a ruler to draw and measure lines to the nearest half centimetre	C	1	11	Made to measure
14	Know the relationships between kilometres and metres, metres and centimetres	a. 1 b. 100 c. 1000 d. 3 e. 4000	1 1 1 1 1	12	Quiz time
15	Record estimates and measurements to the nearest whole or half unit, or in mixed units	203 cm ⤬ 3 m 2 cm 230 cm ⤬ 3 m 20 cm 302 cm ⤬ 2 m 3 cm 320 cm ⤬ 2 m 30 cm	4	13	Quiz time
16	Classify and describe 3-D and 2-D shapes	a. rectangle, 4 sides, 4 right angles, 4 corners b. hexagon, 6 sides, 0 right angles, 6 corners c. triangle, 3 sides, 1 right angle, 3 corners	4 4 4 4	14	At the amphitheatre Arty shapes
17	Read and begin to write the vocabulary related to position	a. B3 b. D6 c. E3 d. A7	1 1 1 1	15	The space battle
18	Know what each digit represents	a. 40 b. 300, 80, 7	1 3	1	Sew it up
19	Identify near doubles using doubles already known	a. 12 b. 13 c. 24 d. 23	1 1 1 1	6	Red roofs
20	Choose and use appropriate operations to solve word problems	Subtraction 23 - 12 = 11 Martin has £11 more than Sue.	1 1 1	10	Cinema problems

Name: _____ Date: _____

1 a. Write this number in figures, six hundred and seventeen: ☐

b. In six hundred and seventeen, the tens digit is: ☐

2 Complete the sequences.

a. 260 270 280 ☐ ☐

b. 872 772 672 ☐ ☐

c. 554 544 534 ☐ ☐

3 Without counting, circle your estimate of the number of sweets in the jar.

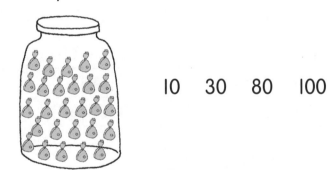

10   30   80   100

4 What number do you estimate the arrow is pointing to on the number line?

0 ———————————————————↓———— 100 ☐

5 Measure the line and write the length in cm to the nearest cm.

☐

Name: _____ Date: _____

6 Fill in the missing numbers.

a. $15 + 5 = \boxed{}$

b. $7 + \boxed{} = 15$

c. $7 + \boxed{} = 13$

d. $9 + \boxed{} = 18$

7 Complete the calculations.

a. $39 + 40 = \boxed{}$

b. $16 + 15 = \boxed{}$

c. $2 + 7 + 8 = \boxed{}$

d. $6 + 7 + 4 = \boxed{}$

8 Complete the calculations. You can use the part of the 100 square to help you.

41	42	43	44	45	46	47	48	49	50
51	52	53	54	55	56	57	58	59	60
61	62	63	64	65	66	67	68	69	70
71	72	73	74	75	76	77	78	79	80

a. $54 + 19 = \boxed{}$

b. $75 - \boxed{} = 64$

c. $\boxed{} + 9 = 53$

9 How much do the swimming things cost in the sale?

a.
45p

10p off!

$\boxed{}$

b.
73p

7p off!

$\boxed{}$

c.
43p

9p off!

$\boxed{}$

10   Write the amounts of money as pounds and pence.

a. 420p   ☐

b. 846p   ☐

c. 205p   ☐

11   Dave used a £5 note to pay for his sticker album which cost £1.50. How much change did he get? Show your working below.

☐

12   Jane had £10. She spent £1.20 on marbles and £1.30 on toy spiders. Read the questions, decide which operations to use, write the number sentences, and show your working below.

a. How much did she spend altogether?   ☐

b. How much change did she get?   ☐

13   Which line measures 6.5 cm? Write the letter in the box.   ☐

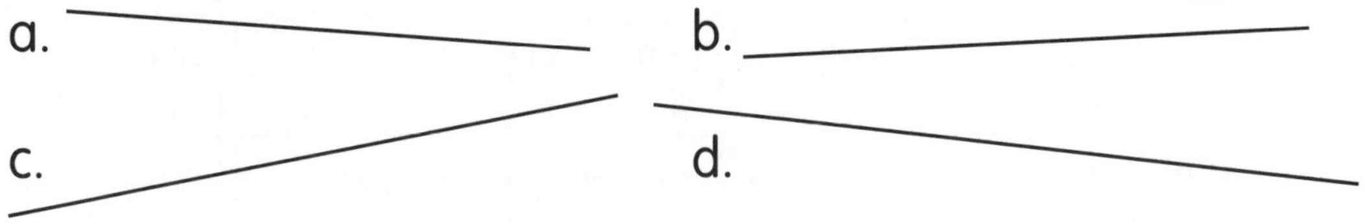

a. _____

b. _____

c. _____

d. _____

Name: _____ Date: _____

14 Fill in the missing numbers.

a. 10 mm = [   ] cm   b. 1 m = [   ] cm

c. 1 km = [   ] m   d. 300 cm = [   ] m

e. 4 km = [   ] m

15 Draw lines to join the measurements that are the same.

203 cm		3 m 2 cm
230 cm		3 m 20 cm
302 cm		2 m 3 cm
320 cm		2 m 30 cm

16 Complete the shape tables.

a.

shape	
name	
number of sides	
number of right angles	
number of corners	

b.

shape	
name	
number of sides	
number of right angles	
number of corners	

c.

shape	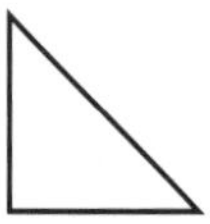
name	
number of sides	
number of right angles	
number of corners	

Name: _____ Date: _____

17 Write the co-ordinates to show where each picture is on the grid.

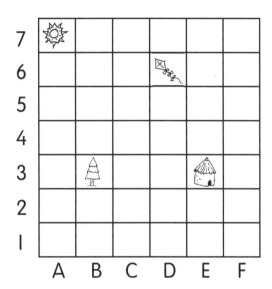

a. Tree [ ]

b. Kite [ ]

c. Hut [ ]

d. Sun [ ]

18 Fill in the missing numbers.

a. $649 = 600 + \boxed{} + 9$ b. $387 = \boxed{} + \boxed{} + \boxed{}$

19 Write the answers.

a. Double 6 [ ]   b. $6 + 7$ [ ]

c. Double 12 [ ]   d. $12 + 11$ [ ]

20 Read the problem, circle the operation needed to solve it,
circle the matching number sentence, and circle the correct answer.

Problem: Mark has £23 and Sue has £12.
How much more money does Mark have than Sue?

Operation: | addition | subtraction |

Number sentence: | $23 + 12 = 35$ | $23 - 12 = 11$ |

Answer: | Mark has £35 more than Sue. | Mark has £11 more than Sue. |

Record keeping chart

1a	Read and write whole numbers to at least 1000 in figures and words	
1b	Know what each digit represents	
2	Say the number that is, 1, 10, or 100 more or less than any given two- or three-digit number	
3	Estimate up to 100 objects	
4		
5	Read scales to the nearest labelled division	
6	Know by heart addition facts for each number to 20	
7	Identify near doubles using doubles already known	
8	Add and subtract mentally a 'near multiple of 10' to or from a two or three-digit number	
9	Extend understanding of the operations of addition and subtraction	
10	Understand and use £.p notation	
11	Solve word problems involving money	
12	Choose and use appropriate operations to solve word problems/ Find totals and give change	
13	Use a ruler to draw and measure lines to the nearest half centimetre	
14	Know the relationships between kilometeres and metres, metres and centimetres	
15	Record estimates and measurements to the nearest whole or half unit, or in mixed units	
16	Classify and describe 3-D and 2-D shapes	
17	Read and begin to write the vocabulary related to position	
18	Know what each digit represents	
19	Identify near doubles using doubles already known	
20	Choose and use appropriate operations to solve word problems	

Aural assessment: Teacher's notes

AUTUMN TERM SECOND HALF

OBJECTIVES	WHAT TO SAY	ANSWERS	MARK	UNIT	CD ACTIVITY
Count on or back in tens or hundreds, starting from any two- or three-digit numbers	1. Write in box 1, the next two numbers, counting on in hundreds from 202.	302, 402	1	16	Special delivery The number screen
	2. Write in box 2, the next two numbers, counting back in tens from 56.	46, 36	1	16	On wheels
Recognise odd and even numbers to at least 100	3. Write in box 3, all the odd numbers between 40 and 50.	41, 43, 45, 47, 49	1	17	Sea captain Ziggy
Derive quickly doubles of all whole numbers to at least 20 and all the corresponding halves	4. Write in box 4, double 14.	28	1	20	Red roofs Space painting
To multiply by 10/100, shift the digits one/two places to the left	5. Write in box 5, the answer to six times 100.	600	1	21	Flying school
Derive quickly division facts corresponding to the 5 times-table	6. Write in box 6, the answer to 40 divided by five.	8	1	22	How sweet! In the sweetshop
Solve word problems involving problems in 'real life'	7. Write in box 7, how much Simon paid for three football cards costing 4p each.	12p	1	23	What's for tea? Ball machine
Know by heart all pairs of multiples of 100 with a total of 1000	8. Write in box 8, the answer to 1000 take away 800.	200	1	26	On track The recording studio
Read the time to 5 minutes on an analogue clock and a 12-hour digital clock	9. Draw the hands on the clock in box 9, so that the time says quarter to two.	(clock showing quarter to two)	1	28	The train station At the airport
	10. It is half past twelve. Write the time on the digital clock in box 10.	12:30	1	28	
Choose and use appropriate operations to solve word problems and appropriate ways of calculating	11. Write the answer to this problem in box 11. It takes me half an hour to walk home from school. If I leave at four o'clock, what time do I get home?	4:30 or 'half past four'.	1	29	Reading clock
Solve a given problem by organising and interpreting data in simple lists, tables and graphs	12. Draw tally marks in box 12 to show that seven blue cars were parked in the car park.	||||| ||	1	30	

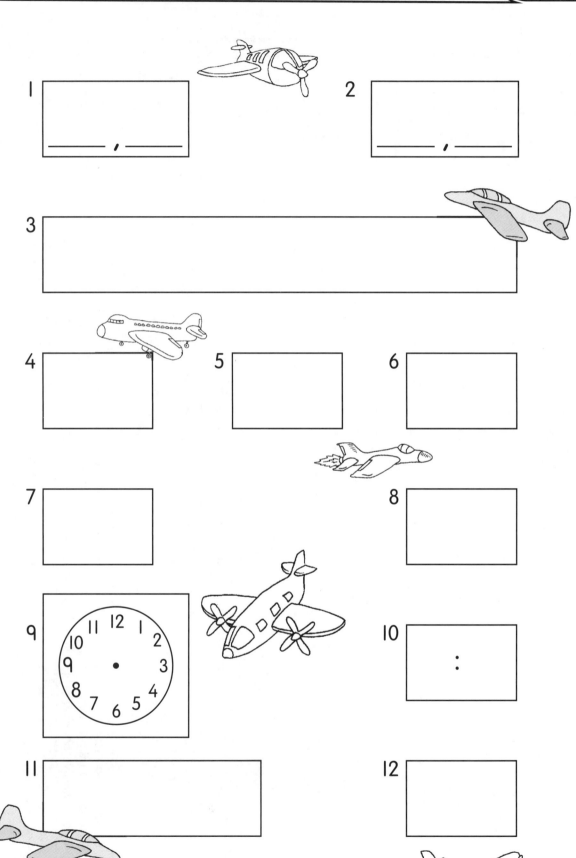

Name: _____ Date: _____

1 ____ , ____

2 ____ , ____

3

4   5   6

7   8

9   10 :

11   12

Written assessment: Teacher's notes

AUTUMN TERM
SECOND HALF

QUESTIONS	OBJECTIVES	ANSWERS	MARK	REMEDIATION UNIT	CD ACTIVITY
1	Count on or back in tens or hundreds, starting from any two- or three- digit number	a. - 74 - 94 104 b. - - 803 793 783 c. - - 775 765 755	3 3 3	16 16	Special delivery The number screen On wheels
2	Recognise odd and even numbers to at least 100	Three from: 64, 66, 68, 70	3	17	Sea captain Ziggy
3	Solve mathematical problems or puzzles	E.g. 3 + 4 + 5, 8 + 3 + 1, etc.	4	18	The coloured planets The automatic food machine
4	Understand multiplication as repeated addition	a. 3 + 3 + 3 + 3 + 3 = 15 or 5 + 5 + 5 = 15 b. 5 x 3 = 15 or 3 x 5 = 15	1 1	19	Ball machine Tooty fruity
5	Extend understanding that multiplication can be done in any order	a. 4 x 3 = 12 b. 3 x 4 = 12 (a and b in any order)	1 1	19	Chart the planets Fishy times
6	Derive quickly doubles of all whole numbers to at least 20 and all the corresponding halves	a. 26 b. 34 c. 18 d. 11	1 1 1 1	20	Red roofs Space painting
7	Say or write a division statement corresponding to a given multiplication statement	a. 7 x 2 = 14 b. 14 ÷ 7 = 2 or 14 ÷ 2 = 7	1 1	21	How sweet! In the sweetshop
8	To multiply by 10/100, shift the digits one/two places to the left	a. 30 b. 300 c. 900 d. 8	1 1 1 1	21	Flying school
9	Say or write a division statement corresponding to a given multiplication statement	a. 4 b. 400 ÷ 100 = 4 4	1 2	21	The law of the jungle
10	Derive quickly division facts corresponding to the 5 times table	a. 20, 20 ÷ 5 = 4 b. 35, 35 ÷ 5 = 7	2 2	22	Flower numbers
11	Solve word problems involving problems in real life	£3.50	1	23	What's for tea?

Written assessment: Teacher's notes

QUESTIONS	OBJECTIVES	ANSWERS	MARK	REMEDIATION UNIT	CD ACTIVITY
12 13	Recognise unit fractions and use them to find fractions of shapes and numbers	12. a. $\frac{1}{8}$ b. $\frac{1}{10}$ c. $\frac{1}{6}$ 13. Show working, 5 blue marbles	1 1 1 2	24	Ziggy's new creations Pizza parlour On the road
14	Recognise unit fractions and use them to find fractions of shapes and numbers	c.	2	25	The TV studio Shape school Ziggy's new creations
15	Know by heart all pairs of multiples of 100 with a total of 1000	500 700 800 400 600 700 300 500 600	9	26	On track The recording studio
16	Say or write a subtraction statement corresponding to a given addition statement and vice-versa	a. $25 - 12 = 13$ b. £13 c. $12 + 13 = 25$	1 1 1	27	Cinema problems
17	Read the time to 5 minutes on an analogue clock and a 12-hour digital clock	a. 11:10 b. (clock showing 9:05) c. 4:55	1 1 1	28 28	The train station At the airport
18	Choose and use appropriate operations to solve word problems and appropriate ways of calculating	45 minutes	1	29	Reading clock
19 20	Solve a given problem by organising and interpreting data in simple lists, tables and graphs	19. ⫴⫴⫴ ‖ (7) ⫴⫴⫴ (5) ‖‖‖ (4) ⫴⫴⫴ ‖‖‖ (8) a. (marble) b. (football) 20. a. 9 b. 6 c. 4	1 1 1 1 1 1 1 1 1	30	Off to space Satellites abound Super survey

Name: _____ Date: _____

1 Fill in the missing numbers to complete the number sequences.

a.

64		84		

b.

823	813			

c.

795	785			

2 Write three even numbers between 63 and 71.

3 Find four different ways to add three numbers so that they make 12.

a. ☐ + ☐ + ☐ = 12   b. ☐ + ☐ + ☐ = 12

c. ☐ + ☐ + ☐ = 12   d. ☐ + ☐ + ☐ = 12

4 The cars in the car park are parked in 3 rows of 5 cars.
Calculate the total number of cars using:

a. an addition: _____

b. a multiplication: _____

5 Write two multiplications to calculate the number of chocolate squares.

a. ☐ x ☐ = ☐

b. ☐ x ☐ = ☐

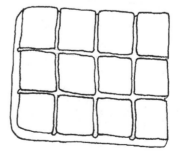

Name: _____ Date: _____

6 Write the answers.

a. Double 13 ☐   b. Double 17 ☐

c. Half of 36 ☐   d. Half of 22 ☐

7 Write a multiplication and a matching division to describe the picture

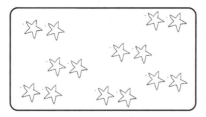

a. ☐ x ☐ = ☐

b. ☐ ÷ ☐ = ☐

8 Complete the calculations.

a. Ten times three equals ☐   b. 3 x 100 = ☐

c. 100 times nine equals ☐   d. ☐ x 100 = 800

9 a. 400 children are sitting in rows in the playground.
There are 100 children in each row. John says, "100 x 4 = 400."
How many rows of children do you think there are? ☐ rows.

b. Check your answer with a division sentence to find out how many rows there are.

☐ ÷ ☐ = ☐

There are ☐ rows of children sitting in the playground.

Name: _____ Date: _____

10 Complete the multiplications and their matching divisions.

a. $4 \times 5 = \boxed{}$

$\boxed{} \div 5 = \boxed{}$

b. $7 \times 5 = \boxed{}$

$\boxed{} \div 5 = \boxed{}$

11 7 children brought 50p each to the school sale. How much did they have altogether?

12 What fraction of each shape is shaded?

a.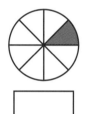

b.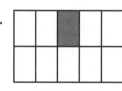

c.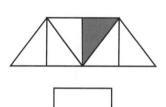

13 Sally has 15 marbles. $\frac{1}{3}$ of them are blue. How many blue marbles does Sally have? Show your working below.

 blue marbles.

14 In which shape is $\frac{1}{5}$ shaded? $\boxed{}$

a.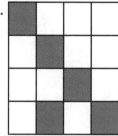

b.

c.

(15) Complete the addition table.

+	100	300	400
400			
300			
200			

(16) Follow the steps to solve the problem and then check your answer using a different operation.

Barry had £25. He bought a book and got £12 change. How much did the book cost?

a. First write a number sentence to solve the problem.

b. The book cost [   ].

c. Check your answer with a different operation.

(17) Write or draw the time on each clock.

a.

Ten past eleven

b.

Quarter to ten

c.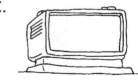

Five to five

Assessment

Name: _____ Date: _____

AUTUMN TERM SECOND HALF

18 Ann left home at 4:15 and arrived at her Aunt's house at 5:00. How long did the journey take?

☐ minutes.

19 Fill in the tally chart and then complete the sentences.

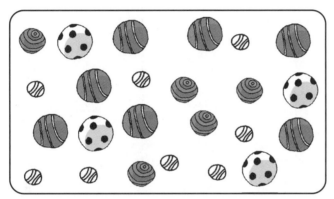

Ball	Tally

a. The balls that appear most often look like this ☐ .

b. The balls that appear least often look like this ☐ .

20 The frequency table shows the quiz scores of a class of children.

Score	Frequency
5	2
6	1
7	3
8	7
9	9
10	4

a. The most frequent score was ☐ .

b. The least frequent score was ☐ .

c. ☐ children scored 10.

1	Count on or back in tens or hundreds, starting from any two- or three- digit number
2	Recognise odd and even numbers to at least 100
3	Solve mathematical problems or puzzles
4	Understand multiplication as repeated addition
5	Extend understanding that multiplication can be done in any order
6	Derive quickly doubles of all whole numbers to at least 20 and all the corresponding halves
7	Say or write a division statement corresponding to a given multiplication statement
8	To multiply by 10/100, shift the digits one/two places to the left
9	Say or write a division statement corresponding to a given multiplication statement
10	Derive quickly division facts corresponding to the 5 times table
11	Solve word problems involving problems in real life
12	Recognise unit fractions and use them to find fractions of shapes and numbers
13	
14	Recognise unit fractions and use them to find fractions of shapes and numbers
15	Know by heart all pairs of multiples of 100 with a total of 1000
16	Say or write a subtraction statement corresponding to a given addition statement and vice-versa
17	Read the time to 5 minutes on an analogue clock and a 12-hour digital clock
18	Choose and use appropriate operations to solve word problems and appropriate ways of calculating
19	Solve a given problem by organising and interpreting data in simple lists, tables and graphs
20	

Aural assessment: Teacher's notes

SPRING TERM FIRST HALF

OBJECTIVES	WHAT TO SAY	ANSWERS	MARK	REMEDIATION UNIT	REMEDIATION CD ACTIVITY
Read and begin to write the vocabulary of ordering numbers to at least 100. Compare two given three-digit numbers	1. Write in box 1, a number that comes between 295 and 316.	Any no. b/n 295 and 316	1	31	Ziggy's toy village Blowing bubbles
Round any two-digit number to the nearest 10 and any three-digit number to the nearest 100	2. In box 2 write 84 rounded to the nearest 10.	80	1	32	Sorting out the warehouse
	3. In box 3 write 150 rounded to the nearest 100.	200	1	32	
Partition into tens and units, then recombine. Use known number facts and place value to add/subtract mentally	4. Write in box 4, the answer to 34 add 15.	49	1	34	On the right track The billboard
Extend understanding that more than two numbers can be added. Use known number facts and place value to add/subtract mentally	5. Write in box 5, the answer to 10 add 20 add 30.	60	1	35	Hatching out! Off the beaten track Load the crates
Solve word problems involving numbers in 'real life'. Choose and use appropriate operations to solve problems, and appropriate ways of calculating	6. Write the answer to this problem in box 6. Daniel is 12 years old and Lisa is 7 years old. What is the difference between their ages?	5 years	1	36 and 37	Country road Cinema problems
Make and describe right-angled turns	7. Write in box 7, how many right angles I turn through when I turn a full circle.	4	1	39	
Recognise and use the four compass directions N, S, E, W	8. I am walking east and then I turn around and walk back the way I came. Write in box 8, which direction I am walking in now?	West	1	40	Desert exploration
Use units of time and know the relationships between them	9. Write in box 9, how many minutes there are in two hours.	120	1	41	Running like clockwork
Know the relationships between kilograms and grams	10. Write the answer to this problem in box 10. I have 300 grams of sherbet. How many more grams of sherbet do I need to make half a kilogram?	200 g	1	42	The strong man Weigh the boxes
Solve word problems involving numbers in 'real life'	11. Write the answer to this problem in box 11. I bought quarter of a metre of ribbon. How many centimetres of ribbon did I buy?	25 cm	1	43	Quizziggy
Know the relationships between kilograms and grams. Record estimates and measurements to the nearest whole or half unit, or in mixed units	12. Write in box 12, 1 kg and 300 g in grams only.	1300 g	1	44	A weighty problem Video evening

Name: _____ Date: _____

SPRING TERM
FIRST HALF

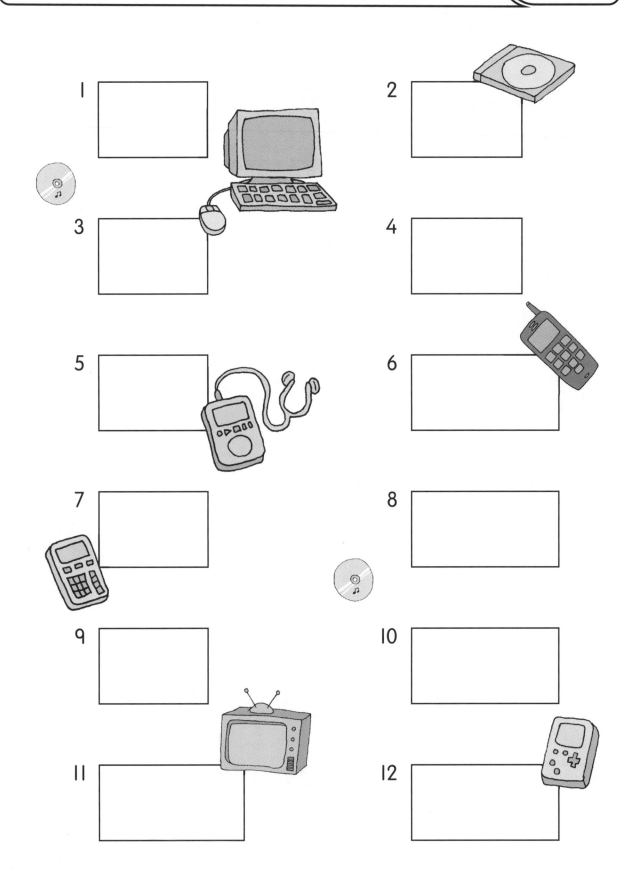

1

2

3

4

5

6

7

8

9

10

11

12

Written assessment: Teacher's notes

QUESTIONS	OBJECTIVES	ANSWERS	MARK	REMEDIATION UNIT	CD ACTIVITY
1	Read and begin to write the vocabulary of ordering numbers to at least 100	1.			
2	Compare two given three-digit numbers	a. 309 b. 298 c. 624 d. 472 2. 280, 290, 300, 310	1 1 1 1 4	31	Ziggy's toy village Blowing bubbles Say cheese!
3	Round any two-digit number to the nearest 10 and any three-digit number to the nearest 100	a. 80 b. 80 c. 60 d. 40 e. 300 f. 600 g. 500 h. 700	1 1 1 1 1 1 1 1	32	Sorting out the warehouse
4	Read scales to the nearest division	a. nearly 4 kg b. between 8 and 9 kg c. just over 4 kg	1 1 1	33	On the scales
5	Partition into tens and units, then recombine	a. Show working, 69 b. Show working, 99	2 2	34	On the right track The billboard
6	Extend understanding that more than two numbers can be added	a. 90 b. 50 c. 99 d. 79	1 1 1 1	35	Hatching out! Off the beaten track Load the crates
7 8	Solve word problems involving numbers in 'real life'	7. Show working, 24p 8. Show working, £1	2 2	36	Country road Cinema problems
9	Choose and use appropriate operations to solve problems, and appropriate ways of calculating	a. + b. × c. ÷ d. –	1 1 1 1	37	In the maths lab

Written assessment: Teacher's notes

No.	Objective	Details	Marks	Page	Activity
10	Make and describe shapes and patterns	a, c, and d	3	38	
11	Relate solid shapes to pictures of them	5 faces, 9 edges	2	38	
12	Make and describe right-angled turns	a. 3 right angles, clockwise b. 2 right angles, clockwise c. 1 right angle, anticlockwise	2 2 2	39	
13	Recognise and use the four compass directions N, S, E, W	(hexagon)	1	40	Desert exploration
14	Use units of time and know the relationships between them	a. 1, 2 b. 3, 4 c. 2, 3 d. week, weeks	2 2 2 2	41	Running like clockwork
15 16	Know the relationships between kilograms and grams	15. a. 1 kg 2 x 250 g b. 2 kg 300 g + 1700 g c. $\frac{1}{2}$ kg 200 g + 400 g + 100 g + 300 g 16. Show working, 800 g	3 2	42	The strong man Weigh in Weigh the boxes
17 18	Solve word problems involving numbers in real life	17. Show working, 3 ½ m 18. Show working, 750 g	2 2	43	A weighty problem
19	Know the relationships between kilograms and grams. Record estimates and measurements to the nearest whole or half unit, or in mixed units	Show working, a, b and d or b, c and e	2	44	A weighty problem The strong man Weigh the boxes
20	Investigate a general statement about familiar shapes by finding examples that satisfy it	b and c	2	45	Maths art

Name: _____ Date: _____

1 Circle the smaller number in each pair.

a. 309 390   b. 829 298

c. 642 624   d. 742 472

2 Write all the multiples of 10 between 271 and 319.

3 Round the numbers to the nearest 10.

a. 81 ☐   b. 76 ☐

c. 55 ☐   d. 40 ☐

Round the numbers to the nearest 100.

e. 342 ☐   f. 568 ☐

g. 450 ☐   h. 709 ☐

4 Write the weight of each bag.
Use the words just over, nearly, and between.

a.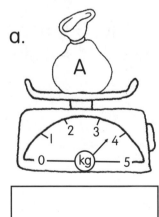

b.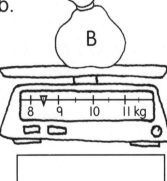

c.

Name: _____ Date: _____

5 Complete the additions and show your working.

a. 43 + 26 = ☐

b. 35 + 64 = ☐

6 Complete the additions.

a. 20 + 30 + 40 = ☐   b. 20 + 30 + ☐ = 100

c. 47 + 32 + 20 = ☐   d. 21 + 46 + 12 = ☐

7 Alisha wants to buy 12 stickers. Each one costs 2p.
How much will she have to pay? Show your working below.

☐

8 Guy and Tim want to buy a book that costs £10. Guy has £6.50
and Tim has £2.50. How much more money do they need to
buy the book? Show your working below.

☐

Name: _____ Date: _____

9 Complete the number sentences. Put +, −, x, or, ÷ in each star.

a. 52 99 = 151

b. 3 8 = 24

c. 18  2 = 9

d. 46 32 = 14

10 Circle the shapes that can be made using only triangles.

a. b. c.  d. e.

11 Complete the table.

Shape	
Number of faces	
Number of edges	

12 Fill in the number of right angles each turn goes through and write if the turns are clockwise or anticlockwise.

a. b.  c.

	right angles		right angles		right angles

Name: _____ Date: _____

13 Follow the instructions and circle the shape you arrive at.

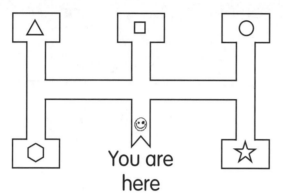

Instructions
1. Go North
2. Turn West
3. Go West
4. Turn South
5. Go South

14 Complete the sentences.

a. 30 hours is more than ☐ day and less than ☐ days.

b. 200 minutes is more than ☐ hours and less than ☐ hours.

c. 130 seconds is more than ☐ minutes and less than ☐ minute

d. 10 days is more than 1 ☐ and less than 2 ☐

15 Draw lines to join the weights that match.

a.	1 kg	2 x 250 g
b.	2 kg	300 g + 1700 g
c.	$\frac{1}{2}$ kg	200 g + 400 g + 100 g + 300 g

16 Paul bought 1800 g of grapes and ate 1 kg of them. How many grams does he have left? Show your working below.

Name: _____ Date: _____

17 A snail crawls half a metre every day. How many metres does it crawl in one week? Show your working below.

☐

18 George bought $\frac{1}{2}$ kg of toffee and $\frac{1}{4}$ kg of chocolate. What is the total weight in grams? Show your working below.

☐

19 Choose three parcels that weigh 2 kg altogether. Show your working below.

a. 600 g   b. 1 kg 200 g   c. 300 g   d. 200 g   e. 500 g

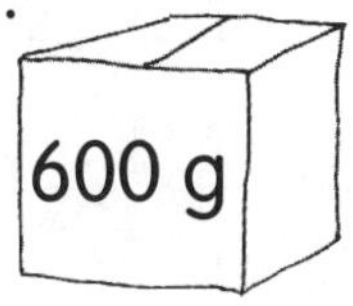

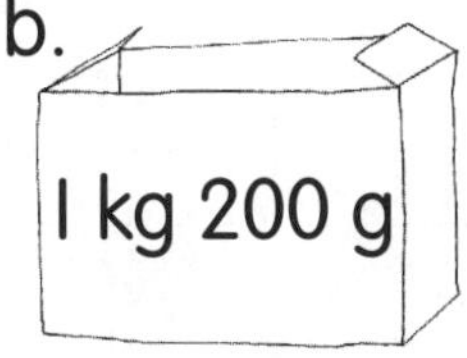

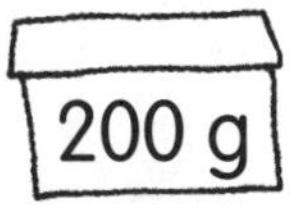

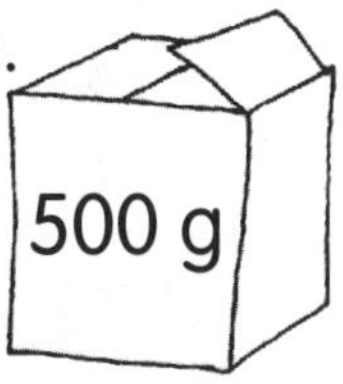

☐ , ☐ , and ☐ .

20 Not all pictures drawn with four sides are quadrilaterals. Circle the pictures that are not quadrilaterals.

a.   b. 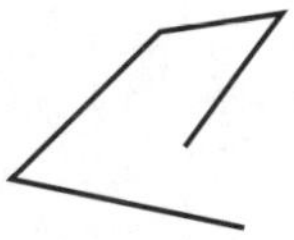   c. 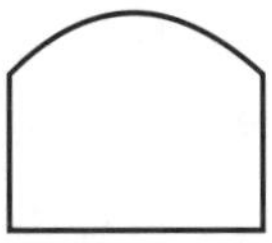   d.

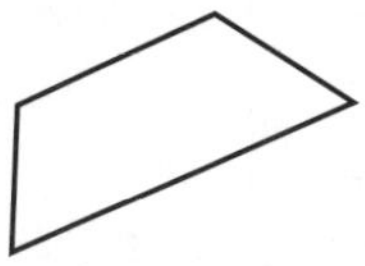

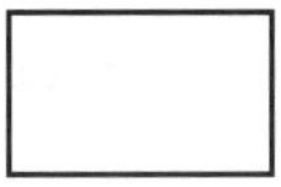

Record keeping chart

1	Read and begin to write the vocabulary of ordering numbers to at least 100
2	Compare two given three-digit numbers
3	Round any two-digit number to the nearest 10 and any three digit number to the nearest 100
4	Read scales to the nearest division
5	Partition into tens and units, then recombine
6	Extend understanding that more than two numbers can be added
7	Solve word problems involving numbers in 'real life'
8	
9	Choose and use appropriate operations to solve problems, and appropriate ways of calculating
10	Make and describe shapes and patterns
11	Relate solid shapes to pictures of them
12	Make and describe right-angled turns
13	Recognise and use the four compass directions N, S, E, W
14	Use units of time and know the relationships between them
15	Know the relationships between kilograms and grams
16	
17	Solve word problems involving numbers in real life
18	
19	Know the relationships between kilograms and grams. Record estimates and measurements to the nearest whole or half unit, or in mixed units
20	Investigate a general statement about familiar shapes by finding examples that satisfy it

mathspace © HarpercollinsPublishers Ltd 2004

Aural assessment: Teacher's notes

SPRING TERM SECOND HALF

OBJECTIVES	WHAT TO SAY	ANSWERS	MARK	UNIT	CD ACTIVITY (REMEDIATION)
Count in steps of 3, 4 or 5 from any small number to at least 50, then back again	1. Write in box 1, the next two numbers after 13 in a 'counting on in threes' sequence.	16, 19	1	46	On wheels / Along the walkway
Solve mathematical problems or puzzles Investigate a general statement about familiar numbers by finding examples that satisfy it	2. Write in box 2, a three-digit number where all the digits are even.	three-digit numbers including only 0, 2, 4, 6, and 8	1	47	
Use known number facts and place value to add/subtract mentally	3. Write in box 3, the answer to 55 add 35.	90	1	48	On track
Extend understanding that more than two numbers can be added Add three or four two-digit numbers with the help of apparatus or pencil and paper	4. Use the working out space in box 4 and find the answer to 15 add 20 add 21.	56	1	49	The automatic food machine / Flower power
Extend understanding of the operation of subtraction	5. Write in box 5, the answer to 93 take away 40.	53	1	50	Target practice / Points make prizes
Derive quickly doubles of multiples of 5 to 100 and all the corresponding halves (Using doubling or halving starting from the known facts)	6. Write in box 6, double 45.	90	1	51	Red roofs / Space painting
Begin to know the three times-table	7. Write in box 7, the answer to six times three.	18	1	52	Tooty fruity
Begin to know the four times-table	8. Write in box 8, the answer to seven times four.	28	1	53	Ball machine / Down on the farm
Solve word problems using numbers in 'real life' and money, using one or more steps Choose and use appropriate operations to solve word problems	9. Circle the number sentence in box 9, needed to solve this problem. Debby spent 20p on four stickers. How much did each sticker cost?	$20 \div 4$	1	55	
Begin to recognise simple fractions that are several parts of a whole	10. Circle the shape in box 10 in which $\frac{3}{10}$ is shaded.	c	1	56	Pizza parlour / Ziggy's new creations
Begin to recognise simple fractions that are several parts of a whole	11. Use the strip and write the answer to this question in box 11. If $\frac{3}{8}$ is red and the rest is blue, what fraction of the strip is blue?	$\frac{5}{8}$	1	58	Dive into fractions!
Solve a given problem by organising and interpreting in simple lists, tables and graphs	12. Look at the bar chart and write in box 12, how many blue cars were sold last week.	5 cars	1	59	Ziggy's survey

Name: _____ Date: _____

SPRING TERM
SECOND HALF

1
```
———— , ————
```

2

3

4

5

6

7

8

9
20 + 4	20 × 4
20 ÷ 4	4 × 20

10
a b c

11

Cars sold last week 12

Cars sold last week

Number of cars (y-axis: 0, 1, 2, 3, 4, 5, 6)
red = 3, blue = 5, green = 4
Colour of cars

Written assessment: Teacher's notes

QUESTIONS	OBJECTIVES	ANSWERS	MARK	REMEDIATION	
				UNIT	CD ACTIVITY NAME
1	Count in steps of 3, 4 or 5 from any small number to at least 50, then back again	a. 40 45 50 b. 24 20 16 c. 18 15 12	3 3 3	46	On wheels Along the walkway
2 3	Solve mathematical problems or puzzles, recognize simple patterns and relationships Investigate a general statement about familiar numbers by finding examples that satisfy it	2. 3 and 2 3. 41, 43, 45, 47, 49	1 5	47	Fact finding tour
4	Use known number facts and place value to add/subtract mentally	a. 15 b. 35 c. 35 d. 15	1 1 1 1	48	On track
5	Extend understanding that more than two numbers can be added... add three or four two-digit numbers with the help of apparatus or pencil and paper	Show working, 74	2	49	The automatic food machine Flower power
6	Extend understanding of the operation of subtraction	a. 54p b. 31p c. 60p	1 1 1	50	Alien maker Target practice Points make prizes

7
8
	Derive quickly doubles of multiples of 5 to 100 and all the corresponding halves	7. a. 90
		    b. 35
		    c. 100
		    d. 45
		8 30 cm
			1
			1
			1
			1
			1
				51	Red roofs
					Space painting

9	Begin to know the three times-table	a. 21 b. 3 c. 6 d. 5	1 1 1 1	52	Tooty fruity What's for tea? Ball machine Down on the farm
10	Begin to know the four times-table	20 12 32 40	1 1 1 1	53	Tooty fruity Down on the farm In the number lab
11	Understand division as grouping or sharing	Show working, 6 sweets each	2	54	The law of the jungle

Written assessment: Teacher's notes

SPRING TERM SECOND HALF

QUESTIONS	OBJECTIVES	ANSWERS	MARK	REMEDIATION UNIT	REMEDIATION CD ACTIVITY NAME
12	Recognise that division is the inverse of multiplication	- 5 12 - - 7 40 -	1 1 1 1	54	How sweet! Chugging along
13	Choose and use appropriate operations to solve word problems	a. multiplication b. addition c. division	1 1 1	55	
14	Solve word problems using numbers in 'real life' and money, using one or more steps	Show working, 12 flowers in each bunch	2	55	Cinema problems Ziggy's space jet
15 16	Begin to recognise simple fractions that are several parts of a whole	15 a. $\frac{3}{5}$ b. $\frac{4}{7}$ c. $\frac{3}{7}$ 16 a. ▭ or any 3 squares b. ◯ or any $\frac{3}{4}$ c. ⬡ or any $\frac{5}{8}$ d. ⬠ or any $\frac{4}{5}$	1,1,1 1 1 1 1	56	Pizza parlour Ziggy's new creations
17	Begin to recognise simple equivalent fractions	a. $\frac{1}{3}$ and $\frac{2}{6}$ b. $\frac{2}{10}$ and $\frac{1}{5}$ c. $\frac{1}{2}$ and $\frac{6}{12}$	2 2 2	57	The architect
18	Begin to recognise simple fractions that are several parts of a whole	$\frac{5}{7}$	1	58	Dive into fractions!
19	Solve a given problem by organising and interpreting in simple lists, tables and graphs	a. 3 b. chips c. yes	1 1 1	59	Ziggy's survey
20	Solve a given problem by organising and interpreting data in simple lists, tables and graphs	a. 2 b. white chocolate c. 18	1 1 1	60	Waiter, waiter!

Name: _____ Date: _____

1 Complete the sequences.

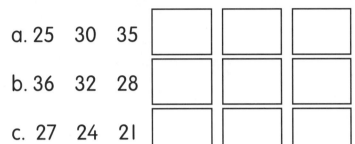

a. 25 30 35 ▢ ▢ ▢

b. 36 32 28 ▢ ▢ ▢

c. 27 24 21 ▢ ▢ ▢

2 Find a pair of numbers with a sum of 5 and a product of 6. Show your working below.

▢ and ▢

3 There are always five odd numbers between two tens numbers that follow each other. Write the five odd numbers between 40 and 50.

▢ ▢ ▢ ▢ ▢

4 Complete the number sentences.

a. 40 + ▢ = 55   b. 65 + ▢ = 100

c. 70 − 35 = ▢   d. 50 − 35 = ▢

5 Find the total by adding the tens, adding the units, and adding the results together. Show your working below.

36 + 15 + 23 = ▢

Name: _____ Date: _____

6 Find the new prices. Show your working below.

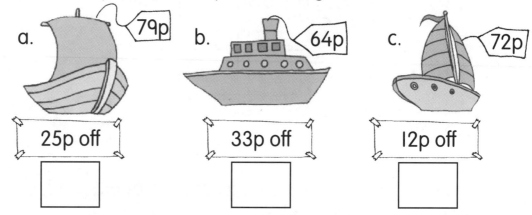

a. 79p
25p off
☐

b. 64p
33p off
☐

c. 72p
12p off
☐

7 Complete the sentences.

a. Double 45 is ☐.   b. Half of 70 is ☐.

c. Twice 50 is ☐.   d. Half of 90 is ☐.

8 Pat's scarf is 60 cm long. Jamie's scarf is half that length. How long is Jamie's scarf? ☐

9 Complete the multiplications.

a. $3 \times 7 = $ ☐   b. $8 \times$ ☐ $= 24$

c. $3 \times$ ☐ $= 18$ d. ☐ $\times 3 = 15$

Name: _____ Date: _____

10 Fill in the 'times 4' machine.

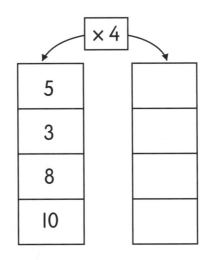

× 4

5	
3	
8	
10	

11 John has 24 sweets. He shares them equally between four children. How many sweets does each child get? Show your working below.

☐ sweets each.

12 Fill in the 'divide by 4' machine.

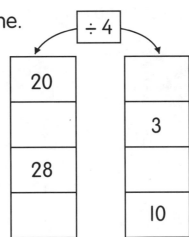

÷ 4

20	
	3
28	
	10

Name: _____ Date: _____

13 Match the problem with the operation needed to solve it.

a.
Mike has £12.
Rod has double
this amount.
How much does
Rod have?

b.
Jack has 79p and
Josh has 58p. How
much do they have
altogether?

c.
Debbie has 12
cherries. She ate
half. How many
cherries are left?

| division | multiplication | addition |

14 Darren picked 11 flowers and Stephanie picked 13 flowers.
They made two equal bunches of flowers. How many flowers
are there in each bunch? Show your working below.

☐ flowers
in each bunch.

15 Match the shaded part of the shapes to the correct fraction.

a.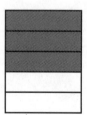

b.

c.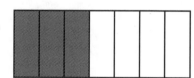

$\frac{3}{7}$ $\frac{3}{5}$ $\frac{4}{7}$

Name: _____ Date: _____

16 Colour the fraction of each shape.

a.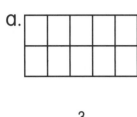

b.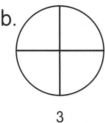

c.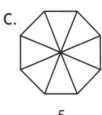

d.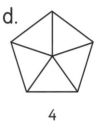

$\frac{3}{10}$

$\frac{3}{4}$

$\frac{5}{8}$

$\frac{4}{5}$

17 Write two fractions that match the shaded part of each shape.

a.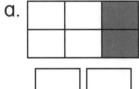

b.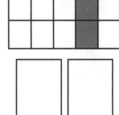

c.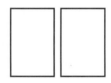

18 $\frac{2}{7}$ of my bookmark is blue and the rest is red. What fraction of my bookmark is red? Show your working below.

 of my bookmark is red.

19 Use the bar chart to answer the questions.

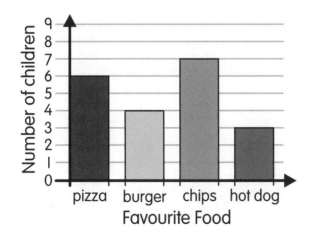

a. How many children like hot dogs best?

b. What is the most popular food?

c. Do more children like pizza than burgers?

Name: _____ Date: _____

(20) Use the pictogram to answer the questions.
Be careful to think about the key!

Favourite type of chocolate

white	
milk	
nuts	
mint	

Key
= 2 children

a. How many children like mint chocolate best?

b. What is the most popular type of chocolate?

c. How many children took part in the survey?

 © HarpercollinsPublishers Ltd 2004

Record keeping chart

1	Count in steps of 3, 4 or 5 from any small number to at least 50, then back again
2	Solve mathematical problems or puzzles, recognize simple patterns and relationships
3	Investigate a general statement about familiar numbers by finding examples that satisfy it
4	Use known number facts and place value to add/subtract mentally
5	Extend understanding that more than two numbers can be added... add three or four two-digit numbers with the help of apparatus or pencil and paper
6	Extend understanding of the operation of subtraction
7	Derive quickly doubles of multiples of 5 to 100 and all the corresponding halves
8	
9	Begin to know the three-times table
10	Begin to know the four-times-table
11	Understand division as grouping or sharing
12	Recognise that division is the inverse of multiplication
13	Choose and use appropriate operations to solve word problems
14	Solve word problems using numbers in 'real life' and money, using one or more steps
15	Begin to recognise simple fractions that are several parts of a whole
16	
17	Begin to recognise simple equivalent fractions
18	Begin to recognise simple fractions that are several parts of a whole
19	Solve a given problem by organising and interpreting in simple lists, tables and graphs
20	Solve a given problem by organising and interpreting data in simple lists, tables and graphs

Aural assessment: Teacher's notes

SUMMER TERM FIRST HALF

OBJECTIVES	WHAT TO SAY	ANSWERS	MARK	REMEDIATION UNIT	REMEDIATION CD ACTIVITY
Compare two given three-digit numbers. Say which is more or less, and give a number which lies between them	1. Write in box 1, a number that is more than 486 and less than 503.	Any no. between 486 and 503.	1	61	Sheep crossing Building blocks
Read and begin to write the vocabulary of estimation and approximation	2. Draw an arrow on the number line in box 2, showing where 387 lies.	Just before the ninth mark.	1	62	Ziggy's toy village
Describe and extend number sequences	3. Circle the rule in box 3 that matches this number sequence. Two, five, eight, eleven.	+ 3	1	63	Special delivery
Add and subtract mentally a 'near multiple of 10' to or from a two-digit number	4. Write in box 4, the answer to 48 take away 9.	39	1	64	The billboard Points make prizes
Use known number facts and place value to add/subtract numbers mentally	5. Write in box 5, the answer to 172 add 400.	572	1	65	
	6. Write in box 6, how much I have to add to 720 to make the next 100.	80	1	66	In the games room On track Switch on additions
	7. Write in box 7, £2 take away 6p.	£1.94	1	66	
	8. Write in box 8, the answer to 129 add 60.	189	1	67	
Know the relationship between litres and millilitres	9. Circle the container in box 9 that has 500 millilitres of liquid in it.	B	1	71	Twin tanks
Read scales to the nearest labelled division					
Identify and sketch lines of symmetry in simple shapes and recognize shapes with no lines of symmetry	10. Draw two lines of symmetry on the shape in box 10.	An '8' shape, symmetry = +	1	73	In Ziggy's workshop In the mirror In the hangar
Read and begin to write the vocabulary related to position	11. Write in box 11, the position of the star in the grid.	C2	1	74	The space battle
Compare angles with right angles	12. Tick the right angles in the shape in box 12.	There are 2 right angles.	1	75	Tangled angles

Name: _____ Date: _____

1 [blank box]

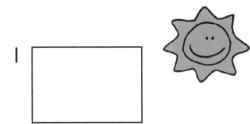

2

300 |———|———|———|———|———|———|———|———| 400

3

+4	+3
−4	−3

4 [blank box]

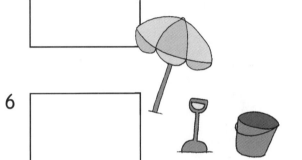

5 [blank box]

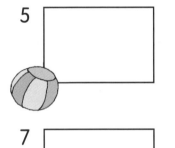

6 [blank box]

7 [blank box]

8 [blank box]

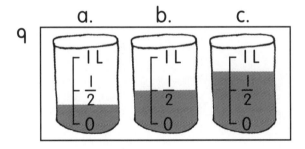

9

a.   b.   c.

[three beakers marked 1L, ½, 0]

10 [box with 8]

11

4				
3				
2			★	
1				
	A	B	C	D

[blank box]

12 [box with kite shape]

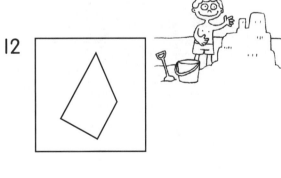

Written assessment: Teacher's notes

QUESTIONS	OBJECTIVES	ANSWERS	MARK	REMEDIATION UNIT	REMEDIATION CD ACTIVITY
1	Compare two given three-digit numbers. Say which is more or less, and give a number which lies between them	a. Any number between 298 and 350 b. Any number between 399 and 410 c. Any number between 860 and 915	1 1 1	61	Sheep crossing Building blocks
2	Order whole numbers to at least 100 and position them on a number line	829 809 298 289 89	2	61	Sheep crossing Building blocks
3	Order whole numbers to at least 100 and position them on a number line Read and begin to write the vocabulary of estimation and approximation	In order from left to right: 220, 245, 275, 286, 292	5	61 and 62	Sheep crossing Say cheese! Ziggy's toy village
4	Describe and extend number sequences	a. 285 305 325 b. 686 683 680	6	63	Special delivery On wheels
5 6	Add and subtract mentally a 'near multiple of 10' to or from a two-digit number	5. a. 378 b. 221 c. 302 d. 178 6. a. +29 b. -21 c. +21 d. -39	1 1 1 1 1 1 1 1	64	The billboard Points make prizes Name that number!

7
8
9
	Use known number facts and place value to add/subtract numbers mentally	7. 525 825 625
		   387 687 487
		   219 519 319
		8. a. 60
		   b. 50, 400
		   c. 70, 900
		   d. 30, 100
		9. a. 339
		   b. 533
		   c. 575
		   d. 813
			1
			1
			1
			1
			1
			1
			1
			1
			1
			1
			1
				65,
				66,
				67
					In the games room
					On track
					In the Maths lab

Written assessment: Teacher's notes

QUESTIONS	OBJECTIVES	ANSWERS	MARK	REMEDIATION	
				UNIT	CD ACTIVITY
10 11 12 13	Use informal pencil and paper methods to support, record or explain HTU + TU, HTU + HTU	10. 539 11. a. 759 　 b. 792 12. 583 13. 613	1 1 1 1 1	68 and 69	Switch on additions On the right track
14	Solve mathematical problems and puzzles	Any three-term calculation that makes 17	1	70	
15	Know the relationship between litres and millilitres Read scales to the nearest labelled division	a.　400 ml b.　300 ml c.　700 ml	1	71	Twin tanks
16 17	Suggest suitable units and measuring equipment to estimate or measure capacity	16 a.　100 ml 　 b.　11 　 c.　1101 17 a. 11 200 ml 　 b. 4 1 100 ml	1 1 1 1 1	72	Twin tanks
18	Identify and sketch lines of symmetry in simple shapes and recognise shapes with no lines of symmetry	a, c, and d	3	73	In Ziggy's workshop In the mirror In the hangar
19	Read and begin to write the vocabulary related to position	a.　orange b.　cherries c.　apple	1 1 1	74	The space battle
20	Compare angles with right angles	a.　smaller than a right angle b.　right angle c.　smaller than a right angle d.　greater than a right angle	1 1 1 1	75	Tangled angles

Name: _____ Date: _____

1 Find numbers to complete the sentences.

a. ☐ is smaller than 350 and greater than 298.

b. ☐ is greater than 399 and smaller than 410.

c. ☐ comes between 860 and 915.

2 Write the numbers in order from the largest number to the smallest number.

298   829   289   89   809

largest   smallest

3 Put the numbers in the correct places on the number line.

275   245   286   292   220

200   300

4 Complete the number sequences.

a. 225   245   265   ☐ ☐ ☐

b. 695   692   689   ☐ ☐ ☐

Name: _____ Date: _____

5 Complete the number sentences.

a. $369 + 9 =$ ☐   b. $240 - 19 =$ ☐

c. $321 - 19 =$ ☐   d. $159 + 19 =$ ☐

6 Complete the number sentences.

a. 51 ☐☐ $= 80$ b. 36 ☐☐ $= 15$

c. 46 ☐☐ $= 67$ d. 60 ☐☐ $= 21$

7 Complete the addition table.

+	200	500	300
325			
187			
19			

8 Complete the additions to make the next hundreds number.

a. $640 +$ ☐ $=$ 700   b. $350 +$ ☐ $=$ ☐

c. $830 +$ ☐ $=$ ☐   d. $70 +$ ☐ $=$ ☐

9 Fill in the missing numbers.

a. $389 - 50 =$ ☐   b. ☐ $+ 60 = 593$

c. $605 - 30 =$ ☐   d. ☐ $= 723 + 90$

Name: _____ Date: _____

10 Find the total. You can use the number line to help you.

$325 + 214 =$ ⬚

325
|————————————————————————————

11 Find the hundreds, then the tens, and then the units, to calculate the additions.

a. 612   b. 263
  + 147   + 529

———————   ———————

———————   ———————

12 Find the total. You can use the number line to help you.

$458 + 125 =$ ⬚

458
|————————————————————————————

13 This year Dan won 365 gold stars and 248 silver stars. How many stars did he win altogether? Show your working below.

Dan won ⬚ altogether.

Name: _____ Date: _____

14 Choose three numbers and any of the signs +, −, x, and, ÷, to write a number sentence that equals 17.

15 Match the measurements to the correct containers.

a.    b. 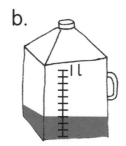   c.

| 300 ml | 400 ml | 700 ml |

16 Circle the nearest capacity.

a.   b.    c.

| 3 ml 100 ml 10 ml | 10 ml 200 ml 1 l | 900 ml 3 l 110 l |

17 Add the capacities and record the results as litres and millilitres.

a. 500 ml + 300 ml + 400 ml = ☐ l ☐ ml

b. 3 l + 600 ml + 500 ml = ☐ l ☐ ml

18 Circle the shapes that have a true line of symmetry.

a.    b.    c.   d.

Name: _____ Date: _____

19 Write the names of the fruits next to their co-ordinates.

a. B6

b. B2

c. F3

20 Fill in the table by putting ticks (✓) in the right places.

a.   b.   c.   d.

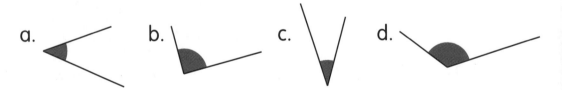

angle	smaller than a right angle	right angle	greater than a right angle
a			
b			
c			
d			

Assessment

Record keeping chart

SUMMER TERM
FIRST HALF

1	Compare two given three-digit numbers. Say which is more or less, and give a number which lies between them
2	Order whole numbers to at least 100 and position them on a number line
3	Order whole numbers to at least 100 and position them on a number line
	Read and begin to write the vocabulary of estimation and approximation
4	Describe and extend number sequences
5	Add and subtract mentally a 'near multiple of 10' to or from a two-
6	digit number
7	Use known number facts and place value to add/subtract numbers
8	mentally
9	
10	
11	Use informal pencil and paper methods to support, record or
12	explain HTU + TU, HTU + HTU
13	
14	Solve mathematical problems and puzzles
15	Know the relationship between litres and millilitres
	Read scales to the nearest labelled division
16	Suggest suitable units and measuring equipment to estimate or
17	measure capacity
18	Identify and sketch lines of symmetry in simple shapes and recognise shapes with no lines of symmetry
19	Read and begin to write the vocabulary related to position
20	Compare angles with right angles

© HarpercollinsPublishers Ltd 2004   257

Aural assessment: Teacher's notes

SUMMER TERM SECOND HALF

OBJECTIVES	WHAT TO SAY	ANSWERS	MARK	UNIT	REMEDIATION CD ACTIVITY
Recognise two- and three-digit multiples of 2, 5, or 10 and three-digit multiples of 50 and 100	1. Write in box 1, the multiples of 5 between 72 and 82.	75, 80	1	76	Lucky numbers
	2. Write in box 2, the multiples of 50 between 130 and 230.	150, 200	1	76	Spacey horses
Derive quickly doubles of multiples of 50 to 500, and all the corresponding halves	3. Write in box 3, double 250.	500	1	78	Red roofs
	4. Write in box 4, half of 700.	350	1	78	Space painting
Begin to know the three and four times-tables. Say or write a division statement corresponding to a given multiplication statement	5. Three children bought a packet of 12 biscuits. Write a division sentence in box 5, to show how many biscuits they will each have if they divide them equally.	$12 \div 3 = 4$	1	79	Ziggy and the beanstalk / In the number lab
Use known number facts and place value to carry out mentally simple multiplications and divisions	6. We know that 1 times 8 equals eight, and 10 times eight equals 80. Write in box 6, the answer to 100 times 8.	800	1	80	Flying school
Begin to find remainders after simple division	7. Write in box 7, the answer to 17 divided by 5. Don't forget to write the remainder!	3 r 1	1	81	Space control
Use known number facts and place value to carry out mentally simple multiplications and divisions. Use doubling and halving, starting from known facts	8. Write in box 8, the answer to 34 times 2.	68	1	82	Red roofs
Choose and use appropriate operations to solve word problems and appropriate ways of calculating	9. Circle the calculation in box 9, needed to solve this problem. Lyn has 15 pens. She shares them equally between her three friends. How many pens will each friend get?	$15 \div 3$	1	83	The law of the jungle
Partition into 'five and a bit' when adding 6, 7, 8 and 9	10. Write in box 9, the answer to 75 add 8.	83	1	86	Points make prizes / The billboard
Use a calendar	11. Look at the calendar page. Sophie's birthday is on Monday 3rd June and Gary's birthday is five days later. Write the day and date of Gary's birthday in box 11.	Saturday 8th June	1	89	That's a date
Solve a given problem by organising and interpreting numerical data in simple lists, tables and graphs	12. Look at the Venn diagram and circle the names of the two children in box 12, who have blue eyes and long hair.	Emma and Liz	1	90	Venn diagram

mathspace © HarpercollinsPublishers Ltd 2004   259

Name: _____   Date: _____

1

2

3

4

5

6

7

8

9

15 + 3	3 ÷ 15
15 × 3	15 ÷ 3

10

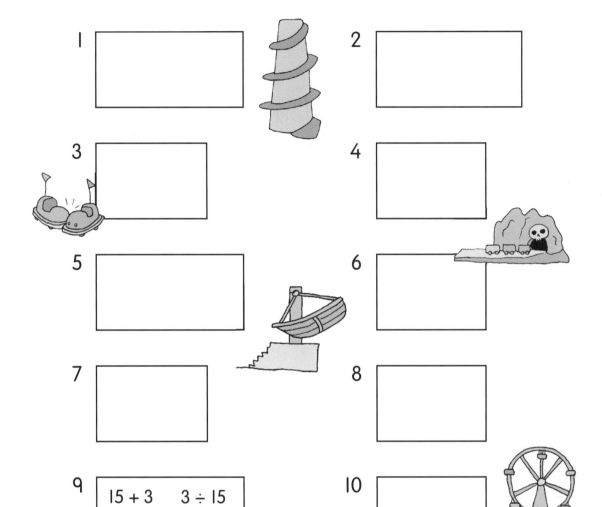

JUNE						
Mon	Tue	Wed	Thur	Fri	Sat	Sun
					1	2
3	4	5	6	7	8	9
10	11	12	13	14	15	16
17	18	19	20	21	22	23
24	25	26	27	28	29	30

blue eyes   long hair

Judy
Robert   Emma
              Liz   Simone
                        Mandy

11

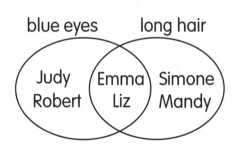

12

Liz	Simone	Robert
Emma	Judy	Mandy

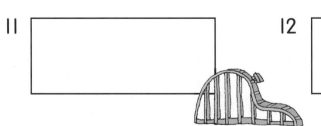

Written assessment: Teacher's notes

QUESTIONS	OBJECTIVES	ANSWERS	MARK	REMEDIATION UNIT	REMEDIATION CD ACTIVITY
1	Recognise two- and three-digit multiples of 2, 5, or 10 and three-digit multiples of 50 and 100	a. multiple of 2, b. multiple of 2, multiple of 5, multiple of 10 c. multiple of 5 d. multiple of 2, multiple of 5, multiple of 10	2 2 2 2	76	Lucky numbers Spacey horses
2	Investigate a general statement about familiar numbers by finding examples that satisfy it Solve mathematical problems or puzzles	a. Show some investigation, yes b. Show some investigation, no	2 2	77	
3 4	Derive quickly doubles of multiples of 50 to 500, and all the corresponding halves	3. a. 600 b. 700 c. 450 d. 250 4. 900 m	1 1 1 1 1	78	Red roofs Space painting
5	Begin to know the three and four times-tables	27 36 18 24 24 32 15 20	8	79	Ziggy and the beanstalk In the number lab Beach scenes
6	Say or write a division statement corresponding to a given multiplication statement	$36 \div 4 = 9$, 9 cows	2	79	Beach scenes The law of the jungle
7	Use known number facts and place value to carry out mentally simple multiplications and divisions	10 100 1000 6 60 600 8 80 800	9	80	Flying school
8 9	Begin to find remainders after simple division Round up or down after division	8. a.Show working, 5 CDs b. Show working, £3 left over 9. Show working, 8 boxes	2 2 2	81	Ask the robot!
10	Use known number facts and place value to carry out mentally simple multiplications and divisions	a. 82 b. 63	1 1	82	

 mathspace © HarpercollinsPublishers Ltd 2004

Written assessment: Teacher's notes

SUMMER TERM SECOND HALF

QUESTIONS	OBJECTIVES	ANSWERS	MARK	REMEDIATION UNIT	REMEDIATION CD ACTIVITY
11	Use doubling and halving, starting from known facts	a. 14 b. 7	1 1	82	Red roofs
12	Choose and use appropriate operations to solve word problems and appropriate ways of calculating	800	1	83	The billboard
13 14	Compare two familiar fractions	13 a. Show working, less b. Show working, less 14 a. 1 b. 2	2 2 1 1	84	
15	Estimate a simple fraction	a. $\frac{1}{4}$ b. $\frac{2}{3}$ c. $\frac{1}{10}$	1 1 1	85	The billboard
16	Partition into 'five and a bit' when adding 6, 7, 8 and 9	a. 43 b. 90 c. 82 d. 73	1	86	Points make prizes The billboard
17 18	Use informal pencil and paper methods to support, record or explain HTU – TU, HTU + HTU	17. 56 18. Show working, 58p	1 2	87 and 88	Points make prizes The billboard Tea time
19	Use a calendar	a. Thursday 2nd October b. Dad goes to France c. second	3 1 1	89	That's a date
20	Solve a given problem by organising and interpreting numerical data in simple lists, tables and graphs		4	90	Venn diagram

Name: _____ Date: _____

1 Tick (✓) the correct spaces in the table.

	multiple of 2	multiple of 5	multiple of 10
a. 472			
b. 570			
c. 235			
d. 900			

2 Investigate the questions and write yes or number.
Show your working below.

a. Is a multiple of 4 always a multiple of 2? ☐

b. Is a multiple of 2 always a multiple of 4? ☐

3 Complete the sentences.

a. Double 300 is ☐ .

b. Twice 350 is ☐ .

c. Half of 900 is ☐ .

d. Half of 500 is ☐ .

4 The distance from Tom's house to school is 450 m.
Tom walks to school and he walks home from school.
How far does Tom walk every day? ☐

Name: _____ Date: _____

5 Complete the multiplication table.

×	3	4
9		
6		
8		
5		

6 Paul counted the legs of all the cows on the farm. He counted 36 legs altogether. He knows that each cow has 4 legs, so how many cows are there on the farm?

There are ☐ cows on the farm.

7 Complete the multiplication table.

×	2	20	200
5			
3			
4			

8 a. CDs cost £4. Alex has £23. How many CDs can he buy?

Alex can buy ☐ CDs.

b. How much money will he have left over?

He will have ☐ left over.

Name: _____ Date: _____

9 5 cakes can fit into one box. The baker bakes 37 cakes and wants to pack them all into boxes. How many boxes does he need? Show your working below.

The baker needs ☐ boxes.

10 Complete the multiplications.

a. $41 \times 2 =$ ☐

b. $21 \times 3 =$ ☐

11 Complete the sentences.

a. Half of 28 is ☐

b. Quarter of 28 is ☐

12 An aeroplane carries 200 people. How many people can 4 aeroplanes carry?

☐ people

13 Fill in the missing words: more or less to complete the sentences. Use the strips to help you decide which word to use.

a.

b.

$\frac{1}{3}$ is ☐ than $\frac{1}{2}$.

$\frac{2}{10}$ is ☐ than $\frac{2}{5}$.

Name: _____ Date: _____

(14) Write the number that comes half way between the two numbers. You can use the number line to help you.

a. $\frac{1}{2}$ ☐ $1\frac{1}{2}$ b. $1\frac{3}{4}$ ☐ $2\frac{1}{4}$

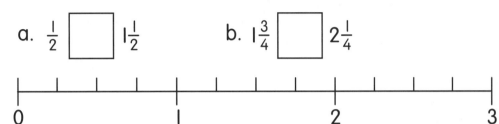

0   1   2   3

(15) About what fraction is shaded in each shape. Circle your estimate.

a.   b.   c.

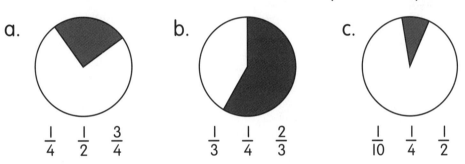

a. $\frac{1}{4}$ $\frac{1}{2}$ $\frac{3}{4}$

b. $\frac{1}{3}$ $\frac{1}{4}$ $\frac{2}{3}$

c. $\frac{1}{10}$ $\frac{1}{4}$ $\frac{1}{2}$

(16) Find the totals.

a. $35 + 8 =$ ☐   b. $25 + 65 =$ ☐

c. $45 + 37 =$ ☐   d. $25 + 48 =$ ☐

(17) Subtract the numbers. You can use the number line to help you.

$83 - 27 =$ ☐

83

(18) Suzy had 94p. She spent 36p on a notebook. How much did she have left? You can use the number line to help you.

94p   ☐

Name: _____ Date: _____

19 Use the calendar page to answer the questions.

a. When is Mike's party?

[ ]

b. What happens on the third Tuesday in October?

[ ]

October						
Mon	Tue	Wed	Thur	Fri	Sat	Sun
		1	2 Mike's party	3	4	5
6	7	8	9 Joe's birthday	10	11 Cinema	12
13	14	15	16	17 Gran's visit	18	19 To the museum
20	21 Dad goes to France	22	23	24	25	26
27	28	29	30	31		

c. Joe's birthday is on

the [ ] Thursday in October.

20 Write the names of the shapes in the correct places in the Venn diagram.

a. 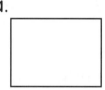 rectangle b. 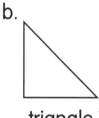 triangle c. 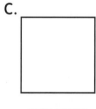 square d. 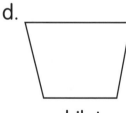 quadrilateral

Has 4 sides   Has a right angle

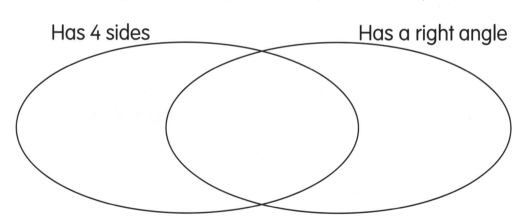

Record keeping chart

1	Recognise two- and three-digit multiples of 2, 5, or 10 and three-digit multiples of 50 and 100																							
2	Investigate a general statement about familiar numbers by finding examples that satisfy it Solve mathematical problems or puzzles																							
3	Derive quickly doubles of multiples of 50 to 500, and all the corresponding halves																							
4																								
5	Begin to know the three and four times-tables																							
6	Say or write a division statement corresponding to a given multiplication statement																							
7	Use known number facts and place value to carry out mentally simple multiplications and divisions																							
8	Begin to find remainders after simple division																							
9	Round up or down after division																							
10	Use known number facts and place value to carry out mentally simple multiplications and divisions																							
11	Use doubling and halving, starting from known facts																							
12	Choose and use appropriate operations to solve word problems and appropriate ways of calculating																							
13	Compare two familiar fractions																							
14																								
15	Estimate a simple fraction																							
16	Partition into 'five and a bit' when adding 6, 7, 8 and 9																							
17	Use informal pencil and paper methods to support, record or explain HTU − TU, HTU + HTU																							
18																								
19	Use a calendar																							
20	Solve a given problem by organising and interpreting numerical data in simple lists, tables and graphs																							

Wiggly snakes

Wash settings

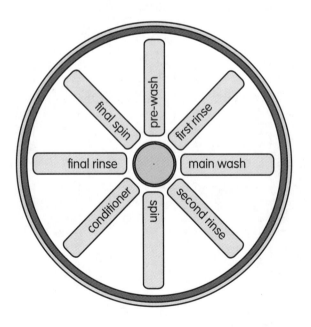

Ladybird bodies

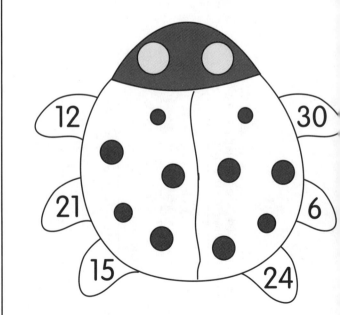

Word problems (1)

1. At my cake stall, each chocolate bun costs £2.50.
Four children buy one bun each.
How much money will I receive altogether?

2. I have 60p less than Jed. Jed has £4.65. How much money do I have?

3. In a toy shop, a calculator is on sale for £4.10. Its original price was £5. How much will I save?

4. In the supermarket, six apples cost £1.05. In the market six apples cost 95p.
What is the difference between the two prices?

5. I have saved £3.05 towards a birthday present for my mother. My brother Ben gives me £1.75.
How much money can I spend?

6. I have saved £1.20 from my pocket money and want to buy a computer game that costs £5.
How much more do I need to save?

Word problems (2)

1 Six people are standing in the garden with both arms up. How many arms are in the air?

2 A lift starts at the 45th floor and drops 7 floors. Which floor is it at now?

3 A rabbit jumps 1 m 60 cm and then the same again. How far has it jumped altogether?

4 Amelia has nine 10p coins. How much money does she have?

5 Joe has eight letters. Each letter has five stamps on it. How many stamps are there on the letters altogether?

6 There are 23 eggs in the fridge. Kezzy takes five out to make an omelette. How many eggs are there left in the fridge?

7 I have a bag of 20 bones and I want to share them between two dogs. How many does each dog get? If there are five or 10 dogs, how many bones does each dog get?

8 Rachel has £2.31 and her brother George has £3.54. How much do they have together?

9 Sophie took 35 minutes to walk home and Lynne took 20 minutes to walk home. How much longer did it take Sophie to walk home than Lynne?

10 The classroom contains tables that sit two children. 18 children walk into a classroom and sit down. They use all the tables exactly. How many tables are there?

Paper and pencil methods for addition

A. Counting in multiples of 100, 10 or 1

For example:

1) $87 + 36 = 87 + 30 + 6 = 117 + 6 = 123$

```
        +30              +3    +3
   ⌒‾‾‾‾‾‾‾‾‾‾‾⌒    ⌒‾‾‾‾⌒‾‾‾‾⌒
   87              117   120   123
```

2) $456 + 518$
$$= 456 + (500 + 10 + 8)$$
$$= 956 + 10 + 8$$
$$= 966 + 8$$
$$= 974$$

```
        +500           +10    +4    +4
   ⌒‾‾‾‾‾‾‾‾‾⌒    ⌒‾‾‾⌒‾‾‾⌒‾‾‾⌒
   456            956  966  970  974
```

B. Adding the most (or least) significant digits first

For example:
$$54 + 37 = (50 + 30) + (4 + 7) = 80 + 11 = 91$$
or:
$$54 + 37 = (4 + 7) + (50 + 30) = 11 + 80 = 91$$

	54			54
	+ 37			+ 37
	80			11
or	11			80
	91			91

	367			367
	+ 56			+ 56
	300			13
or	110			110
	13			300
	423			423

Paper and pencil methods for subtraction

A. Complementary addition - counting up from the smaller to the larger number

For example:

1) 85 - 47   47 + 3 + 30 + 5 = 85

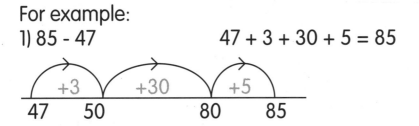

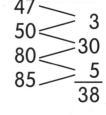

```
47 ──┐
50 ──┤  3
     ├ 30
80 ──┤
85 ──┘  5
        38
```

2) 574 - 356

```
      +4      +40      +100      +74
  356   360       400       500       574
```

```
  574
- 356
────────
    4   to 360
   40   to 400
  100   to 500
   74   to 574
────────
  218
```

B. Compensation - take too much, add back

1) 85 - 57 = 85 - 60 + 3 = 28

```
              -60
         +3
  25    28              85
```

2) 735 - 468   = 735 - 500 + 32
                    = 235 + 32
                    = 267

```
  735
- 468
────────
  235   take 500
+  32   add 32
────────
  200
   60
    7
────────
  267
```

C. Decomposition

```
   72   = 70 + 2  =  60 + 12
-  45     40 + 5     40 +  5
                   ──────────
                     20 +  7 = 27
```